ROAD
SIDE

ROAD SIDE

MY JOURNEY TO IRAQ AND THE LONG ROAD HOME

DYLAN PARK-PETTIFORD

Lawrence Hill Books
Chicago

Published by Lawrence Hill Books
An imprint of Chicago Review Press Incorporated
814 North Franklin Street
Chicago, Illinois 60610
ISBN 978-1-64160-977-7

Library of Congress Control Number: 2025932370

All images are from the author's collection

Typesetting: Jonathan Hahn

Printed in the United States of America
5 4 3 2 1

To Hannah, Story, Brody, and Hendrix.

To my mother, father, and brother—we had a good run.

And to my ancestors, for saddling me with this generational trauma.
Thank you for ruining my life, and making this book possible.

"We were eighteen and had begun to love life and the world; and we had to shoot it to pieces."
—Erich Maria Remarque, *All Quiet on the Western Front*

"You are a [man] marked for sorrow."
—Sophocles, *Electra*

CONTENTS

―――――

ACT III: SOMEWHERE IN BETWEEN

AUTHOR'S NOTE

I **LIKE TO THINK** of myself as a reliable narrator, but between all the concussions I suffered during fistfights at recess, my military service, and dabbling in recreational drug use in the late 2000s, things can get a bit foggy on occasion. Aided by candid conversations with mutuals and the journals I kept between 2004 and 2014, I promise I'm telling these stories to the best of my recollection.

Jokes and self-deprecation aside, for legal reasons and the privacy and protection of those involved, names, dates, and other details were changed during the writing of this book.

PROLOGUE

ON A GRAY and gloomy morning that followed in the wake of another gluttonous Thanksgiving weekend, Rory Pettiford leaned up against a pay phone in a dimly lit corridor of San Jose's Good Samaritan Hospital. A chilling draft carried the wail of sirens and the smell of wet pavement down the hallway like a wind tunnel whenever the automatic entrance doors opened for another weary visitor. For a second time, Rory's call would go unanswered. With the only quarter he had left, he gave it one last shot. He clutched the receiver, listening to the trill repeatedly, and was just about to hang up again when a boy with a heavy Israeli accent answered.

But the person on the other end wasn't a child. The diminutive voice belonged to Eliyahu, an adult man with the stature and physical features of someone twenty years younger due to focal segmental glomerulosclerosis, the same genetic disorder that made Gary Coleman a lovable pint-sized onscreen figure for decades. Eli, as Rory called him, could hear the layers of excitement and panic in his closest friend's voice. More than anything, Rory wanted Eli to join him in celebrating the birth of his first child. What would be a simple request for most was a logistical uncertainty for Eli because of his health. The arthritis made it painful for him to move, and the periodic seizures saw to it that he didn't drive too much these days. He shouldn't have been driving at all, but his license had not yet been revoked.

However, if there was one person Eli would do anything for, it was Rory, a man who expected nothing of him and had always been there for him, even when Eli's own family hadn't. If there was one place he'd venture to go out of the house, it was the hospital where he spent a good amount of time anyway. Eli agreed to come after his daily afternoon nap, so that he'd be rested and would have the energy to make the twenty-five-mile drive.

Elated, Rory rushed back to the cramped confines of a sterile room where his wife, Young-Ae, a petite Korean woman, was nearing the finish line of a thirty-six-hour marathon of labor. After experiencing the heartache of two miscarriages during previous pregnancies, Young-Ae refused to receive painkillers of any kind, despite assurances from the doctor of the statistically low risk of complications they posed to the child. Her refusal to take any chances only heightened her suffering. Rory hated seeing her in pain, and implored her to consider an epidural. Like her own parents, Korean immigrants who barely escaped the clutches of war under a violent Communist regime decades earlier, she would suffer through anything to ensure her family was safe.

For weeks, Rory and Young-Ae debated on what they would name their son. Rory wanted to name him Satchel after his favorite baseball player, Satchel Paige. For Young, that was completely out of the question. Young joked she'd file for divorce before she named her son after a purse. A strong Korean name like Bong or Deok-Su might be nice, she suggested. *Bong or Duck Soup?* Rory bristled at this. How about naming the child after one of the Beatles? John, Paul, and George were boring, Young countered. And she wasn't going to call her son Ringo. Rory was a natural born salesman and offered a compromise.

His favorite musician, a Jewish man named Robert Zimmerman, had a fantastic stage alias—Bob Dylan.

Bob Dylan was a white boy who broke all the rules. He didn't buck authority for show. In a time when championing civil rights was more likely to get someone killed than it was to gain them clout or coin, Dylan incorporated taboo sociopolitical themes in his music. Harsh nasally vibrato be damned, Dylan was going to strum his guitar and sing his heart out, and he was going to make sure people heard him. He defied convention and sang about things people weren't supposed to be singing about. Rory was a Black man who had escaped the hostilities of the Deep South as a child, and Dylan's rebellious streak held his attention.

Rory didn't know it at the time, but Dylan's latest album, *Infidels*, was almost prophetic. His first son would be called an infidel in foreign countries by bearded men waving black flags. On *Infidels*, Bob Dylan sang of jokers and sweethearts, honorable men and neighborhood bullies. He sang of killers and men of peace. Rory's first son would be all of those things too.

When the child finally came, there was a serene, almost eerie quiet. There was no crying. There was no kicking or screaming. The sleepy-eyed newborn didn't do much except let out the long sigh he'd been holding in for nine months while urinating all over himself and his exhausted mother.

Young-Ae watched her son stare apathetically into the distance and asked the nurse if something was wrong with the child. As far as the medical staff could tell, she had just given birth to a totally healthy baby boy. The doctor said they would run a series of tests to help allay her fears, and the child was whisked away by the accompanying nurse. Rory kissed Young-Ae on the forehead, told her not to worry and to try and get some sleep. The hard part was over.

While his wife rested, Rory made himself as comfortable as possible in a bedside chair with worn cushions and unforgiving ergonomics.

Released only one week earlier, John Lennon's latest posthumous single, "Every Man Has a Woman Who Loves Him," which was included on a tribute album to Yoko Ono, played in the headphones of Rory's second-most prized possession, the Sony Walkman it took him months to save up for. Four years earlier, to the week, Rory was in Oakland at the Coliseum with Eli and Rory's older half brother Troy at a Stevie Wonder and Gil Scott-Heron concert. In the middle of his set, Wonder stopped the show to make an announcement to the audience. Rory looked up at Eli, who was sitting on Troy's shoulders, and they shared a smile.

"I want you all to understand that I'm not a person who likes to be the bearer of any bad news." The crowd fell silent. The smile on Rory's face disappeared. "Someone has recently been shot. He was shot tonight—three times," Wonder said with his voice cracking. "I'm talking about John Lennon." A collective audible gasp reverberated through the arena. Eli squeezed Troy's neck and buried his face in the man's Jheri curl to hide his tears.

But this was not that.

Today's announcement was different. It was one of life, not death. Rory spent the rest of the day in that hospital room with his eye on the door, expecting Eli to walk through it at any moment with a smile and a warm embrace. Hours passed. Rory listened to the album front-to-back—twice. Then he grabbed lunch from the cafeteria, returned to the room with his sleeping wife, and listened to the album front-to-back twice more.

When his friend didn't show during the agreed time, Rory stopped the cassette player and removed his headphones to keep an ear open for a ringing phone at the nurse's station, thinking Eli might call with an update. A half-dozen more hours passed and neither happened. Eli never made it at all.

At home two days later, with his newborn son in his arms, Rory received a phone call that Eli died in a car accident on his way to the hospital. Rory held his newborn son and cried.

Eliyahu's death was certainly an ominous way for me to start my life. It's a black mark never to be forgotten as long as the name on my government-issued identification card reads DYLAN ELIYAHU JAFAR PARK-PETTIFORD.

Jafar was the name of my father's other closest friend, an older gay Muslim man who was also an outcast in his own right. A hyphenated last name is what happens when your mother refuses to surrender her name and subscribe to patriarchal norms. (Defiance runs in my DNA.)

Young-Ae worked as an administrative assistant at a small tech startup called Intel, for Gordon Moore and Andy Grove, the company's founders (and forefathers of Silicon Valley). Eli and Jafar were engineers there. Rory was a janitor. Over the years, Gordon Moore became a paternal figure of sorts to our family. I crawled around on his floors as a child, did my homework in his conference rooms, and even worked at Intel for a short spell after college. But even before I was alive, Mr. Moore gave my parents opportunities they likely would've never had. He didn't give my parents handouts, but they worked hard for him, and eventually Rory was able to trade in his mop and coveralls for a bunny suit and a slightly larger paycheck, where he would help manufacture chips and befriend Eli and Jafar.

The odd trio became fast friends and spent every waking moment together, whether it was at work, after work, or on the weekends. Rory, Eli, and Jafar loved debate and discourse over home-cooked meals, and because there was always something to debate or discuss, they often did it late into the night. Young-Ae found their pseudointellectualism exhausting most days and completely insufferable others. But the three young men were inseparable.

That is, until Eli's death. Jafar abruptly left for Buffalo shortly thereafter to be with his dying mother.

I never met Eliyahu or Jafar, so when I was old enough to inquire about the origin of my peculiar, over-syllabic, Semitic double middle name, my old man told me the day I was born was the most bitter-sweet day of his life. Now, bittersweet isn't exactly how you'd want your parents to describe your existence, but I was named after the people my old man loved and lost. And I found a small amount of solace in that.

There were what-ifs he thought about regularly over the years. Rory asked Eli to make the drive that day, so, by transitive proper-ties, Eli's death was technically his fault. The blame he put on himself didn't let me fully absolve myself either. I felt guilt by association. I found myself thinking about the small details that could've altered the course of our lives. I wondered how different things would be had I come on my actual due date. I wondered how my parents' lives would've been had I not been born at all. I could feel the resentment and the passive-but-sometimes-aggressive animosity my father har-bored toward me until the day he died.

———————

We didn't talk too much in the years before his death. Every attempt at a cordial conversation was derailed by paranoid accusations and unwarranted hysteria. According to him, his things were always being stolen by people who held grudges against him, or he was being watched by nefarious forces who wanted him dead. I'd later learn this behavior was attributable to early-onset dementia. I wanted to place him in a facility so he'd have the support I couldn't give him from four hundred miles away in Los Angeles. When I proposed this to him, he refused, then stopped answering my calls altogether.

Ironically enough, the last time I saw my father was at his brother Troy's funeral. I drove from Los Angeles to San Jose, picked him up, and drove him to Sacramento, where the service was held in an Elks

Lodge banquet hall. Many of the people there that day were distant relatives who, to me, may as well have been strangers. Spending one afternoon in a cramped room with them quickly highlighted the prevalent mental illness and dysfunctional constitution running through our gene pool. Those born to our bloodline were born agents of chaos.

My great uncle Virgil gave the same eulogy three times because, like my father, he too had dementia. He'd speak, sit down, then after other friends or family spoke, he'd stand up again—"I'd like to say a few words." Back to step 1. Others would try to usher him off the stage, but I urged them to let the man finish. He wasn't harming anyone. And I thought it was hilarious.

For the entirety of the memorial, my father sat in the back, adding his very audible commentary and ad-libs. He regularly reminded the other service-goers that Troy still owed him money and that Troy's death didn't relieve those debts. He expected someone to make good. During one eulogy, my father looked at me and said he had better things to and wanted to go home. I told him to stop being rude. Then, while I was at the podium speaking a few words of remembrance, I looked toward the back of the room and my father was asleep and snoring. Rory's half sister threatened him with physical violence, to which he responded, "I wish you would. You'll be laying in that casket next to that ugly motherfucker."

It was time to go home.

On our way out, my father yelled, "When I die, I'm going to haunt all of you."

And he kept his promise.

My father's last day on earth wasn't too different than my first. On a gray and gloomy autumn day, just weeks before another Thanksgiving weekend—this time in the midst of a global pandemic that had already claimed hundreds of thousands of lives—he sat on his couch coughing uncontrollably in a cramped one-bedroom apartment. These fits were a regular occurrence following a kidney and pancreas transplant a decade prior. Even then, he was never completely healthy, and there was always some new malady.

On that day, like many before, Rory placed a delivery order for orange chicken, chow mein, and egg drop soup from his favorite Chinese restaurant around the corner. When the food was delivered an hour later, he wouldn't be alive to receive it. My father's landlord noticed the to-go bag had been sitting on his doorstep for weeks, and the neighbor began complaining of strange smells. During a wellness check, police found my father's decomposing body sprawled out on the living room floor.

Nearly two weeks later, I received an enigmatic voicemail from the Santa Clara County Medical Examiner's Office that left no details. It was a call I almost didn't want to return. It meant that someone I loved was gone, and I didn't want to spin that wheel to see which name the arrow would land on. When I called back, they informed me my father had passed away "some time ago." The cause of death: complications due to COVID.

My father had been on ice in one of their freezers for weeks, but because their facility was now at capacity, I needed to claim his remains. If I didn't, they'd be forced to "dispose" of him. Living in Los Angeles ensured I had no way of making arrangements in the next twenty-four hours, so I agreed to pay a daily fee to keep his body in a refrigerator like some morbid Airbnb listing until I was able to fly back to the Bay Area.

On my first attempt to enter his apartment, the smell of death floored me. I drove around to several different Home Depots to find a gas mask and a protective coverall—items that were in short supply during the ongoing pandemic. On my second entry into the apartment, I first made a beeline to the bedroom to look for the important things: official documents, family heirlooms, jewelry, and the keys to his car. On his bedside table, next to a stack of photos of me and my younger brother, was a gold signet ring with a large inlaid jade stone, the one he called his Jedi ring when I was a child. I took it.

The living areas were stuffed with unopened boxes that had not been touched since he moved in after his divorce with Young-Ae a decade prior. The kitchen counters were piled with half-eaten TV dinners, buckets of discarded chicken bones, and fast-food bags. The sink was overflowing with plates and bowls covered in mold and maggots. Piles of dusty paperwork, books, and DVDs covered every available inch of real estate that was left.

I knew my father's mental health had deteriorated, but for a man who could be considered a germaphobe with mild to moderate symptoms of OCD, this was incomprehensible to me. After growing up in abject poverty with no sense of security, as an adult my father put an emphasis on his cleanliness, his appearance, and his material possessions.

This was the man who organized the multilingual books in his office library in alphabetical order of the author's last name. The same man who had a color-coordinated closet full of bespoke English and Italian suits. The same man with an impeccably curated cufflink and cologne collection he put on display. This was the same man who reorganized the garage twice a month—for fun. Everything had a place and a purpose in our household. Somewhere along the way, he lost his home, his place, and his purpose. Then he locked himself away from the pain of the outside world.

Like the day I was born, Rory spent his last days quietly wishing and waiting for someone to come over and keep him company. All of the invitations, visits, and phone calls dried up over the years. The only hobby he had after he retired was burning bridges and running everyone who had ever loved or cared about him out of his life. No one walked through that door, and his phone never rang. The most charismatic and outspoken man I've ever known died quietly. And like Eliyahu, he died alone.

ACT I

HOME

———

"Home is where the heart begins, but not where the heart stays."
—Hanif Abdurraqib, *They Can't Kill Us Until They Kill Us*

1

TELL ME WHEN TO GO

THE ECHOES OF a bouncing basketball and piercing squeaks of sneakers on freshly polished hardwood were drowned out by a restless crowd. Like on many nights before, Rory Jr. and I sat in the nosebleeds of the Oracle, an aging basketball arena in Oakland, watching our favorite professional basketball team blow another lead in the final minutes of a game. My younger brother's big brown eyes never left the action on the court. Despite the forgone conclusion, he remained hopeful. He always did. That's what made us different.

Outside the arena, the occasional bolt of lightning lit up the sky while the rain fell. Inside the arena, boos rained down on the home team clad in white uniforms lined with orange lightning bolts. The final buzzer sounded, and the entire crowd groaned in unison. Game over. Trailblazers 78, Warriors 75. We sat there for a bit watching grumbling men, some covered in face paint, as they descended the stairs toward the exit like a sad circus. It was the start of a new season, but the results were the same as the last.

Long after a majority of the crowd had already filed out of the stands, Rory and I stayed in our seats, taking it all in, imagining what it would be like to be down on the court instead. A security guard in a vinyl yellow jacket whistled at us and told us to beat it. We didn't have to go home, but we couldn't stay there.

Rory apologized, and I followed as his large frame cleared a path down the tight aisles. He was technically my little brother, but that was in age only. Even though I was four years his senior, he stood taller and wider than me. Every time I looked at him, it was like seeing a newer version of myself. As teenagers, we were so similar in appearance that people often confused us as twins.

At a logjam in the lobby, we watched an angry fan yank off his jersey in disgust, threatening to throw it in the trash and vowing to never watch another game again. Seeing an opportunity, Rory asked how much he'd take for the newly discarded colors.

"Fifty bucks," he replied, thinking that he might be able to take advantage.

"What? I can buy one on eBay for that much. I'll give you twenty dollars. You were just about to throw that rag in the trash. I'll give you thirty," Rory countered. The man's chin crinkled in contemplation for a brief moment.

"Fuck it. Deal."

I'd seen transactions like this happen a thousand times before. Rory was an avid curator of sports memorabilia and a shrewd negotiator. The proof was in the jersey and shoe collection that lined the walls of his room and our parents' garage.

When we exited the building, we were hit by a cool and crisp Northern California breeze, raising goosebumps in places on my skin that were covered in a layer of sweat just moments before. A massive glowing sign on the side of the circular building cast cardinal shadows down on the labyrinth of the parking lot, illuminating it like some seedy red-light district.

Rory and I navigated our way through the maze, zigzagging through aisles strewn with trash. We walked by a girl throwing up as her friend held her hair. We quickened our steps and laughed with our forearms over our noses and mouths. At the end of another row of cars, a skirmish had broken out between rival fans, and we slowed our pace to watch for a bit. They were drunk and sloppy, yelling words as hollow as their bottles. Moments later they were shaking hands and patting each other on their sweaty gravel-covered backs as they hugged it out, saying things like, "It's all love, baby."

Finding my car in that muddle of metal and concrete always proved difficult. I held the key fob above my head, clicking the alarm button repeatedly as we walked. At the end of every column, I would stop and look up at the light poles, each with different numbers, trying to determine if we were headed in the right direction.

After a few minutes of parking lot futility, I finally heard the familiar wails of my old Jeep Grand Cherokee. I let her scream her sad siren alarm song in the distance until we could figure out exactly where she was hiding. Rory spotted the flashing lights, and we followed them through the murky haze like a light tower guiding our ship through a rocky bay.

When we finally sat in the car, I panicked while patting my empty jean pockets, thinking I had lost my cell phone. Then I realized I'd put it in my jacket pocket while paying for hot dogs at halftime. I was embarrassed at myself and looked over to see if Rory had noticed my mini panic attack. He was too busy taking pictures of his newly prized possession with his cell phone.

When I turned the key in the ignition, the old SUV didn't come to life like she was supposed to. Instead, she groaned and let out a sigh before quitting altogether. This wasn't the first time, but it was always just as infuriating as the time before. Sometimes I imagined that one day she'd work her own problems out, because I didn't have the money to fix whatever it was that was ailing her. I glanced over at Rory again, and he couldn't be bothered. He was still fixated on the blue and yellow jersey.

"The tag says 1991 and this thing is near mint. It doesn't even look like it's been washed." He held it closer to my face to confirm his discovery. It smelled like it had not been washed since 1991. "I don't wash mine too often either. It ruins the screen printing," he replied matter-of-factly while looking out the passenger window as if saddened by the memories of past mistakes.

I waited for another moment, then patted the dash for some encouragement, and turned the key again, this time pumping the gas pedal repeatedly. Slowly but surely, the engine mustered enough strength to start up. *Fuck yes. There we go.*

We crept cautiously through side streets of dilapidated neighborhoods, looking for a way around all the closed roads. All of the exposed brick and mortar had been veiled in layers of painted-over graffiti, with every new veneer of paint like a ring on a tree marking the years.

My head was on a slow, deliberate swivel to spot any police cruisers or potential carjackers. I was driving with expired tags in a common car that could be easily flipped for parts in a chop shop somewhere—a nice target for all participating parties. My love for this place did not blind me to the truth. Oakland is a lion of a city known for eating its young, which is exactly why my father took me away from that place when I was a cub.

Back on the main streets, colorful crowds congregated on every corner. The air of the city gave it life, almost as if it were its own living, breathing being. He'd moved us away from there at a young age to lessen our chances of being statistics, as many of his friends had been when he was growing up. I tried to picture my father as a teenager growing up here, and I wondered about the things he did and all the trouble he got into. For us, it was a school night, and if I didn't have Rory home by a decent hour, I wouldn't have to imagine the trouble we'd be in.

We drove down the 880, a long stretch of ugly highway that connects the East Bay to our home in the South Bay. The gray blur of concrete walls waved like a never-ending flag beyond the streaked glass of my windows. Other than the glowing green numbers on the dash, we sat in complete darkness with the radio turned down so low that it was barely audible above the growl of the tires conquering each imperfection in the unfinished road.

Rory was now fast asleep, clutching his jersey the same way a child might find comfort in their favorite blanket or stuffed animal. Beneath his tough exterior—the broad shoulders, scarred cheek, and bruised face—he was just a kid. He'd always be the giggly kid who did the funniest impressions of Andy Kaufman or an angry Donald Duck. He'd always be the chubby kid who could find any reason to dance in public, embarrassing everyone but himself. My parents often forced Rory on me, thinking that having a younger brother with me would severely limit the amount of trouble I could cause, so he'd always be the kid who tagged along wherever my friends and I went. They must've known that having an eleven-year-old shadowing me would drastically decrease my chances of run-ins with the law or getting one of my teenage counterparts pregnant, and they were right. More than my safety, they probably just wanted both of us out of the house for their own rest and relaxation.

Over the years, the involuntary camaraderie between Rory and I blossomed into an unbreakable friendship. Later on, as an adult, I was glad that he still thought I was cool enough to be seen with. He never told his friends how much he hated being around me, like I had said on countless occasions about him when he was younger—quite the opposite, actually. Whenever I bumped into one of his friends, they always told me how much he bragged about me, which I thought was strange, because I didn't feel like there was anything to brag about.

I turned up the radio and interrupted Kanye West calling some poor girl a gold digger by switching the station to National Public Radio.

"The war in Iraq rages on. Four more US service members were killed in Taji when their patrol came under enemy fire."

The program hosts talked about foreign policy. They named cities in countries I could not point out on a map. I tuned everything out and stared into the two white cylinders of light that illuminated the void in front of me for the rest of the drive.

A little while later, I pulled onto a dark street with an entrance so small that it seemed to open only when you approached it. It was lined with colorful houses, from different eras, of all shapes and sizes, a neighborhood close enough to Oakland that one could drive there in thirty minutes, but so far removed from Oakland that it could be a foreign country.

Stopping in front of a cream-colored house with a white picket fence bordering a well-manicured yard set off a motion sensor above the garage door. Floodlights lit up the house, warning would-be intruders. The only intruders this house had ever seen were Rory and I sneaking in and out on weekends in the middle of the night, after our parents had fallen asleep. A blond cat took heed and scampered under the blue Volvo sedan with a discolored quarter panel and flat tire sitting in the driveway.

That house on South Milton Avenue had been my home for a majority of my life, but it no longer felt that way, and it hadn't for some time.

"Aye, Ro. Wake up, we're here." I tapped Rory's arm once to no response. Then tapped it more forcefully a few more times in rapid succession. Rory sat up in a groggy fog.

"Already? That was quick."

We did the same elaborate handshake we'd been doing for longer than I can remember. Rory slid out of the passenger seat and exited the car.

"Hey, you forgot something," I yelled as he made his way up the driveway. I was holding the jersey he'd forgotten while he was likely fretting about the lecture he might receive when he crossed the threshold back into our parents' home.

He returned to the idling vehicle, grabbed the jersey, and thanked me. Then I watched him head for the house and close the door behind him as quietly as possible.

I could have stopped him to tell him I'd enlisted in the military. I was awaiting my orders to ship off to basic training any day now, and I'd be gone for the next six months to a year. But Rory was having a good night, and I didn't want to ruin it. So I didn't say anything.

2

SEMI-CHARMED LIFE

I **STOOD AT ATTENTION,** making a point to avoid eye contact with anyone. I could feel myself swaying back and forth, trembling uncontrollably, possibly from the frigid Texas winter air but more likely from the volatile energy radiating off the cadre of screaming drill sergeants. I was nervous and already questioning my decision to enlist. But more than anything, I was trying my hardest not to vomit all over one of the drill sergeant's impeccably polished combat boots. In order to keep myself from retching, I closed my eyes and thought about all the laughs and love I'd received from my favorite people less than twenty-four hours prior to whatever shit show this was.

The day before I shipped off to basic training, my high school sweetheart Claire threw me a farewell party at her parents' sprawling house in the rolling hills of South San Jose. I tended to the hot dogs, hamburgers, and wings on the grill, pausing only to acknowledge the congratulatory back slaps and handshakes from a bunch of people I didn't really know. If enlisting in the military hadn't completely garnered Claire's father's approval, I knew my barbecuing skills would. And if that didn't earn his acceptance, Olive, Claire's Great Dane puppy, appreciated the chunks of meat I snuck her on the side.

My best friends Brian, Kyle, and Adrian played basketball in the pool with my brother. When they got bored with that, they challenged each other to a diving competition. After every cannonball, Claire and her friends would squeal when a rogue wave splashed them while they laid out next to the pool. Claire's melanin-free skin wasn't built for long (or even short) durations in the sun, but that didn't stop her from trying to get herself a little color. She was a sunburnt shade of pink, and her freckles were so pronounced they were no longer distinguishable from what could be melanoma. She joked the cancer would be worth it if she was able to get my golden-brown complexion. I threw her in the pool. She pretended to hate me for it. The smile on her face told me she didn't. We roughhoused for a bit, then snuck away and fucked in her bedroom, and then roughhoused in the pool some more until the sun went down.

When the water was too cold to enjoy, we sat around the bonfire talking about the promises of the future. Rory Jr. was halfway through his junior year of high school, preparing to take the SATs, even though he didn't foresee college in his future. He wanted to be an artist—not the starving kind, though, but the type with a big house and endorsement deals.

Claire was entering the second semester of her sophomore year of college. She was smart enough to go to a better college but followed me to San Jose State University, the same institution I had just dropped out of to join the military. Being close to home would allow her to help her parents with her younger sister, who suffered from Prader-Willi syndrome, a neurocognitive disorder in which the afflicted have an insatiable appetite, leading them to eat themselves to death without the proper supervision.

Kyle was the oldest of all of us. A former Jehovah's Witness who escaped the clutches of the church's cult-like indoctrination, he found himself on the streets as a teenager and hustled to survive. He always had a wallet full of cash but relished in petty theft.

Brian, my closest friend, was the most pragmatic of all of us. He wasn't a dreamer with grandiose visions of being rich or famous. He just wanted security—to have a decent job, a picture-frame family, a house with a white picket fence, and a black lab. His wants stemmed from a series of losses he'd endured in his short time on the planet. His older brother got into the medicine cabinet as a child, overdosed on prescription meds, and died. His mother, who was in and out of halfway houses, was killed by a car that ran a stop sign. Then, during our freshman year of high school, his house burned to the ground after the washer and dryer caught fire in the garage.

Despite being dealt several bad hands during his formative years, Bad Luck Brian never folded. His trajectory was slow and steady, but it was always upward. While the rest of us were in a hurry for greatness, he was in the process of transferring from West Valley, the local community college affectionately known as Breast Valley for producing an abnormal amount of porn stars, to a four-year university to major in accounting.

And then there was Adrian. Coming down from the high of the relative success of his band's last album, he was getting ready to record another studio album in England and making plans to go on another world tour.

Me? I was getting ready to go on a tour of my own.

Claire's father interrupted our bonfire by screaming at Rory for peeing on the toilet seat and floor in the guest bathroom. And even though Rory explained it wasn't pee—he was just grabbing a towel and it was water from his swim trunks—the mood was effectively killed. The party was over.

Earlier that evening, in a ravenously intoxicated state, I ate some shrimp cocktail that had been sitting out in the sun, then spent the rest of the evening paying for it. As everyone filed out to go home, they each stopped to check in on me, patting me on the back and wishing me good luck while I was on my knees in the bathroom, crying out to the heavens and praying to the porcelain gods.

Claire dropped me off at a local motel after everyone else left. Her father forbade me from spending the night under his roof, saying things like "I have a wife and three daughters to protect, surely you understand."

I didn't understand. I was good enough to date his daughter for four years, but he still saw me as a potential sexual predator? It was strange logic that didn't quite camouflage the racist trope of the sex-crazed Black man preying on an innocent white girl.

Early the next morning, running on no sleep, I mustered what little strength I had to get myself to the airport. The entire flight from San Jose to San Antonio was spent in a claustrophobia-inducing lavatory while flight attendants continually knocked on the door, checking to see if I was OK or to make sure I wasn't a terrorist getting ready to hijack another plane. That, ironically, was the reason I was on that flight in the first place. I was another teenager recruited by Uncle Sam to preserve freedom and democracy and the American way of life by fighting the war on terror.

As the plane descended, I was forced to return to my seat. A large man in a corduroy jacket standing outside the door, presumably waiting for an open lavatory, followed me back, taking a seat across the aisle from me where a mother and her small child had previously been sitting for a majority of the flight. I smiled wryly at the air marshal as he not-so-nonchalantly eyeballed me. With my seat belt securely fastened and my seat back and tray table up in an upright position, I continued to retch into one of those skinny white bags that are always stuck between the pages of the *SkyMall* magazines in the pouch on the seat back in front of you. Not exactly the start to my military career I was hoping for.

Later that evening, I found myself standing in formation with dozens of other wide-eyed recruits on a concrete pad somewhere on Lackland Air Force Base, a sprawling military installation right down the road from the Alamo, as a group of drill sergeants circled us like sharks in the water. I was delirious and waited patiently for my turn

to get berated. I didn't have to wait long. Out of the corner of my
eye, I could see a short, red-faced drill instructor making a beeline
toward me, stomping the whole way to make his presence known.
He stopped with his nose millimeters from mine and snarled. Below
a strawberry blond mustache were teeth stained yellow by decades of
cigarette smoke and chewing tobacco.

At five foot nine (and three-eighths of an inch), I'm not what
society would consider a tall man, but I towered over him. The brim
of his cap, or Smokey Bear as they're called, pressed firmly against
my forehead, leaving a temporary indentation. It was the most intense
staring contest I'd ever been a part of. The drill instructor was analyz-
ing everything about me, and I knew he was formulating a plan to put
me through as much pain as I could take before the night was over.

Like the iconic scene in *Alien³* when the Xenomorph has a cow-
ering Ripley pinned up against the wall and its secondary mandible
protrudes from its mouth to give her a little kiss, I turned away and
retched every time I caught whiffs of his coffee-covered halitosis. I
could taste the bile building up in the back of my throat, then felt it
on my tongue, and I swallowed it. He eyed my makeshift name tag
while I struggled to keep my composure and hide the fear in my eyes.

"What kinda name is Park-*Peddyferd*? How do you say your name,
recruit?" he said with a thick Southern accent somewhere between
Colonel Sanders and Yosemite Sam.

For as long as I can remember, roll call for any event has been
more difficult than it need be. Explaining how to pronounce my full
name with a double middle name and hyphenated last name has
always been met with confusion or curiosity.

"You got it right the first time, sir."

"Where you from, recruit?"

"San Francisco, sir."

I'm not actually from San Francisco, I'm from the San Francisco
Bay Area. But no one knows where or what Campbell, California, is,

so this is the easiest response to keep conversation about my origins as short as possible.

"San Francisco, huh? Just what we need, another faggot in the service. Don't even think about sucking any dicks while you're here, Park. Not in my Air Force. Now get on your face and push until I'm tired of watching."

Admittedly, sucking dick had not crossed my mind, mostly because I'm not gay. But even if I was, nothing about the ambience was remotely sensual. This was not the proper environment for fellatio of any kind.

I placed my palms on the cold concrete. My muscles were achy and I could feel myself shaking even before I began doing some comically pathetic pushups. Before I got to my fifth, he spun on his heels to go harass another poor bastard. Around the fourteenth or fifteenth rep, I puked everywhere, to the horror of everyone in the vicinity. No matter how hard I tried to keep it in, I couldn't stop the flow of vomit pouring from my face. The drill instructor stood over me and screamed at me to finish twenty, then to report to the nurse for an IV. I've never been waterboarded, but those next five pushups were torturous. Seeing and smelling my own puke from such a close proximity made me throw up even more as I struggled to lift my body. Rinse and repeat for five more reps.

At the end of that first night of basic training, I lay in a bottom bunk, physically drained and mentally exhausted, staring at the metal grid and mattress above me. Despite being in a barracks surrounded by dozens of other young men, it was dead quiet, a silence occasionally broken up by a cough or sniffles coming from the next bed over. In the pitch black, I couldn't see the kid in the bunk next to me, but I could hear him trying to keep it together. He eventually cried himself to sleep while I continued to stare into the void.

I imagine we were all thinking the same thing: *How the hell did I get here?*

3

FORTUNATE SON

——————

MY ENLISTMENT CAME a few years after that world-changing day in September 2001. Instead of expounding on where I was that day—we've all heard that story from a million different people a million different times—I'll just say that I, an impressionable teenager, became swept up in the gross manufactured patriotism that emerged from the rubble and cancerous ashes of those fallen towers. It wasn't the far-right, red-hat-wearing nationalism that's disguised as the patriotism we see on television today. It was the red, white, and blue bald eagle Bud Light commercial kind of patriotism. The lifted Chevy Silverado with a yellow SUPPORT THE TROOPS magnet and truck nuts kind of patriotism. The please rise from your seats, remove your hat, and place your hand over your heart to recite the National Anthem before you watch young men give each other CTE on the gridiron kind of patriotism. And to quote Lee Greenwood, I was "proud to be an American."

I graduated high school a couple years after the war on terrorism in Afghanistan was declared, which happened to be around the same time that George Dubya and Team America World Police announced Iraq had world-ending weapons of mass destruction. Patriotism was at an all-time high, and I, just like many of my peers, wanted to do my part. My senior year, I walked into a Marine Corps recruitment office and began the process of enlisting. A few weeks later, the recruiter picked me up from my house to give me a ride to the nearest MEPS (military entrance processing station) for a physical and to take the ASVAB (Armed Services Vocational Aptitude Battery), an SAT-like test administered by the government to ensure the recruits they're planning on entrusting with weapons of mass destruction have a pulse and a basic grasp of the English language. When the recruiter knocked forcefully on the front door, it was my old man who answered. My father turned and looked back at me, betrayed. Then he turned his attention back to the recruiter and threatened his physical well-being.

"How many Purple Hearts do you have, Sarge?" my dad asked, rhetorically.

"None, sir. I've been very fortunate."

"Well, do you want your first, motherfucker?"

Pops beating his ass wouldn't have gotten the poor guy a Purple Heart, because that's not how it works, but the message was received loud and clear—10-4, good copy. My father's behavior didn't seem to surprise him, as he'd probably gone through this regularly, but for his own safety, he did an about face and retreated off my front porch faster than the Fourth Marines at Bataan.

My first attempt to enlist failed, so attending college or learning a trade was really my only other option. My soft, moisturized hands had never seen a real day's work, so becoming a contractor, plumber, mechanic, or electrician was out of the question. I knew I didn't have the grades or academic acumen to attend a school like Stanford or Cal Berkeley, so I enrolled at the local commuter college, San Jose State University.

Thinking I was going to join the military, I hadn't even bothered applying for scholarships, and my parents refused to let me take out loans. My mother took pity, though. She loosened her purse strings a bit and paid the tuition for my first semester. She made it very clear, however, that after that I was on my own. They gave me two weeks to move out (which turned into several months). I wasn't angry about my parents cutting me off. I knew that they would never actually let me go hungry or homeless—not as a teenager anyway. Still, I needed to learn how to adult—and fast.

Step 1: Find my very unqualified self a job.

Dylan Park-Pettiford, Sustenance Associate. That was the title the owner of Blendz, a hip smoothie and salad joint in downtown Campbell, assigned me. It seemed a little over the top, but I didn't argue, because it sounded better than the other options: Panini Press Engineer or Smoothie-lier. And while I enjoyed the short commute, the free meals, and the low-stress atmosphere, I wasn't Blendz material. My boss kept saying I didn't show enough enthusiasm while offering spirulina shots, and I absolutely refused to upsell add-ons for drinks. It probably did not help that every time I was asked to toss a customer's salad, I giggled with my coworkers. Sophomoric? Perhaps. But I was still a freshman.

One of my high school classmates, Brandon, was a regular at Blendz. After a "gnarly sesh" at the skate park up the street, he'd skate over for his usual Red Bull Energy Blend—a diabetes-inducing smoothie that consisted of frozen yogurt, strawberries, raspberries, apple juice, and half a can of Red Bull—to go along with his grilled chicken and cheddar panini. It didn't take long for him to recognize how out of place I was, and he asked if I wanted to pick up shifts at the skate shop he worked at.

Five-Oh, the local skateboard shop, was owned by a member of the Faction, a celebrated punk band from San Jose, and was a popular hangout for teenagers. More important, it was walking distance to my house. There, I was surrounded by other like-minded youth, and we spent most of our workdays in the back alley practicing our kick flips, listening to indie rock or underground rap, getting stoned, and eating bánh mì from the Vietnamese deli next door. All the employees gave their friends steep discounts on merchandise, if they charged them at all, so the shop went out of business real quick. And while that was sad, we never got paid on time, if at all, so the merchandise and the friendships made were our salary.

I worked at a surf shop in the mall for a bit. Again, the entire staff consisted of teenagers led by a manager who was only a few years removed from being a teenager himself. It was in the back room where I met Mike Nichols and Chris Laurel. They were like real-life versions of Bert and Ernie if Bert and Ernie were covered in poorly thought-out tattoos, listened to Eminem, and sold drugs on the side. But they were some cool white boys, and we became thick as thieves, as they say. Well, *I* wasn't a thief. I was way too afraid to steal—if my soft little body survived any amount of time in county lockup, my Korean mother surely would've ended my life, and that was a chance I was not willing to take for a fifty-dollar Santa Cruz hoodie. But Mike and Chris relished the thrill of doing anything that defied authority. Swiping tees and snagging sneakers was sport for them.

It didn't take long for the manager to figure out the missing merchandise and register shortages weren't just clerical mistakes, as we often reported them. There was a thief among us, and he was going to catch them. He zeroed in on Mike and Chris and pulled me aside to act as a mole. Instead, I explained the missing clothing was likely due to an accidentally discarded shipment box.

I'm a lot of things, but I'm no snitch.

Mike and Chris didn't do everything by the book, or anything really, but they were fiercely loyal to those who looked out for them. In their trade, loyalty was currency. When Mike and Chris learned my parents kicked me out before I was eighteen, they offered up their spare bedroom in their trap house off Moorpark Avenue—a neighborhood where one would now be hard-pressed to find a home for sale under seven figures—as a way to repay me for keeping them out of trouble (and jail) on a handful of occasions.

However, the small room was not charity. They didn't charge me for my first month's stay to help get me back on my feet, but they made it clear they were expecting rent money the following month. The number they proposed was far more than I could afford—likely to help subsidize their growing drug trade. Even if I worked full time selling T-shirts for minimum wage at a retail store in the mall (I worked part time), I still wouldn't be able to afford the rent, so I was back on the job hunt.

I borrowed one of my dad's suits and went from store to store in the mall canvassing retailers, and eventually landed a gig as a greeter at Macy's. From there, I transitioned into its loss-prevention department. That didn't last too long either. I was fired, along with the rest of the team, after my partner Benny followed a Black gentleman into the fitting room, stalked him around the store, then tackled the unsuspecting man as he exited the mall. I sprinted from the camera room to the entrance to assist, and the poor man looked at me as if to say, *How could you do me like this? I'm one of your own, you Uncle Tom.*

As it turns out, the man didn't steal anything at all. The shirt Ben accused him of lifting was under a pile of clothes in the fitting room. *Oops.* Ben went on to become a cop for the Oakland Police Department, which was fitting, because profiling Black people is kinda their thing.

Right down the street from the mall, Claire worked as a tour guide at the Winchester Mystery House. And Brian worked at the hot dog stand there. It seemed like a logical place for me to work, and they got me free passes to go on a tour to check it out. The Mystery House is a massive Victorian-style mansion on the border of San Jose and Campbell that once served as the residence for Sarah Winchester, the wealthy widow of the firearms dealer William Winchester. In 1881, after her husband's death, Sarah inherited a majority stake of ownership in the Winchester Repeating Arms Company and upward of $20 million, which today would be the equivalent of over half a billion dollars.

Built on 162 acres, with forty rooms, indoor toilets and plumbing, heating, electricity, elevators, and windows designed by Charles Lewis Tiffany of Tiffany & Co., Winchester spared no expense on her new home in Northern California. And she never stopped adding on to the home. If the legends are true, Winchester believed she was haunted by the ghosts of all the people killed by her husband's invention, and the only way to appease them was by building never-ending expansions on her home. There was the labyrinth-like construction to confuse bad spirits and a bell tower to summon the good ones. Ghostly music was played on a pump organ in the ballroom at night, and the number thirteen was found all over the property. Thirteen bedrooms, thirteen bathrooms, and rooms with thirteen windows. A very peculiar place.

Following Sarah Winchester's death, a couple business partners purchased the property with the intention of capitalizing on the poor (rich) woman's mental illness by turning it into a tourist attraction.

After witnessing the inside of the home firsthand and listening to Claire expound on all the eccentricities of the mansion, I was having second thoughts. First off, there was no way I could memorize all of the lines during an hour-long tour, and there's absolutely no chance I'd be able to do that several times a day with a straight face. Public speaking in a haunted house for eight dollars an hour?

Yeah, no thanks. *Pass.*

There was the short stint as an emergency medical technician. During a drunken heart-to-heart at a house party, Mark Shriver convinced me to take a semester's worth of night classes with him to become an accredited EMT. The sales pitch was simple enough—in a few months we'd be driving around in ambulances, gaining some real-world work experience to slap onto our deficient résumés. More important, we'd actually be making a positive contribution to society. I was in.

A few weeks after finishing the program, Mark and I were both hired by Pacific Coast Ambulance, a medical transportation startup serving Oakland and Richmond. The office was off Franklin and Fourteenth in the Financial Center, a gorgeous fifteen-story, 1920s-era art deco building covered in brass and marble, which didn't seem like the obvious choice to house an ambulance company, but nothing about the company made sense. And outside of our sharp uniforms, nothing about the company was very professional.

Pacific Coast was accredited as a nonemergency "basic life support" transportation company, so we picked up the easy calls AMR (American Medical Response) couldn't when they were too busy actually saving lives. Essentially, we transported old people and dead bodies to and from nursing homes and medical facilities and only rendered lifesaving medical care in rare instances. The job was mundane, and the promise of blood, guts, and mayhem never materialized like we thought, so we found ways to keep ourselves entertained. And with a crew of eight eighteen-to-twentysomething-year-olds running a fleet of three aging ambulances, things went as one might expect.

We drove Code 3, sometimes to avoid traffic but usually just for the thrill of driving fast with lights and sirens on. There were joyrides outside of our jurisdiction. On nights with no scheduled pickups, we partied. We smoked and drank. And because we were a group of virile, semiattractive coeds, the overnight shifts often led to fucking in the office or ambulances. Pacific Coast was a frat party on wheels.

As it turns out, Pacific Coast Ambulance was also a front for some not-so-legal business dealings. After a late shift one night, Mark and I returned to the office to discover the locks had been changed. Not too long after that, the owner was charged with insurance fraud, tax evasion, drug possession, and a laundry list of other crimes. He went to jail, and I was back in the unemployment line.

When Claire wasn't at volleyball, track-and-field practice, or the Mystery House, she worked part time as a dog groomer. Her store was looking for someone to unload trucks during the graveyard shift. The pay was fifteen dollars an hour, which was twice the amount I was making to toss salads and tackle shoplifters, so I figured, *Why not? How bad could unloading pallets stacked with fifty-pound bags of dog food be?*

The answer: *extremely.*

Every night I clocked in at 9:00 PM and unloaded trucks until I physically couldn't anymore. Then, if there was time, I had the pleasure of mopping floors and kennels covered in dry dog shit, piss, and vomit until 5:00 AM. Before the sun was even up, I'd clock out, drive home with heavy eyelids, and stumble through the front door of that trap house I was still living in. I'd collapse on a twin-sized mattress with no box spring, where I made a futile attempt to get a couple hours of sleep.

It was like that every day for a year. I was completely burned out. On top of that, I was failing most of my classes—working my ass off to pay for school but flunking out because of it. It was a Joseph Hellerian catch-22. My bank account balance was probably lower than my GPA, which was pretty damn low.

Yet somehow things would still get lower. After an exceptionally strenuous shift at the pet store, I came home from work to find anything and everything of value in my room had been stolen. Things like this happen when two of your roommates are drug dealers and the third roommate has a brother who's a crack addict who lives in a van in front of the house.

I wasn't willing to find out if there was a basement below rock bottom.

———————

For the first month or so of college, every day was a carbon copy of the previous one: wake up, take a shower, get dressed, hop in my Jeep, then drive sleepy-eyed through the back streets of downtown San Jose. If I didn't arrive to school early enough, the parking lots would be full, and I'd jockey up and down one-way streets to find a parking space large enough for my SUV. This wasted hour or so of parking-lot futility generally led to one of three things: a parking ticket, showing up to class exceptionally late, or just giving up and going home.

All the things I expected of college were absent. The parties were abysmal, the football team sucked, and the few friends I had joined the Greek system—something I refused to participate in. (I wouldn't join a fraternity, but I joined the military. Go figure.) There were no inspirational professors like Sean Maguire as played by Robin Williams in *Good Will Hunting*. I didn't experience those moments of clarity or mind-awakening epiphanies that other students shared. College felt like a chore, which was a selfish way for me to feel. My parents had sacrificed so much so that Rory and I would have opportunities they never did. I wanted to do right by them. Really, I did. So I went through the motions, thinking that one day something might click and I'd get my shit together. That never really happened.

Admittedly, things like poor parking, limited cafeteria options, and a subpar social scene are all First World problems that only matter to immature eighteen-year-old boys, but they were just enough to have me considering other options. And that's where military recruiters come in. Still only a few years removed from 9/11, the patriotism, nationalism, and all the other -isms were still very much at their peaks. Military recruiters roam college campuses to convince confused teenagers who are seeking a sense of purpose that Uncle Sam will fill that void. And it works.

I'd had a few run-ins with the same recruiter on campus. He never remembered he'd already approached me until I reminded him I'd already declined several times. The polite rejections never deterred him, though. In the same way a man will sidle up next to a woman in a bar as nonchalantly as possible, he struck up a conversation with me at the counter of the Burger King in the student union while I waited for my order of French toast sticks. He asked if I had ever considered joining the Armed Forces. I told him about my father threatening to kill a Marine recruiter. He laughed, saying that happens fairly often—just another one of the many occupational hazards. But I wasn't joking. And much like the woman being hit on at the bar, I attempted to rebuff him to no avail.

"A lot of parents feel that way, and understandably so," he said, "until they see you wearing that uniform. They'll be too proud to be angry at you. Trust me. My parents were the exact same way."

When a complete stranger asks you to trust them, that's typically a red flag. In fact, it's an indicator that you should probably *not* trust them. I told him I promised my mother I'd finish college.

"And you still can," he countered. "The educational benefits are outstanding. The military will pay your tuition if and when you decide to go back." It's like he had a mental flowchart for every response imaginable.

We walked and talked. He told me I'd travel to corners of the globe I'd probably never see otherwise. And, if I was lucky, I might even get to kill some bad guys or blow some shit up.

"But wait, there's more," he said like Billy Mays selling me Oxi-Clean. The recruiter offered me a signing bonus of *at least* ten grand. I stopped dead in my tracks. Ten thousand American dollars? Legal tender? I'd barely passed algebra in high school, and I wasn't doing so hot in my precalculus class, but it didn't take me long to calculate how much I could use that much cash. I'd never seen that much money in one place ever—and certainly not with my name on it. More than anything, I was tired of working odd jobs.

He drove a hard bargain, but even with all the benefits laid out on the table, I wasn't sold. Well, I didn't *think* I was.

He asked for my phone number. I lied and said I didn't have a cell phone. My father was a salesman, and I'd watched him cold call entire phone books, turn his Bob Costas voice on, and sell shit to people and corporations with big pockets, by any means necessary. This recruiter was just another salesperson with a good sales pitch. He handed me a card and told me to give him a call if I wanted to talk about it some more.

A few days later, I hopped off the bus on my way to work, when I saw a large crowd and news vans gathering outside of the San Jose Municipal Rose Garden. I made my way up to the tall cast iron fence to catch a glimpse. Hundreds, maybe thousands, of people were seated in chairs while someone spoke at a podium. Next to the podium was a large painted portrait of a handsome man next to a row of American flags. A woman with an uncanny resemblance to Maria Shriver was speaking into the microphone.

"Pat, your family doesn't have to worry anymore. You are home, and you are safe, and you will not be forgotten," she said.

It dawned on me that this was Pat Tillman's memorial service. A week earlier, Tillman, a San Jose native and local celebrity, was killed in action in Afghanistan.

I watched for nearly an hour as celebrities and politicians all took the podium to recite canned one-liners and clichés. Toward the end, a younger man approached the podium and cracked a joke I didn't hear, which garnered a few uncomfortable chuckles.

"I didn't write shit because I'm not a writer. . . . It was amazing to be his little baby brother." His voice began to crack. "Thanks for fucking coming. Pat's a champion and always will be. Uh, just make no mistake, he'd want me to say this, he's not with God, he's fucking dead. He's not religious. Thanks for your thoughts, but he's fucking dead."

There was something excruciatingly heartbreaking about a man who gave up fame and fortune to serve his country only to die overseas. But there was something even more honorable about a man who gave up fame, fortune, and ultimately his life for something that he believed in.

The following day, I made my way down to the recruiting station and walked into the Army office.

"Change your mind?" he asked rhetorically with a smile. He knew I'd be back.

He gave me some material on Army jobs and a study guide for the ASVAB. He asked if I wanted a few weeks to study, but after flipping through the practice quiz, I was confident enough to take it on the spot. And I did. I scored within the 90th percentile of all applicants and could choose from nearly any enlisted career field in the Armed Forces. The recruiter handed me a pamphlet with a list of jobs, their training requirements, minimum commitments, and, most important, the bonuses attached to each.

Sitting on a bench in front of the station, my eyes scanned the reading material with photos of men with guns, men in helicopters, and men in tanks underscored by captions like "Always ready, always there," "Be the one your country looks to in times of need," "A modern day knight," "Your choice, your future," "Join the team that makes a difference," and other platitudes that belong on those motivational posters with bald eagles flying over snowcapped mountains.

In the middle of a completely unrealistic daydream about wearing a green beret and killing terrorists, I saw an Air Force recruiter step outside to smoke a cigarette and then eyeball my pamphlet.

"Army, huh? Those your ASVAB scores?" He gestured toward the paper on the bench next to me. "Mind if I take a look?" He grabbed the sheet and gave it a quick once-over. "You're too smart to join the Army."

I asked what he meant by that.

"I'm not trying to disparage my brothers in green. I was just saying you're an exceptional candidate and you could do better than being a grunt. Anyone can be a grunt. They're the lowest common denominator. Shit, most grunts probably can't even spell *denominator*."

"Well, I was thinking I wanted to go Special Forces," I said, which is probably something he heard from every other recruit who stepped into his office.

"You're one of those high-speed recruits, huh? What makes you think the Air Force doesn't have operators? We've got pararescue and combat controllers."

I didn't even know what those titles entailed. I'd never heard of them.

"That's because they're silent professionals. They do the real work and don't need all the accolades. They don't need movies, TV shows, and video games like the Navy SEALs do to stroke their egos. Let me ask you this—who do you think saves the SEALs when they need rescuing? I'll give you a hint: they wear Air Force uniforms. Hang tight."

The Air Force recruiter made his way indoors and returned a few seconds later with a pamphlet and a card. He scribbled his cell phone number on it.

"Don't make any rash decisions. This is your future. There's a pararescue unit ten minutes up the road in Mountain View. You wouldn't even have to leave home to join. Look that over, then give me a call. And when you're ready, I'll take you out to lunch, and I'll introduce you to the guys at Moffett."

4

SWEETHEART LIKE YOU

CHERISE WAS A fair-skinned and freckle-faced twentysomething white girl from Iowa who preferred to be called Cherry. Cherise sounded like the name of a stuffy, middle-aged white woman. Sometime in 2004 she was slapped with an unexpected rent increase by her landlord. It was an amount she couldn't possibly afford, and she only had thirty days to figure something out before she ended up on the street or a bus back to Des Moines.

Cherry didn't want to share her space with a stranger, so, like me, she worked several odd jobs on the side. At one point, she even considered stripping. After an audition with a sleazy strip club owner at the Pink Poodle, Cherry decided she'd just put an ad up on Craigslist for someone looking to sublet her extra room until she figured something out. A day later, I responded to that listing for a cozy bedroom in a quaint apartment on a quiet street.

When I showed up to that fourplex on a crowded street lined with other aging multifamily complexes to meet Cherry and tour the digs, I pretended not to be surprised by the shoebox-size room with asbestos-lined popcorn ceilings and discolored carpeting, in a two-bedroom apartment with appliances that were likely installed before the first season of *Growing Pains* aired. There was nothing cozy, quaint, or quiet about it. The place was a shithole in one of the few neighborhoods in San Jose not yet fully gentrified by the incoming throngs of well-paid nerds during the tech boom. But, like Cherry, I had few other options.

The first time I met her, I could tell she wasn't completely sold on me. I'm not sure I'd be sold on me either. Surely, there had to have been another woman with similar interests or goals looking for a place. The only folks who answered the ad were the type of people who usually answer Craigslist ads looking for a room to rent—people who are completely out of options. Of the pool of applicants who responded, I was the closest in age, didn't have a rap sheet, and didn't make any hints about sexual favors.

Claire wasn't exactly excited by the idea of me having a room-mate of the opposite sex. But her father refused to even entertain the notion of letting me stay at their house despite me having dated his daughter for the better part of four years, so her protests were short-lived. As long as I promised to "be good"—which was Claire's way of saying *Don't cheat.* Claire was cordial but brief with Cherry. And she remained suspicious of my new roommate, saying things like "I can tell by the way she looks at you that she wants to fuck you."

During sex, Claire was especially vocal, making sure her best porn-star impression could be heard through the apartment's thin walls. For Claire, it was a way of marking her territory and establishing an imaginary hierarchy with my new roommate. It was actually just good marketing for me.

Cherry worked as an elementary school teacher, so we rarely saw each other on weekdays. Occasionally, however, we caught each other on the weekends, and when we did, the exchanged pleasantries sometimes evolved into long, semi-deep conversations that didn't end until the sun came up. Cherry admitted she was sheltered and well-to-do for a majority of her life, but she dreamed of moving to

California. When she did, she suddenly found herself cut off and out on her own.

While our stories weren't exactly the same, they were similar enough. We were both struggling young adults and learning things on the go while using each other as a support system in the meantime. She would cook dinner, because she liked to, so I'd do the dishes. She would make sure the common areas were clean, and I'd take out the trash. She would buy the drugs if I rolled the joints for her, because she didn't know how (and I liked to). We were an odd couple fit for a sitcom.

The living arrangement was only supposed to last a couple months until I shipped off for basic training, but the background check for my security clearance was taking longer than anticipated. With recruitment numbers not seen since World War II, the military enlistment process turned into a long and arduous one. Lines stretched out the doors of recruiting stations, and the Department of Defense utilized a battery of aptitude testing, physicals, medical screenings, mental health evaluations, and extensive background checks to turn people away. All those hurdles still weren't enough to slow the flow of candidates from showing up, so Uncle Sam had to find other reasons to disqualify folks from service. Tattoos? Disqualified. Below average credit rating? Disqualified. Too many cavities? Disqualified.

Although I was told I'd be on a plane to San Antonio in weeks after I signed the dotted line, I still hadn't received a date to ship off to basic training. I was promised a slot as a pararescue recruit, but there were no current openings for the foreseeable future. It was the good ol' bait and switch. I was told by the recruiter I could enter a different career field and "cross train" into the job I wanted after a year or two of good service. That was mostly a lie, but I didn't know it at the time. He said the same wing had a Security Forces unit that was undermanned.

"Security Forces?"

"They're somewhere between law enforcement and light infantry," he replied. "Chuck Norris is a Security Forces alum. They're pretty fucking bad ass," he added, which was also mostly a lie.

I reluctantly agreed because I couldn't wait another year. Even then, it'd likely be another three to six months before I reported to Lackland Air Force Base, and I was running out of money. To cover the next month's rent and keep my cell phone on, I sold my Jeep. I downgraded to an old Daewoo Lanos and took a job working as a barista at a quiet coffee shop off Winchester Avenue. I just needed enough money to cover rent until I left for San Antonio—whenever that would be.

Andrea, my manager at the coffee shop, was an upper-class college student only a few years my senior. She constantly reminded me how courageous I was to enlist and how my "selflessness" was such an attractive quality. Bravery didn't really have anything to do with me being broke, bored, and wanting something better for myself. Nothing I said stopped her from regularly telling me she would pray for my safety every night when I went overseas. I tried to tell her my chances of actually deploying to a theater of combat were slim to none. And if I did, it wouldn't be for a long while.

The more likely scenario was that I'd do years of training and, by the time I was finished, the wars in Iraq and Afghanistan would be over. I mean, how long could it take to catch Bin Laden and straighten Saddam out? As far as wars go, these were supposed to be relative cakewalks.

Andrea took me downplaying my future military service as me being humble and told anyone and everyone who would listen that I was a hero. It was awkward for me, but the tip jar with the SUPPORT THE TROOPS sticker on it was constantly overflowing. It took me some time to realize I was "the troops" and she was quietly adding those tips to my paycheck to help supplement my low wages. (To this day, that might be the most support I've ever actually received for my military service.)

Andrea routinely scheduled me to work the closing shifts with her, but I didn't mind because I hated waking up early for the morning rush. While she punched numbers and closed out the register, I would organize the food displays, wash dishes, and mop the floors. She didn't like cleaning the restrooms for the obvious reason—people are fucking disgusting—so I did it for her. And she didn't like taking the trash out at night because there was a man who loitered in the alley behind our store. He made her uncomfortable, and understandably so. So I always volunteered for trash duty too.

The man in question was a transient who took shelter with his emaciated Rottweiler in a nook between a concrete wall and a dumpster in a dark corner. During one of our regular run-ins, the trash bag I was lugging split open and soggy, coffee-stained refuse spilled all over the puddle-lined pavement. When I returned with a new trash bag, the man and his dog were rummaging through the pile of expiring and half-eaten pastries. Embarrassed, he grabbed what he could, tugged his companion's leash, and backed away apologetically.

I told him an apology wasn't necessary, right before apologizing for not having any warm drinks or food to offer him. All the machines were cleaned out and shut down. Instead, I gave him two bottles of water and a bag of hard vanilla-bean scones. I told him I usually worked the night shift on weekdays and if he was ever hungry to find his way to our back door around 9:00 PM, and I would make sure to get him a hot beverage and the leftover pastries we usually just throw out. Claire would give me sample baggies of dog food and treats from her work to bring them as well. The man and his dog were in rough shape, and it's easy to see how they could make folks uncomfortable, but they were just trying to survive in a world trying to throw them away.

After an unusually hellish shift in which someone used their feces to finger-paint all over the walls in the restroom, an angry patron dumped her drink all over the counter because the temperature was not to her liking, and Andrea's angry ex-boyfriend decided to pay her a visit, we locked up and made our way to our cars. Andrea gave me a long hug, and with her face nestled in my shoulder, she cried. Then she thanked me for helping her get through the day. I told her it was the least I could do, as she'd been helping me get through most of my days. Her ringing phone interrupted the moment we were having, and the same look of panic I'd seen her wearing when her ex-boyfriend walked into the store found its way back onto her face. He was calling again. I made my way back to my car, and even with the windows fogged up, I could see her getting berated through the phone. She looked back at me as I cranked the ignition repeatedly with no luck.

"I'm closing up now. I'll be home soon. We can talk about this later," I heard her saying.

She hung up, tapped on my window, and offered to give me a ride home. Less than two minutes later, Andrea and I were parked in my driveway. My apartment was squarely between her house and the café. She said she didn't mind picking me up and dropping me off until my car was fixed. I had no intention of getting it fixed. I couldn't afford it. The car didn't even have a title, so it was more trouble than it was worth. And I'd be gone soon enough.

I thanked her for the ride, which is the part where I usually would've turned and exited; instead, we sat and stared at each other in the dark for a few seconds too long. Just like the drive there, we were silently marinating in our frustrations. The right words might've been nice, but the companionship was more than enough in the moment.

I was in the middle of telling her how much I appreciated everything she'd done for me when the bright yellow beams of a car pulling in directly behind us ended the party like the lights coming on in a bar at the end of the night. I recognized the square headlights of the black Volkswagen Jetta. It was the same car Claire and I had fucked in, fought in, or made late-night food runs in thousands of times before.

I panicked, thanked Andrea again, and quickly exited the vehicle. She didn't have to go home, she just couldn't stay there.

Claire kicked open the car door, then approached Andrea's driver's-side window like an overzealous officer during a traffic stop. Claire had some questions, and they weren't about Andrea's license and registration. Andrea started her car but wasn't going anywhere as long as Claire had her blocked in. I intercepted my angry girlfriend before she could do anything we'd both regret. I hadn't cheated, but I couldn't say that I wouldn't have given the opportunity, so I guess she had a reason to be upset. I calmed her by telling her Andrea had just given me a ride home because my car broke down. Claire's frown softened, and she retreated back to the Jetta to move it out of the way so Andrea could leave.

While Claire and Andrea jostled parking positions, I made my way inside. Cherry was sitting on the couch in a dimly lit room in a lace bralette and mismatching lace panties, smoking the joint I had rolled for her the night before. Again, I panicked.

"What're you doing?!"

"Nothing. Just getting comfortable after a long day of chasing shitty kids around. You don't want to join me?"

She wrapped her lips around the tip and took a long drag. This felt like a trap. I told her I would join her later. But I really *really* needed her to remove herself and her unexpectedly very fit body from the room. I was already skating on thin ice, and if my girlfriend walked in on me entertaining Cherry with her cheeks out, it would've been the inciting incident for World War III. And I wasn't ready for combat just yet.

Cherry didn't put up a fight and did as I asked. She wasn't the confrontational type either.

After Claire and I fucked, fought, and ate like we did most Friday nights, she left, and I made my way to the couch and watched the late-night news in a daze. I rolled another joint, and when I looked up, Cherry was sitting in the chair adjacent to the love seat.

"Is the coast clear?" she asked sarcastically. "Can I join you now or is she still on a rampage?"

"This is your house. You can do whatever you want."

She'd actually paid for the weed I was smoking, so I tried to hand her the joint. She waved me off. Instead, she laid back, made herself comfortable by propping one leg up on the arm of her seat. She looked me directly in the eyes, pulled her panties to the side and touched herself in front of me. This was not the reserved elementary school teacher I thought I'd moved in with.

"Why are you doing this?" I asked.

"You just said I could do whatever I want." She had me there. "And I like when people watch."

At least she was honest about it. My better judgment told me to get up and leave the room. The blunt I'd just rolled was packed with a strain called Gorilla Glue #4 I'd gotten from Mike and Chris. And like its moniker suggested, it made me one with the couch. I couldn't get myself up if I wanted to. I pretended not to watch Cherry, but I kept glancing over through the gray haze separating us. There was no point in protesting. When she was done, she stood, collected herself, then kissed me on the top of my head as she made her way back to her room.

The following Monday, I received my work schedule. I'd been moved from night shifts with Andrea to the day shift. I understood completely. Andrea was already dealing with her psychotic ex-boyfriend; she didn't need to deal with my understandably insecure girlfriend as well.

A few days later, in the middle of a lunch rush hour, I was paid a visit by two NSA officers. (I believe they were actually agents from the National Background Investigations Bureau's Office of Personnel Management, but that's a mouthful.) They looked like Tommy Lee Jones and Will Smith in *Men in Black*: black glasses, black suits, black ties, a black government car—they even ordered their coffee black.

I asked the new shift lead if I could take an early break, and she agreed without hesitation. She wasn't going to say no to a couple of guys carrying guns. My years of illegal Napster and LimeWire downloads had caught up with me, and I was ready to accept a plea deal for lesser charges.

The agents sat me down on the patio and went through a three-inch thick dossier of my personal and financial affairs. They had copies of my credit reports, noting every late card payment, every overdraft fee, and essentially every poor financial decision I'd ever made, which usually stemmed from being poor. Some days I had to decide between eating and paying my credit card bill. Some days I couldn't do either.

They asked me about some of the girls I dated. They also asked if I dated boys. I didn't date boys, and although I knew the answer, I wanted to ask why that would be a problem if I did, but I kept my mouth shut. They asked if I liked animals. I said of course. Who doesn't like animals? They clarified that they were inquiring if I was interested in animals sexually. No, obviously. But that question got me thinking—how many military recruits admit to fucking livestock? The answer is nonzero if they even had to ask.

The agents also had copies of both my high school and college transcripts. They'd interviewed some of my teachers, professors, and classmates. They had my employment records. They'd spoken with bosses and coworkers. Big Brother knew everything about me. It was equal parts terrifying and impressive.

They asked me about my history of drug use. My friend Eric had a brother who was addicted to meth, or maybe it was crack. I wasn't well versed in the particulars of street narcotics, but the occasional run-ins with him were enough to scare me straight. I'd only "experimented" with alcohol, marijuana, and mushrooms "once or twice," I said. I would've failed a polygraph test had I been given one. I thought this a reasonable enough answer and was expecting the agents to be on their way. They were just getting warmed up. One of the agents asked if I was a Communist sympathizer. *A what now? Why would I be?* They followed up by asking if I had contact with anyone in North Korea, China, or Russia.

Huh? To be honest, I wasn't even totally sure what Communism was or what it entailed. I knew that being called a Commie generally had negative connotations, but I must've slept through that chapter in AP History. My mother was born in Korea, but she grew up in a suburb of Seoul, and she'd since become an American citizen. Me, a Communist? It was such a bizarre accusation I actually laughed. Which is exactly when they dropped the bomb on me. I, Dylan Park-Pettiford, am the grandson of Kyu-Man Park, a documented Communist and former combatant for the Korean People's Army. And they didn't find that funny in the least. This made me a potential threat to national security. If there was evidence I was a foreign agent attempting to infiltrate the Department of Defense—and they were doing their damnedest to find that evidence—I'd be staring down time in Fort Leavenworth federal penitentiary.

After the agents left, I went back to going through the motions of making overpriced lattes while staring off into the distance thinking about what had just happened. The sound of approaching sirens in the distance caught my attention. They weren't cop cars coming to apprehend me. Two fire engines followed by an ambulance cut through the parking lot and made their way behind the building. I poked my head out the back door and watched as the medics carefully approached the same Rottweiler I'd given cups of water to so many times before. I assured them the dog was friendly and called the dog over. It didn't move, so I went to go grab him.

On the other side of the dumpster, paramedics were attempting to revive the homeless man.

5

SEOUL MEETS BODY

ON FEBRUARY 6, 1919, just days after the emperor's death and weeks before the March First Movement—the prologue to Korea's declaration of independence from Imperial Japan—my grandfather Kyu-Man Park was born to Kim Myeong-Sun in a sleepy mountainside village in Pyongyang. While Korea's cries for freedom were being brutally suppressed by the Japanese government and demonstrators were being executed in the streets—over seventy-five hundred people were killed and another fifty thousand were arrested during the protests—Kim was hiding away from her own abusers.

Birthing a son in secret during a violent revolution was a fitting progression for the rebellious young woman who is regarded as being Korea's first feminist author. Sun's first published work came at twenty-one in the form of a short story called "A Girl in Doubt" (or "Suspicious Girl," depending on the translation). Two years later, she joined *Creation*, an influential magazine credited with setting the stage for Korea's literary style. In 1925, under a pseudonym, Kim sold a book titled *The Fruit of Life*, making her the first woman from the isolated peninsular country to publish a book of poetry.

Kim was also multilingual. When she wasn't writing her own prose and poetry, she produced the first Korean translations of Western poets like Edgar Allan Poe and Charles Baudelaire. In an era when the concept of feminism did not yet exist, she argued that increased involvement by women in the political sphere could bring about world peace. Kim was an open champion of free love and may have been bisexual, making her the subject of unrelenting abuse by both her seniors and her peers, some of whom she had once considered friends.

Kim's sociopolitical leanings rubbed everyone around her the wrong way, but she would not be silenced, and she refused to change her stance. She worked as a journalist for a local newspaper and even tried her hand in cinematography two decades before the Golden Age of Cinema in Asia. But no matter how many truths Kim wrote on paper or told on the screen, she couldn't outrun her own truth. She was the daughter of a comfort girl, and my grandfather was likely the product of rape, which only made the criticism from those around her worse.

In the early stages of Kim's artistic awakening, her writing carried a hopeful tenor. In a poem titled "Pomegranate," Kim submits that "whether [she] loves or hates, life merely flows." As Kim's mental health devolved over the years, so did the topics of her poetry and prose. In "Battle," a more political piece, she tells the tale of an old soldier "paralyzed in sleep" by "heavy thoughts." In the last stanza, the soldier dies and people turn their heads to ignore him. She was writing about PTSD and veterans issues decades before PTSD was even recognized by the *Diagnostic and Statistical Manual of Mental Disorders* as a legitimate medical ailment.

Cast out by society for her radical beliefs, Kim was eventually forced to flee to Japan, where she would spend the rest of her life in a psychiatric ward on the outskirts of Tokyo, penniless and alone. Before departing Korea for the last time, she penned a poem forebodingly titled "A Will":

Joseon,* when I part from you,
Whether you knock me down by a creek
Or yank my blood in the field,
Abuse me more, even my dead corpse.
If this is still not enough,
Then abuse her as much as you can
When someone like me is born henceforth.
Then we, who despise each other, will be parted forever.
Oh, you ferocious place, you ferocious place.

Shortly before her death in 1951, Kim's estranged adult son was conscripted into the North Korean military to fight Americans and his fellow countrymen south of the 38th parallel for no other reason than living on the wrong side of an arbitrary line when Korea was divided into two following World War II. The story goes that when American GIs ambushed Kyu-Man's squad, killing several of his comrades, Kyu played dead and was lucky enough to escape with some frostbite and bullet fragments in his ass.

During the tail end of the Forgotten War, he defected across the border under a hail of gunfire—this time from his North Korean counterparts—hoping that one day he would be able to send for his family. Young-Ae's biological mother and siblings never escaped North Korea.

As with many other Koreans, the line cutting the country in half fractured our family. Kyu was never able to reunite with his first wife or the rest of his children. My mother has siblings she hasn't seen since she was an infant. And it's unlikely she'll ever see them again, as they're likely all dead now.

---

* Joseon was the dynasty that preceded the Korean Empire. However, it was still commonly used as a moniker for Korea into the early 1900s.

I called my mother the evening after being interrogated by the alphabet agents. The answer was an obvious one, and it may have been ill-mannered to ask her why she never told me about our family's true origins, but I did anyway. In the moment, I wasn't concerned about the trauma I may have been unlocking; I was more worried that I was unknowingly lying about being the descendant of an enemy of the state. *Ignorantia juris non excusat.* In court, "ignorance of the law excuses not," and I easily could have found myself disqualified from military service. I told her I wanted to know everything she knew about her family.

She answered all the questions she could. She showed me the time-stained black-and-white pictures that had been tucked away for decades in the back of family photo albums. She let me dig through her father's belongings locked away in public storage. She did her best to accommodate me during my newfound mission of existential self-discovery.

I soon realized that in order to unlock the truth of my family's history, I needed to work my way from the present backward. To understand my grandfather's story, I first needed to know the details of my mother's upbringing, which started with my mother emigrating from South Korea to Los Angeles. After a few years in Southern California, Kyu-Man, Young-Ae, and Oak-Sim, my grandfather's new wife, ventured to the San Francisco Bay Area, where they would join other immigrants in a newly burgeoning Korean community in a small town called Campbell, California.

The Campbell, California, Rory and I called home wasn't the rustic Rockwell painting of my mom's youth. To those who had lived there long enough, Campbell was known as the Orchard City. As a teenager, my mother walked past farmland and through groves full of colorful fruit trees on her way to and from school. Over the years, my mother watched as high-rise buildings appeared on the horizon. Expressways took the place of the unincorporated dirt roads, crisscrossing the city, dividing it into quarters. Old farm houses with acres of land began to disappear; in their place apartments, condos, and homes rose from the dirt.

The stories of the old Orchard City sounded nice, but that place was completely foreign to Rory and me; it was *long* gone. Nowadays, the only reminders of Campbell's agrarian past are seen every Sunday at a vibrant farmers' market; at night on the town's skyline, in the form of a colorful water tower; and down below on the old railroad tracks that once led to and from the city's canneries, where the world's first fruit salad was invented in 1893, but now only served to ruin the suspension and alignment of cars passing through.

Despite all of its changes, some heirlooms from prior generations remained for us to relish. After getting out of class, Rory and I would cross the bridge that led over the expressway into John D. Morgan Park, where my mother would sit in the fields and draw sketches of the ever-changing landscape. From the park, I would walk down Rincon Avenue, stop at the Korean-owned hot dog stand at the intersection with Winchester Boulevard, and buy some curly fries and root beer floats for Rory and me, just as my mother and her sister did when they were teens. My mother's unfamiliarity with the new Orchard City did not dissuade her from starting a family there. She grew up to love Campbell, and she tried to make sure Rory and I would too.

But the Campbell I knew was no longer where Jack Kerouac spent time loading boxcars for gas money to continue the cross-country road trip he wrote about in his postwar novel *On the Road*. Four decades later, Kerouac's rhythmic Beat prose would be replaced by the gravelly screaming of Rancid's lead singer Lars Frederiksen, who recounted his time growing up in Campbell on the group's hit track "Roots Radicals": "Took the 60 Bus, out of Downtown Campbell. . . .

Somethin' struck me funny when we ran out of money. Where do you go now when you're only fifteen?"

Rory and I drifted back and forth between Black culture and a growing counterculture consisting mostly of jaded, lower-middle-class Caucasian kids. We grew up listening to both rap and punk rock, and if we weren't shooting hoops on the courts with our basketball coach Raymond Townsend—a biracial man who would go onto be the first Filipino American to play in the NBA—we were imitating the moves of the local skateboarding legend Steve Caballero down at the skate park at the Campbell Community Center.

From the outside, the old Campbell was a quaint suburb in the San Francisco Bay Area, with picturesque homes on shady tree-lined streets. Fancy restaurants and expensive boutiques lined Campbell Avenue, but it wasn't out of the ordinary to find a heroin addict or two slumped over in the shadows of dumpsters in the back alleyways. Like a lot of small American towns, drugs found their way into the Orchard and took hold. This mini epidemic went unchecked for years because so many of its residents were willfully ignorant of the growing problem. Admitting to the problem would only bring attention to it and drive housing prices down.

Drugs were becoming readily available, and for a lot of these kids, experimentation with narcotics quickly turned to addiction. That addiction often led to desperation, and desperation transformed into a subsection of forgotten youth who relegated themselves to lives of petty crime. At the time, the police presence in the Orchard was almost nonexistent, so groups of restless teenagers did whatever they wanted and ran roughshod in the background of the quiet community, like bad movie extras. The dropout rates rose exponentially, so much so that the Campbell Union School District opened up a continuation school for the droves of teenagers who were at risk of not graduating.

Our parents saw to it that we wouldn't have enough free time to even contemplate getting in trouble. They both took on extra jobs to pay for the tuition to send us to St. Lawrence Academy, a private Catholic K–12 school two towns over. After school, Rory and I had basketball or football practice, followed by tutoring. After tutoring, we'd go to tae kwon do lessons or whatever bullshit extracurricular activity my mom's work colleagues were making their kids do at the time. It was a lot.

While their logic was sound, placing Rory and me into a private school introduced us to the depravity they sought to hide us from. I'd never seen drugs in the flesh or had access to alcohol before being surrounded by a bunch of rich kids. My parents had unknowingly opened the fast lane to our delinquency.

Because St. Lawrence was a private school exempt from the regulations of the California public school system, corporal punishment was legal. I found myself being paddled or smacked with rulers in the principal's office on a regular basis. In sixth grade, Sister Murphy caught me writing a note to Becky Westover and launched a chalkboard eraser at my head with surprising accuracy. It was funny to the class until the nun followed that up by declaring I was acting "niggardly." Even a classroom full of privileged white kids who said racist shit to me all the time knew that was a no-no.

The next day my father walked into the office and did his best Johnnie Cochran impersonation. He and the diocese agreed that my junior high and high school education would be tuition-free for the foreseeable future, lest they find themselves on the wrong side of a very ugly lawsuit.

The truth is, Rory and I didn't belong in a Catholic school. We were the only two non-Catholics in attendance, and though we were encouraged (with threats of eternal damnation) to accept the three sacraments—baptism, confirmation, and the Holy Eucharist—I absolutely refused.

As a curious child sitting in the pews of the church during weekly mass, I had a lot of genuine questions about my God-fearing environs.

I couldn't have been the only one who thought it was strange to be talking to an invisible guy who lives in a cloud. In any other institution outside of religion, hearing voices and talking to invisible people would ensure you were committed to a psych ward, right? Also, the symbology was terrifying. Why are we praying to a twelve-foot-tall statue of a guy stapled to a cross? Why are we drinking his blood and eating his body? Isn't that cannibalism? Is it true that every Catholic Church houses relics? If so, why are they keeping the toe of Saint Thomas in a glass box behind the altar? This didn't strike anyone else as odd? I wasn't going to submit myself to the Lord and Savior until I got some answers. And I never really did.

Over the years at St. Lawrence, I learned to go through the theological motions. Then, during my sophomore year, I'd decided I'd had enough. During a mandatory monthly prayer service at school, I was randomly selected to lead the invocation. I didn't really know any prayers outside of a few lines I'd learned watching *Sister Act* as a kid. I stood up in the front of the entire school, took a deep breath, and began to recite the Lord's Prayer. When I began to stumble and stutter somewhere around "thy kingdom come," a group of nuns shot me death stares that could cut though the armor of an M1 Abrams main battle tank. And that was the spark that lit the fuse to my anti-hero origin story.

I thought *Fuck it* and went full heel. I was tired of pretending, so I directed my attention to the priests and asked why Christians were always so fucking judgmental. Sister Murphy stood and walked toward me, telling me to choose my next words more carefully. The next words that came from my mouth would determine the length and severity of my punishment. I chose to tell her I was pro-choice and they might be too if they knew that two of my classmates had already had abortions. I took it one further and told the faculty to stop condemning homosexuality, because another kid in my class spent the weekend in a halfway house for trying to kill himself after being told repeatedly that being gay is a sin. Then, I followed that up by admitting I didn't even believe in God.

Father Milkemeyer yanked my Black ass off that stage with divine speed, and as I was ushered off, some of my classmates wished me Godspeed. Meanwhile, my brother and his friends were in the crowd laughing hysterically.

Even after all of that, I was only suspended for a week. Blessed are the merciful, for they will be shown mercy or some shit like that, right? That mercy didn't last long after an altar boy walked in on me getting a hand job in the church rectory from a chubby Mexican girl. That was the last straw for Father Milkemeyer and Sister Murphy. They gave me a choice: I could remove myself from St. Lawrence voluntarily, or they could expel me, which would make getting into any decent college nearly impossible. I didn't even want to be there, so the decision to transfer to Westmont High School, the local public school my mom and aunt had attended as teenagers, was an easy one.

For the following year, our parents gave Rory and me an impossibly long list of weekly chores to do to teach us a lesson. If we somehow managed to complete that list, we had mandatory reading time or Bible study—especially ironic for a non-churchgoing family, with a son who was just kicked out of a Catholic school for denouncing religion (and getting jerked off in the back of the church). I think the idea was that we wouldn't have idle hands like some of the other troubled kids in our neighborhood. As we grew older, some of those other troubled kids would eventually get their shit together. Others would move into their parents' basements or join gangs.

There were the Nortenos on Cadillac Drive who jumped my brother as he was walking out of a McDonald's. There were the Sobrato Drive Surenos who jumped me in front of my school because I was wearing red, all while the students and faculty watched in horror. There were the Lost Boys, a bunch of rich kids who drove around in tricked-out cars and lowered trucks. (The first installment of *The Fast and the Furious* franchise had just kicked off in theaters, so souped-up Japanese cars with ridiculous paint jobs were very in. Rest in Peace, Paul Walker.) Then there were the white supremacists who called themselves SPG—MAGA members before the MAGA movement had a moniker. They were the Ku Klux Klan's junior varsity team.

Being two of a handful of Black residents in the Orchard presented a problem for Rory and me. We found ourselves getting into a lot of fist fights with a lot of racist white boys. Under the rare circumstances the authorities actually intervened, Rory and I were always labeled as the aggressors. During my first of many encounters with SPG, two of those assholes—Chunk, a skinhead, Carhartt-wearing, steel toe–booted big body, and Oswald, a goofy-looking motherfucker who looked like he'd repeated the twelfth grade several times because he had a full beard and tattoos—pinned me up against a wall as I was walking out of class and warned me not to fuck with SPG.

"What's SPG stand for?" I asked.

"Savage Pimp Gang," Chunk said without a hint of irony before flashing a gang sign.

I probably shouldn't have laughed, but I did. They beat my ass, and instead of crying or screaming for help, I laughed more. That made them angrier, so they kicked and punched me harder, and in return I laughed even harder. They started calling me the "funny nigger" after that.

I quickly made a reputation for being a class clown and was always making fun of myself to the delight of others. Clowning myself took the ammo away from any would-be bullies. I didn't know it at the time, but my self-deprecating sense of humor would become a defense mechanism for me that was stronger than any Kevlar body armor I ever wore.

6

STRANGE FRUIT TREES

AS WITH MY mother's family, the roots of my father's family tree were buried deep, and I'd have to do a lot of digging to find anything at all. I knew nothing about the Pettifords, which meant there were things I didn't know about myself. My old man wasn't an immigrant, but growing up in Leesville, Louisiana, during the heart of the civil rights movement, he may as well have been. My father's mother, Dolores Maedelle Cobbs, was an Army nurse at Fort Polk, a military installation that served as a training ground for soldiers before they shipped off to Vietnam. The swampy, jungle-like vegetation, heat, humidity, and precipitation of Louisiana made it the perfect place for infantrymen to become acclimated to the extreme conditions they would face in Southeast Asia. My old man was the byproduct of one of the hundreds of thousands of troops who passed through during the twenty-year-long conflict.

Pops never mentioned anything about his own father, and the few times I asked, I was told he died when my dad was a child. I assumed this was code for Gramps being a deadbeat. He'd probably just up and left his baby mama and kids as men are known to do from time to time. Eventually, I stopped probing for details, because I stopped caring. My old man would fill me in when he was good and ready, but that never happened.

As a child, it was difficult hearing my closest friends talk about their grandparents with loving reverence. I loved going to Brandon's grandparents' house after school and listening to his grandpa's World War II stories. Every so often Maca, Brandon's grandma, would enter the room and chide Papa, saying his war stories weren't appropriate for children. Papa would feign remorse and stop to appease her wishes, then as soon as she exited, he'd start right back up again with a smile.

Papa had a faded tattoo of Donald Duck on his forearm that he'd gotten during his time in the Marine Corps. I would hold his hand and trace the art with my finger while he told me about fighting on islands in the Pacific I'd never heard of. I would ask him to tell me about the time he sprayed Japanese soldiers with flame throwers, not knowing that I was making his lifelong trauma my entertainment. Papa knew I was young and that I didn't know better, and if telling his stories put a smile on my face, he was more than glad to do so no matter how hard that might have been for him.

Nearly twenty years later, I went over to Brandon's house for Thanksgiving. His entire family was there: his father, his mother, his stepfather, his aunts, his uncles, his cousins, his nieces, his nephews, and of course Papa and Maca. They'd all watched me grow from adolescence to adulthood, and they'd often introduce me as their son or a cousin to their friends. I'd spent more time with them than my own extended family.

When I arrived that evening, Brandon pulled me to the side to tell me Maca was suffering from late-stage Alzheimer's. She didn't know who her own children and grandchildren were, and she wasn't too sure about Papa either. Brandon apologized in advance and told me not to take it personally if she said something insulting or was afraid of me.

I wasn't sure what to expect, and I was cautious to approach Maca, but when she saw me, her eyes lit up. She held my face. Brandon's family watched in awe, while Maca talked to me with a clarity and exuberance they rarely saw anymore. I hadn't seen her in decades, and Maca remembered me like I'd never left.

Papa and Maca were the favorite of all my friends' grandparents. I found it intriguing how different all of my friends' families were. All of their grandparents had divergent backstories and circumstances. Some were rich, some were poor. Some of them were racist, others held signs on picket lines as champions of civil rights. Some were still functioning, while others needed supervision around the clock. However, the one thing they all had in common was that they liked to spoil their grandkids for any occasion imaginable, and as a child it was hard for me not to be envious.

But the thing about grandparents is they die. As we grew older and the list of obituaries lengthened, conversations changed from birthday presents to inheritances. I watched other teenagers divvy up their grandparents' estates. Brian got an old Toyota Camry with no miles on it and some money for college. Eric got a cherry '69 Cadillac Coupe de Ville and $10,000 in cash, which he promptly spent on a drum kit and weed. Brandon got the keys to the house I'd spent many afternoons in, which would later sell for millions. Me? I didn't even know my grandfather's name. I resigned myself to the fact that I'd have no help in the future. And to me, that was fine. I couldn't miss something I never had, so I thought about my absentee grandfather less and less until he was all but forgotten.

Then, in college while working on a family-history research assignment for an anthropology class, I went down the Pettiford family rabbit hole. Over the years, the advent of ancestry websites and DNA technology assisted in this search for my beginnings, and I was able to travel back to the 1800s in search of my people. (Anything before that was nearly impossible to track down, because of that whole slavery thing.)

Evidence of the first Pettifords in the United States can be found in the North Carolina State Public Record in a legal paper called the

Pettiford Treason Document. The report states that in August 1732, three slaves named Tom, Primus, and Hannah Pettiford were freed after their owner, Captain John Pettiford, was "murthered" by his wife, Anne, with the help of an overseer named Joseph Haynes. Both Anne and Joseph were found guilty, then burned at the stake and hung, respectively.

Just a few decades later, several more Pettiford men would earn their freedom by fighting in the Revolutionary War for their white landowners, according to censuses taken in 1790 and 1810 in both North Carolina and Virginia. (Poor people of color in America have been fighting wars for white benefactors since day one—more on that later.) William, George, and Phillip Pettiford, along with a man named Valentine Locus, the husband of one Rachel Pettiford, all applied for their pensions for service during the Revolution.

And thus began a tradition of Pettiford men fighting in every one of America's major conflicts. It's even in our name. The name Pettiford is derived from a Norman house established after the Conquest of 1066. From the Old French word *pedefer*, or *pied de fer*, meaning "iron foot," the name is thought to have been given to a knight who lost his foot in battle, which is fitting. My father joked that Pettiford men do two things extremely well: fight wars and die young—a familial prophecy, or curse, I'd much rather break than fulfill. Even if that makes me the Black Lieutenant Dan.

Nearly a century after the Revolutionary War, Confederate soldiers in Fort Pillow, Tennessee, slaughtered an all-Black regiment of the Union Army—most of whom were former slaves—as they attempted to surrender. A few months later, my ancestors Edward, Reuben, and Wiley Pettiford would return the favor. As members of the Twenty-Eighth Regiment of the Colored Infantry, they fought at the Siege of Petersburg. This time, when the Confederates tried to surrender, the Union Army gave no quarter to the Rebels and bayoneted every last Gray Coat. Edward was wounded from a shell blast at the Battle of

Crater and, starting in 1911, spent most of his last days in the National Home for Disabled Volunteer Soldiers in Danville, Illinois, passing away in 1926, a little over a month after leaving the facility.

In 1873, less than two decades after the end of the Civil War, William R. Pettiford—a businessman, educator, and minister—opened the First Colored Baptist Church of Birmingham. That church would later be known as the 16th Street Baptist Church—yes, *that* 16th Street Baptist Church. It was the same church that served as the organizational headquarters for the civil rights movement, the same church that was bombed by the Ku Klux Klan on September 15, 1963, taking the lives of four young girls—Addie Mae Collins, Cynthia Wesley, Carole Robertson, and Carol Denise McNair. The attack was recounted by Martin Luther King Jr. as "one of the most vicious and tragic crimes ever perpetrated against humanity." *That* church.

During my extensive research, I learned about a number of the interesting characters I share blood with, having legacies that will live forever, like the aforementioned William R. Pettiford, who was described as the Black man who did more to "elevate his race" during that era outside of anyone not named Booker T. Washington. There's the legendary jazz musician, Oscar Pettiford, who was the bandmate of Dizzy Gillespie, John Coltrane, Duke Ellington, Miles Davis, and Thelonious Monk. He also discovered Cannonball Adderley. But for every William or Oscar, there's a much longer list of Pettifords that history would much rather forget, as evidenced by their rap sheets, mugshots, and cause of death listed on their death certificates. One of those Pettifords was my grandfather.

On an overnighter in the school library, I stumbled across an article about a cold case murder in Killeen, Texas. The photo of the victim showed a man who looked like a carbon copy of my father. Up until that moment, I knew nothing of the man. The only thing I was certain of was that his name was Joseph Pettiford. I didn't know he was a sergeant in the US Army stationed at Fort Hood—one of the bases I would eventually train at. I didn't know he was a combat veteran. I didn't know he enlisted when he was eighteen and fought in Korea. I didn't know he reenlisted and served in Vietnam. And I definitely didn't know he was gunned down in cold blood one night while sitting on his couch watching television after putting his children to bed.

Another photo on the website showed Joseph standing next to a white woman, surrounded by several different light-skinned Black children. To the dismay of local residents, Joseph married a wealthy Caucasian woman whose family had political clout. Interracial marriage had only been made legal seven years earlier in Texas, and in a place like Killeen it was still very much frowned upon. And despite having a larger Black population because of the military installation next door, Killeen was, and still is, a successful recruiting area for the Ku Klux Klan.

Immediately following his nuptials, Joseph received several threats on his life. If my grandfather was anything like I am now, he likely laughed them off or told them to go fuck themselves. And they probably didn't like that. Folks who were close to my grandfather posit his death was at the hands of police officers who were members of the local KKK chapter. His murder is still listed as a cold case by the Killeen Police Department. Texas Attorney General Ken Paxton's office has blocked several of my attempts to gather information on my grandfather's murder, citing it as "an open investigation" nearly fifty years later. The more likely explanation is that Paxton is just another good ol' boy holding the thin blue line.

Following his father's death, my old man ran away from home, forged documents saying he was eighteen, then joined the Navy. After being out in the middle of the ocean for months, young Rory was seasick and homesick. He gave himself up to his commanding officer, admitting he was underage and had joined illegally. Rory was kicked off the boat the second the ship reached port. After returning to the South, he packed a truck with his older half brother and drove across the country from East Texas to Oakland, California, to stay with some of their cousins.

Just a few years later, while attending high school at Castlemont, Rory laid eyes on Young-Ae at the disco. Although my mother was only a few years removed from emigrating to America and spoke broken English, it was not enough to dissuade my father from trying to strike up a conversation. My father would say, "Love is a universal language," but in reality, he was just a horny teenager who followed her around all night until she agreed to go on a date with him—which, in hindsight, is really predatory, and dudes really need to stop doing that shit, but I digress.

They quickly fell in love and eloped at eighteen. Cultural differences (read: racism) saw to it that my mother was estranged from her family after marrying a Black man. The rift between the Black and Korean communities in California had been growing for decades and reached cataclysmic levels following the L.A. Riots. And it's one that I've experienced firsthand my entire life. I was never accepted by my Korean peers as one of theirs—or by my Black peers, for that matter. I was stuck somewhere in the void in between for a majority of my youth.

Socially and culturally, my folks could not have been more different. Geographically, they came from opposite ends of the planet. My father's people were slaves brought over from West Africa to Haiti, the poorest country in the Western Hemisphere. My mother's people were the products of a violent Communist regime in the most isolated country on the planet. And somehow Providence brought them together. Had things gone a little differently, the universe might've seen to it that my grandparents killed each other on a battlefield somewhere in East Asia, and I wouldn't be sitting here writing about generational trauma and how peculiar the Park-Pettiford family dynamic is.

Uncle Sam doesn't care about cute stories or kismet either. As long as I was physically and mentally fit, he'd hand me a rifle to wage war under his banner.

7

TO THE COLORS

ILLUMINATED BY A wall sconce, a lonely vending machine filled with candy, chips, cookies, and other treats sat on a dark concrete paddock, beckoning us. Across the sprawling field to our right, the golden arches of a McDonald's peered over a twelve-foot-high concrete wall topped with razor wire. Lit up like a beacon in the early morning darkness, it was a reminder of simpler times. Surrounded by dozens of other bald, zit-faced recruits in neat columns and rows, I stood at attention inhaling the aroma of the french fries I wouldn't taste for months. We weren't being waterboarded or anything, but this was torture.

After another long day of physical training and verbal berating, we were dismissed and retreated back to our barracks for the evening. The fifteen minutes of free time before "lights out" was the only time we had to ourselves. There were a few loners here and there, but for the most part, others used the time to socialize. Those fifteen minutes a day were the only real social normalcy we got. We joked, talked a little shit, told each other about our backgrounds, and shared photos of our girlfriends with one another.

Every once in a while, one of the fellas had a lady who was a smoke show waiting for him back home, but more often than not, photos of women or children who aren't what society would consider classically attractive were passed around, and we'd all say something like, "Aw, beautiful family man" and kept it moving. Basic training was already hard enough. There was no need to tell some guy his loved ones were ugly.

When I bragged about how hot my girlfriend was with a wallet-sized bikini photo I kept in my locker, the white trainees joked that they wanted to borrow the pic before they went to bed. Jonesy, one of the few Black airmen, said he was disappointed I was dating a vanilla white girl and asked why I couldn't find myself a wholesome Black woman. It's not that I wasn't attracted to Black women—I'm not some self-hating Negro. The town my parents moved me to as a child didn't have many Black folks. I was one of a handful of Black kids in a high school with twelve hundred students—so, statistically, the chances of me even finding a Black girl were slim to none. Then there's the part where she actually had to like me. I was just dating a girl who treated me decently.

Plus, Claire had a booty like a Black girl. Jonesy asked for photographic proof to corroborate these claims. When presented, he was somewhat satisfied with my assessment. Then he countered that Claire probably smelled like wet dog. And I couldn't help but laugh.

Greco, an airman we called Gecko for his slender, almost-amphibian appearance, took a seat on the bunk across from me. "I have fire watch tonight," he said with a whisper.

"I'm not trading with you, so don't even ask," I replied.

Fire monitors were a rotation of sad souls assigned to stand guard for a few hours in the middle of the night while everyone else slept. They were the first line of defense for any potential threats and were there to sound the alarm in case of an emergency like a fire. I was already the acting "latrine queen," a title given to the recruit designated to make sure the restroom facilities were cleaned immaculately. This wasn't my favorite job, but it was certainly better than being assigned to the kitchen patrol, or KP duty, for which a recruit spent their mornings or evenings working directly under the kitchen staff. Duties typically included food preparation, bussing tables, and washing the dishes. The "house mouse" was the drill instructor's personal assistant and secretary. The "dorm chief" was the kid, or kiss-ass, who ran the day-to-day operations when the DIs weren't present and reported back to them with any grievances. In other words, they were snitches.

The contrived hostility coming from the drill sergeants was designed to elicit a response from the recruits to get an idea of our personalities, and they'd assign us to different positions accordingly. Everyone had a role.

"That's not what I'm asking. I'm taking orders," Gecko said with his hand partially covering his mouth like we were two spies in a clandestine meeting.

"Orders for what?" I asked, slightly confused.

"I'm raiding the vending machine." I sat up a little straighter. He had my attention. "Twenty bucks, and I'll get you whatever you want."

Twenty dollars was a steep price, but Gecko was essentially risking his neck to make a few bucks. It was dumb, but I respected the hustle. The vending machine was strictly off limits to anyone but the drill instructors and training cadre. And there was no honor system here. The vending machine was located right next to their office and was under the watch of two security cameras. This was a *Mission Impossible*–level heist, and if Gecko was caught, he was looking at being recycled back to the first week of basic training at best, and possibly an other-than-honorable discharge for theft.

I told him if he was caught, I would disavow all knowledge of his antics, then gave him twenty dollars for a Snickers bar, shook his hand, and wished him well, like he was about to parachute into Nazi Germany under the cover of darkness. Gecko went around the room asking anyone who he thought might be interested in his offer, ignoring the recruits who looked like they would snitch. I crawled into my bunk and watched as Gecko quickly stuffed hundreds of dollars into his locker. The drill instructor entered moments later to make one last check on us before shutting off the lights.

"Good night, ladies!" he yelled.

"Good night, sir!" we responded in unison.

A few hours later, I was awoken by Gecko standing over me, smiling like the Cheshire cat with a Snickers bar in hand. He placed it on my chest and then moved on to his next customer. I rolled out of bed, quietly opened my footlocker, hid the candy bar in a roll of socks, then got back in my bunk and closed my eyes.

Hours later, a blaring bugle jarred us from our sleep. Like lemmings, we all poked our heads out from under the bunks one by one to look at the clock on the wall: *4:00 AM. You have got to be shitting me.* The obnoxious reveille was followed up by two equally obnoxious drill instructors who were foaming at the mouths—Technical Sergeant Zurita and Staff Sergeant Odom—flying into the room, flipping beds, and screaming at anything with a pulse.

Taylor, the airman in the bunk next to me, was slow to rise. When he turned toward me, he had chocolate smeared all over his face and sheets. He saw the fear in my eyes and began to panic. If he was caught, the instructors would've torn the room apart from the floors up, likely would've discovered our illegal contraband, and we all would've been hemmed up. I had to think of something quick.

"Clean your fucking face up. I'm going to tell the DIs you shit yourself," I whispered to Taylor.

"What?!"

"Clean your face and pull the sheets off your bed and act like you're sick," I repeated, this time through clenched teeth. "Just fucking do it, man."

I made a beeline to intercept Sergeant Zurita. I stood in front of him at attention.

"Sir, Airman Park-Pettiford reports as ordered!"

"What is it, shit stain?" The response was so topical it threw me for a loop.

"Um. Uh . . ." I couldn't formulate a sentence.

"Get it out, or get the fuck outta my way."

"Sir, Airman Taylor came down with a stomach bug in the middle of the night. And he, uh, he soiled his sheets."

We both turned and looked at Taylor, who was hunched over doing a comically bad job feigning illness. He had his sheets balled up in his arms and the brown stains were partially visible. Zurita took a step toward him and decided against it. Instead, he ordered me to escort Taylor to the medics.

Having a semester's worth of college credits earned me an extra stripe on my sleeve and a negligible pay increase to go along with it. But being nineteen years old made me a senior citizen in basic training. As such, I was constantly trying to guide other young men in the right direction. Getting a bunch of teenage boys to act right was a fool's errand, but I tried anyway. I was just tired of having to pay for everyone else's fuck-ups. Eventually, my assertiveness was misconstrued as having the traits of a natural-born lower-level supervisor, and I was appointed the role of element leader. Like the title suggests, each EL was assigned to marshal a handful of airmen called an element or a fire team.

We were divided by last names, so my fire team consisted of Montgomery, a hulking goofball with thick glasses and a thicker Midwest *dontchaknow* accent; Olsen, a Mormon kid who regularly tried to convert me under the guise of pretending like he wasn't trying to convert me after I asked him about the nature of his strange-looking undergarments that everyone else called "magic panties"; and Paguaga, the immigrant from South America who we called Goo Goo because of his serious fascination with Western pop culture, most notably American alternative rock bands like the Goo Goo Dolls.

Monty, Olsen, Goo Goo, and I all came from different places and grew up in different cultures, but I treated them with respect, and they did the same for me. They knew if they fucked up, I would be subjected to endless amounts of abuse for being their leader, and in turn I would do everything I could to return the favor. As the popular military idiom goes, shit rolls downhill.

I quickly learned that no matter how hard we scrubbed the toilets, no matter how many times we mopped the floors, no matter how organized our lockers were, it was never good enough. That was a part of the military pedagogy—always striving to do better. Before Uncle Sam versed us on the ins and outs of killing terrorists and defending the Constitution of the United States against all enemies, foreign and domestic, we were given an edification in military bearing—or the embodiment of professional standards the United States requires its warfighters to uphold. Every service member is expected to display an attitude and appearance to bring a certain credit and cache to the uniform. Those who adopted these ideals fervently were called "shit hot." Those who did not were referred to as "shit bags."

I was somewhere in the middle. I took pride in my appearance, but I didn't really give a fuck about the performative nature of it all. It was difficult to buy into the contrived prestige of the uniform, because a majority of the people wearing them around me were white kids from flyover states, some of them with zero life experience, and even more of them were very vocal bigots. In time, I would display the flag on my shoulder with pride, and I would stand a little straighter when wearing my uniform. It just wasn't during basic training.

For the next nine weeks, the idea that the smallest details of every job, from the cooks to the combat controllers, are critical to mission success was drilled into us. Every single component needed to work together to keep the war machine moving. If one can't press a dress shirt and slacks with the proper creases, how could one be entrusted to handle weapons capable of great harm? If one couldn't make one's bed with straight lines and impeccable hospital corners, how could one be relied upon to pack a parachute correctly? If one can't march in formation in perfect lockstep, how could one be expected to lead troops into combat? I didn't buy it, but that was the rationale. Basic training followed by extensive technical schooling for specific career fields was designed to rid us of our bad civilian habits. It was brainwashing indoctrination labeled as tradition and wrapped in colorful ribbons with ornate medals.

For as much as they lectured us on teamwork and accountability, or expounded on fighting for the Land of the Free and the Home of the Brave, I'd never seen more bigotry than during my time in the military. The racism was rampant. There was the causal, mostly harmless racism that gave me slight pause, like the time a drill instructor said Black troops make for better fire watch personnel because they have built-in camouflage in the dark. And there were what-the-fuck moments, like the time a fellow trainee said he wasn't going to invite his girlfriend to our graduation ceremony because he didn't feel like fighting off all the Black men in our class. It was not unusual to hear someone or something being called a nigger in casual conversation. And, as such, it was not unusual that the few Blacks in basic training congregated with each other socially. Unless the racism led to physical violence, it mostly went ignored. And even then, it was chalked up to boys being boys.

During physical training, I wasn't too concerned about the trainees around me. I didn't think of it as a competition with the others around me. I ran cross-country in high school in between other sports to keep myself in shape, and I applied the same practice I learned doing long-distance running in basic training: I focused on pacing myself throughout the day so I didn't burn myself out. However, that seemingly sound logic was quickly discarded. The drill instructors *made* everything a competition. And if you weren't first, you were considered last.

And that's where the misogyny came into play. Our basic training units weren't coed, but we often drilled side by side with our female counterparts. "Losing" to a female airman was considered absolutely unacceptable. If a female airman was faster than a male during a run, the male was run into the ground. If a female airman did more sit-ups or pull-ups, the males were berated, then put through a gauntlet of additional calisthenics. We were punished so that we didn't forget and didn't let it happen again. How could we be expected to fight war-hardened terrorists in foreign countries if we were being embarrassed by someone with a pussy?

Conversely, we were also trained to handle female trainees with kid gloves, like they were lesser than us, to be their saviors if they fell behind on marches or runs or were struggling during an obstacle course. It was blatant sexism hidden behind the guise of teamwork. One could argue that things are better now, but when I was in basic training, it was over a decade before all military occupations and specialties were opened to women in the US Armed Forces. Until 2015 women were disqualified from a majority of the combat roles. They were considered physically inferior or too emotional for the stressors of combat. That is complete horseshit, obviously. But if a young man hears something enough times, he begins to believe it.

Then there was the homophobia. Ironically, for the amount of casual homophobia that occurred daily around me during my military service, homoeroticism was on full display during basic training. While only a few of us were called queens, several times we were all ordered to clean the barracks wearing nothing but tighty-whities, combat boots, and yellow rubber dishwashing gloves. It was a scene the production designer for the Village People would've been proud of. These cleaning sessions were called GI parties and, at their core, they were meant to emasculate us. The toilets and showers in some of the barracks were open and without privacy, to desensitize us to the male figure, but the lack of privacy led to fellow airmen accusing others of looking at their genitalia, often followed by shouting and sometimes shoving matches.

When the cadre didn't get the rise they wanted out of us, the insults and treatment got worse and would only continue as such for the duration of our time at Lackland. Those who weren't able to tolerate the artificial hostility exhibited by the drill instructors in order to make us as uncomfortable and compliant as possible had a helluva time in basic training. Some were recycled multiple times throughout the nine weeks and would have to start over from the beginning until they got it right. Others were deemed unfit and discharged altogether.

Then there were those who took things into their own hands. One recruit punched a drill instructor. One tried to run away and was found eating a Big Mac and fries at the McDonald's right outside the base's main entrance. Another thought the best way out was by attempting to hang himself with his shoe laces. At the time, it seemed insane to me that these kids were having such a hard time. But we were exactly that—kids. Many of us had never experienced the "real world."

Outside the barracks, things weren't much better. Stress is one thing, but the Texas heat was another. The San Antonio sun had kids fainting as they stood in formation. They told us locking our knees restricted blood flow to the brain, but we were also screamed at if we weren't standing up straight. Clenched assholes lead to locked knees. The 110-degree weather made heat exhaustion very real, and we were ordered to hydrate at every available opportunity. Our canteens were made of plastic, and when it was hot enough, the chemical leaching had me reeling worse than the heat stroke. I also learned that one can get violently ill and even die by drinking too much water. Hyponatremia is what they called it, I think.

And don't get me started with the bugs—Jesus Christ, the bugs. Spiders so big you could make eye contact with them. Flying cockroaches the size of mice. Kamikaze June bugs that seemed to revel in dive-bombing unsuspecting targets. Everything is bigger in Texas, including the misery.

For me, it wasn't the ultra-strict regimen and routine in basic training I found difficult. It wasn't the getting screamed at either. My father and mother raised me in a household that was one degree away from boot camp. I was yelled at constantly and expected to address my parents as "sir" and "ma'am," so addressing my seniors as such was right at home for me. It wasn't the physicality of training either. Sure, waking up at 4:00 AM every morning to run or do backbreaking calisthenics while some drill instructor screamed shit like, "Get on your face and push until I get tired of watching you," because he enjoyed seeing you in pain was tough, but it wasn't going to make me quit. I played basketball, football, and hockey; ran cross-country in high school; and was also on the swim team, so I was in decent enough shape, and over the years I'd had my fair share of overzealous coaches. For me, the most difficult part of basic training was learning to become a war fighter.

I'm from the Bay Area, a city kid, through and through. When we took our training to the outdoors, I was out of my element. I wasn't much of a camper growing up. To me, paying to be homeless in the wilderness for days on end seemed like a Caucasian extracurricular activity. I'd been fishing at Lake Vasona once or twice, but I cut myself while skinning a catfish and vowed never to do that shit ever again.

Shooting guns wasn't my cup o' tea either. Hunting was completely out of the question for me. I didn't have it in me to take a living being's life. As a small child, I'd poured salt on a snail once and then cried about it after it died. Possibly having to kill someone was a position I'd failed to thoroughly examine before joining an organization whose mission statement is to end lives. To me, firearms were (and still are) terrifying. Sure, I'd rubbed elbows with troubled kids in the neighborhood who carried guns, and on one occasion my friend showed me his dad's gun after school, but I'd never actually handled a gun, let alone shot one. I absolutely was not about "that life."

Initially, I was slow and methodical on the firing range, something my peers might've seen as a weakness or confused with a lack of talent. It was neither. The weight of responsibility I felt holding a weapon was enormous. That ten-pound assault rifle may as well have been ten thousand pounds. The understanding that every time I squeezed the trigger I was practicing to take another life forced me gather myself between every shot fired.

For potential conscientious objectors and peaceniks like myself, the military has a way of making death a little more palatable. When you're in the field, you're not murdering people, you're "neutralizing" targets or threats and accomplishing mission objectives. The more one dehumanizes the enemy by likening them to inanimate objects, the easier it is to end them. And if we still couldn't come to peace with that, we could always turn to religion.

On Sundays we had the option of attending church or staying in the barracks for more PT (physical training) or cleaning. A majority of us, religious or not, chose church. Those sixty or so minutes of sitting, reflecting, and listening to a pastor drone on about salvation and the word of the Lord were a much-needed break for our bodies and minds. Airmen caught violating the sanctity of prayer service by sleeping, talking, or acting inappropriately in any way were blessed with a litany of additional duties and backbreaking physical training that would have them pray to their Lord and Savior for forgiveness. Attending Catholic schools for the better part of a decade during my formative years all but ruined theology for me, but church was the devil I knew. I feared the drill instructors more than I feared eternal damnation.

Days before Claire flew out to Texas for my graduation, she cut all her hair off and donated it to Locks of Love, a nonprofit that makes custom hair pieces for disadvantaged children who've lost their hair from cancer treatment, alopecia, burn trauma, or any other medical condition that might cause hair loss. Her selflessness is one of the reasons I loved her. But after bragging about how hot she was for nine weeks, I had some explaining to do when she showed up with a bob haircut that was two degrees away from being bald. The other recruits joked that Claire was my beard and that I had her cut her hair short because I liked to fuck boys. Again, the homophobia.

8

WHITE RABBIT

A CLOUD-LINED, BABY BLUE sky sat atop the rolling green hills of Bexar County, Texas, stretching out for as far as my sore BCG (birth control glasses, the nickname given to government-issued eyewear for its uncanny ability to keep its wearer from engaging in intercourse)–covered eyes could see. The serene, picturesque landscape was something from an early-'90s Microsoft Windows desktop. I stared off into space for a few moments at a time, almost forgetting where I was until the crack of another violent explosion pierced the air. We'd been at Camp Bullis for Hell Week, and on that particular day we were learning how to set up claymore mines and throw hand grenades.

A Black female airman named Best was being prepped by a member of the cadre in a small concrete bunker down below us. Out in front of Best and the instructor was an open field, dotted with craters and scorched earth from the dozens of live grenades that had already been thrown by other trainees that morning. Best had a gentle nature about her. I didn't talk to her often, but when I did, she was polite and soft-spoken. As with a good amount of us, the military was a way out of her situation back home. She'd enlisted to pay for college. I didn't get into the specifics, but I was curious as to why she joined Security Forces. She didn't. She joined the military with an open enlistment with an understanding that she'd be placed in any of the available medical or administrative career fields. The recruiter lied, and now she was covered in camo faceprint, crawling around in the dirt next to a bunch of young men who'd barely graduated high school.

"You ready?" the instructor asked her.

"Yes, sir!" she yelled back with a false confidence that wasn't fooling anyone. Best held her shaking hand out to receive the frag.

"Proper grip!" he yelled as he placed the grenade in her hand. Her large eyes stared at it through her thick Coke-bottle glasses.

"Proper grip!" she echoed.

"Thumb to clip!" he yelled.

"Thumb to clip!" she repeated, putting her left thumb through the ring.

"Twist pull pin!"

"Twist pull pin!" she replied, yanking the pin out. She was now holding a live grenade. I was holding my breath.

"Strike a pose!" he ordered.

"Strike a pose!" Best yelled back, standing in an awkward position somewhere between an Olympic shot-putter and the Heisman trophy.

"Frag out!"

"Frag o—"

Time seemed to slow as we watched the grenade fall out of her hand, then roll down the back of her arm into the bunker. *Oh fuck.* The instructor grabbed Best and threw her over the concrete wall of the bunker and jumped on top of her. The three to five seconds it took for the frag to detonate could've been an eternity. A violent pop followed by a cloud of dust and smoke enveloped the two, and when it cleared they both laid motionless. I had just witnessed my first two casualties.

Jonesy and I sat watching in shock as other members of the cadre and medics rushed toward the downed airmen. Slowly the instructor lifted his head. He was obviously still dazed from the concussive blast. He continued to lie atop Best, who was also now moving. When the instructor came to and determined both he and Best were alive and in one piece, he grabbed the strap on the back of her helmet and slammed her Kevlar-covered skull into the ground twice, unleashing a string of obscenities.

Class dismissed.

———————

I had just gotten out of the shower and couldn't find my towel. I patted myself down the best I could, followed up with a little shimmy to shake off more of the loose water. I peeked around the corner to make sure my roommate wasn't there. I was alone, but the window blinds were pulled back and the interior of my dorm room was on display for everyone to see. When the coast was clear, I quickly tiptoed across the living area with an exposed ass to draw the blinds, leaving a trail of watery footprints from the bathroom to the front door and back to my closet. I was digging through a basket of unfolded laundry when a violent pounding on the door sent me scrambling in seven different directions to cover my nude body and simultaneously clean my mess.

Surprise room inspections could and did happen at any time of the day. If we failed, we were assigned to extra duties during the workweek. Or even worse, we had our rare weekend liberties revoked, and I couldn't risk that. Those two or three days off were the only thing that gave me hope. I wasn't yet twenty-one, so I couldn't even go out for drinks, but getting off base and exploring the town without a group of drill sergeants breathing down my neck was all the respite I needed. Weekends off were the light at the end of a long, dark tunnel full of mud and covered in barbed wire.

The pounding on the door continued. I quickly threw on PT shorts, mopped the floor with my towel, kicked it under the bed, then opened the door and stood to the side at attention.

"Airman Park-Pettiford reports as ordered."

Monty and Goo Goo were standing in my doorway like Christmas carolers dressed in their finest Oakley glasses and boot-cut True Religion denim. With them was Jonesy. Jonesy and I had a similar demeanor and looked so alike that our peers often asked if we were related.

"What the fuck, Negro? Why aren't you ready?" Jonesy asked with a wrinkled brow.

"We said 1800 on the dot. You're still down to go, right?" Monty queried with genuine disappointment.

"We're all going to get tattoos," Goo Goo added, as if that's what it would take to convince me. Our weekend had officially started, and they were trying to exit the base before that could change.

"Yeah, yeah. Give me a second," I replied.

I had a *we need to talk* text from Claire, but I ignored it and stuffed a duffel bag with a few changes of clothes and the Nintendo GameCube I purchased at the commissary but never had any time to actually enjoy.

If basic training was high school, technical school was a well-funded state college for future warfighters. After boot, airmen were shipped off around the country to different installations to be trained in their specific job fields. Fortunately, my Air Force Specialty Code, not too dissimilar from a college major, kept me at Lackland in San Antonio. Because I wasn't willing to wait a calendar year for a slot in the pararescue pipeline—one that most kids washed out of anyway—I found myself going to the University of Security Forces.

The Security Forces career field was transitioning from local base law enforcement to a specialized light infantry for the Air Force. Similar to our Army counterparts, there were several different specialties in the Security Forces sector. The Phoenix Ravens were specially trained teams tasked to provide flyaway security for aircraft and important personnel landing in hostile territory. We called teams assigned to guard nuclear weapons facilities Nuke Troops. It sounded prestigious, when in reality they were a bunch of teenagers babysitting nuclear warheads and the crews operating them while living in dorm-like underground bunkers stocked with DVDs, video games, and high-fructose corn syrup snacks. Security Forces K-9 teams were often attached to units in other branches to provide bomb detection support. Security Forces Combat Arms instructors trained other Air Force personnel in the plethora of weaponry we deployed with. And then there were CPET troops—Close Precision Engagement Teams. They were our force multipliers, countersnipers who stalked the enemy snipers that stalked us. But, as a member of the Air Force Security Forces family, chances are you'd be the poor bastard standing on a flight line or gate in negative-degree weather or guarding some three-star general's bathroom, like Paul Blart with a machine gun. There was a little of something for everyone.

But we'd figure all that out later. At that moment we were loading up our luggage into the back of the Dodge Magnum station wagon Jonesy rented for us. Monty booked us a couple of rooms in a budget-friendly hotel. Goo Goo bought us tickets to see Papa Roach at a bar called the White Rabbit. And I—well, I was the tour manager, designated driver, and babysitter.

Hangovers permitting, we planned to drive to Austin the next morning. Austin was technically a location just outside of the approved travel area for trainees, but rules were made to be broken. We wanted to grab some food and see the sights, then we'd wrap up our freedom tour with a trip to Corpus Christi to lie out in the sand for a while before our Sunday-evening curfew. We had three days of liberty and we were going to use every last second of it. At least that was the plan.

After dumping all our luggage off at the hotel, we walked into a tattoo shop. Goo Goo got a tattoo of a guitar with a banner that read,

Savor Every Moment of This from the Used's song "The Taste of Ink." Jonesy got a tattoo of an ornate gothic cross. I got a tattoo of a koi fish surrounded by waves and lotus flowers. Monty couldn't decide between flames on his forearm or a tribal armband.

We left the shop and strolled around the River Walk. We tried to sneak into a couple of bars but were immediately rebuffed by the bouncers. They probably went through this dozens of times a day with other underaged military recruits. I looked young for my age and even more so with a freshly shaved face and head.

We stopped for a bite and mocktails at a tourist trap called Dick's. Dick's is the type of place where waiters in eccentric outfits walk around insulting patrons, known as Dickheads. They'd draw crude doodles on tall phallic paper hats resembling the Pope's mitre, then they'd crown an unsuspecting guest, before insulting them some more. For whatever reason, visiting families from the Bible Belt loved that shit. I didn't personally get the humor, but everyone else enjoyed it, and that was enough for me not to put up a stink about it.

At dinner, my phone rang and it was Claire calling. Still wearing my dick hat, I stepped outside to answer.

"You can't text me back?" she asked.

"Sorry, I was packing and it skipped my mind," I answered.

"I'm glad I skipped your mind." I could tell she was in the mood to fight, which was a pretty normal occurrence.

"Claire, what is your deal? I have liberty this weekend, so I was trying to get off base."

"Well, I guess I'm just calling to say you can have all the liberty you want."

"Huh? What does that even mean?"

"I'm giving you the freedom to do whatever you want because I don't think we should date anymore."

"What? Where is this coming from? You're dumping me because I didn't respond to your text fast enough?"

"No, I'm breaking up with you because I need something else."

"What are you talking about? I've given you everything you've ever asked for. Or at least tried to." She didn't say anything. "We've been together for four years."

"Exactly," she replied. "I don't want to waste any more time with someone who I'm not sure I want to spend the rest of my life with."

"Why don't you want to spend your life with me? Everything was fine the last time we talked," I said, sounding like Pádraic Súlleabháin in *The Banshees of Insherin.*

"I don't know. I just don't."

I walked back into the restaurant with my stupid hat on and tears in my eyes. If there was ever a moment where I felt like a dickhead, it was that one. When I returned back to our table, two female air(wo)men, who we regularly trained with, were sitting with Jonesy, Monty, and Goo Goo. Courtney was a bubbly redhead from New Mexico. Lacey was a Black girl from Alabama with a heavy Southern drawl.

I quickly wiped my tears, pulled off the hat, and forced a smile. Both girls stood and gave me long hugs. It was always strange to see our peers outside of their uniforms. Lacey paused and gave me a look. "Have you been crying, Park?"

"No," I responded, unconvincingly.

"Yes, you have. What's wrong, sugar?"

"My girl just broke up with me over the phone. Four years down the fucking drain."

"That white girl? I'm sorry. Well, what're you doing after dinner? Can we hang out with y'all tonight?"

"We're going to a Papa Roach show."

"A Papa whatnow?"

"Papa Roach, the band?"

She stared at me blankly. For some reason, I thought singing their hit song to her might jog her memory: "Cut my life into pieces, this is my last resort. Suffocation, no breathing . . ."

She responded with a series of blinks that essentially said, *I have no idea what the fuck you're saying right now* in Morse code.

"Yeah, you boys have fun with all that." She leaned in a little closer. "Give me your phone." She dialed her number and pressed call, so I'd have it saved. "Text me after and maybe we can meet up."

Monty and Goo Goo didn't want my breakup to ruin the weekend we all needed so desperately, so when we got to the White Rabbit they gave forty dollars to a homeless man standing in front of a liquor store to buy us a half of tequila and a plastic flask, and for doing so, they gave him a shot and let him keep the change. We snuck it into to the club, and I spent the rest of the night singing about cutting things into pieces and making out with a Hot Topic Goth chick. Her two friends weren't as attractive, but Jonesy and Monty didn't mind. "Sometimes you have to jump on a grenade for your boys," they'd say. Besides giving your life for the man next to you, taking one for the team by entertaining the ugly friends was the best way to be a wingman. In their minds, anyway.

The following morning, after exchanging contact info with our new muses, we drove to Wimberley, a quiet pioneer town an hour north of San Antonio. We spent hours jumping off rope swings hanging from cypress trees into a crystal blue watering hole. Then we laid out on rafts floating down a lazy river, talking about our future, which was mostly talk about war and women.

When we were sun-kissed and satisfied, we drove another hour north to Austin and ate BBQ until we were sick. We made our way through the streets of downtown Austin toward the river, where we noticed a large crowd forming up ahead. Folks were holding signs we couldn't read, screaming at something we couldn't see. As we got closer, we noticed a line of police. Behind the police were a few dozen men and women dressed in black, white, or red. They were waving Confederate flags and had homemade wooden shields painted red with black crosses on them. One woman with stringy blonde hair and leathery skin waved a flag that said, WORLD CHURCH OF THE CREATOR. Another man held a sign that read, AMERICAN WHITE KNIGHTS OF THE KU KLUX KLAN.

They yelled about God and "white Christian values," but nothing about the hate in their eyes and the foamy spit that flew from their mouths while they screamed said *Christian* to me. They were there in support of Proposition 2, a referendum banning same-sex marriage. Across from them were hundreds of peaceful counterprotestors waving rainbow flags.

"Why are the police protecting the Nazis?" Monty asked. Oh, my sweet summer child.

We made our way to the beach park and took a nap on a grassy slope along the water. Again, we woke to another crowd forming along the river under the bridge. We asked what was going on, and a lady told us they were waiting for the bats. When night fell, a colony of thousands of screeching, flying rodents appeared from beneath the Ann W. Richards Congress Avenue Bridge. We watched in wonderment as the amorphous cloud changed directions in the sky as if being pulled by invisible strings, shifting into different shapes with the setting Texas sun as a backdrop.

The hotels in Austin were too expensive, so Monty suggested we drive a little farther north to Fort Hood. Killeen was a military town, and we'd be able to get rooms for damn near free. Jonesy was skeptical. He warned us that we should stay away from Killeen after dark. And by "we" he meant him and me, the two Black men in the party.

A city with roots going all the way back to the nineteenth century, Killeen was an isolated trade hub where more cotton, wool, and grain passed through than people. During the onset of World War II, Killeen's rural roots would all but disappear. In 1942 Camp Hood, named after the notoriously lousy Confederate general John Bell Hood, was commissioned to meet the training demands for the

Department of Defense. The farms, ranches, and cotton gins were leveled to make way for training grounds and barracks. In return, the Army provided the locals with other business opportunities in service of the government. And Killeen became a military boom town. It also became the recruiting grounds for a resurgent Ku Klux Klan.

"Taylor said Killeen stands for 'Kill Each and Every Nigger,'" Jonesy said, without a hint of the humor I'd come to know from him.

"Papi, don't be saying that word around me. It's racist," Goo Goo rebuked.

"You're not even fucking Black, Goo Goo. You're a white dude with a weird accent," Jones countered.

"Why are you being racist to me now? If you want the racism to stop, you shouldn't say it either. Nobody should say it."

Jonesy fired back: "I can fucking say it—I'm Black."

"Well, if you can say it, everyone can say it."

Jonesy balled his fists. "Then say it. I dare you."

"I'm not going to, because I'm not racist—like you."

Monty gave me a look. I stepped between the two. "Would you idiots relax? Goo Goo, I know you mean well. But this ain't Argentina, brother. Niggas can say 'nigga.' You can't. Those are the rules."

Monty stepped in. "So what's the call? We going to Hood?"

"Before Evita over here started crying about Argentina, I was trying to tell you Killeen used to be a sundown town," Jonesy replied.

"Don't joke about Eva Peron, papi," Goo Goo warned. His grandparents were exiled political refugees of the Argentine Revolution.

"OK. What's a sundown town?" Monty asked genuinely, trying to get things back on track.

I filled him in: "They're places in America where Black folks aren't allowed to be after sundown."

"Why? Or what?"

"I can give you the full history lesson later, but it goes back to slave patrols. If Black folks were wandering around at night, they thought we were either runaway slaves or committing crimes. So we'd get beaten, arrested, or lynched," I explained.

"'We,' he says."

"Yes, 'we.' We as in Black people. In some places, shit hasn't really changed."

"*Las estadounidenses son tan jodidamente estúpidos*," Goo Goo mumbled under his breath.

"It's 2005, man. Things are aren't like that anymore," Monty said with ignorant confidence.

"Are you serious? We *literally* just walked through a fucking Klan rally in the middle of Austin, Texas, earlier today. And Austin is the most liberal city in this fucked-up state. What do you think it's going to be like in the place they call 'Kill Each and Every Nigger'?"

"Who's they? And there were only like twenty of those racist idiots. There were way more people shouting them down," Monty reasoned.

"OK, now imagine me or Park walking down a dark street by ourselves, bumping into twenty Klan members. How do you think that would end for us?"

"But you aren't by yourselves. You're with us."

"Holy shit. You just don't get it, do you?" Jonesy replied, exhausted. "Look, I don't wanna go. Let's go somewhere else," Jonesy pleaded.

"It's a military town. We're *in* the military. Nobody's going to fuck with you. And if they try to, Goo Goo and I will step in. Stop this victim bullshit, you fucking pussy. Once we leave this place, our job is to go to places where people want to fucking kill us. So you better fucking get used to it."

They looked to me for the final decision. After all, I'd been their leader for the past few months. Admittedly, it was a bitch move, but to appease both parties with some bipartisanship, and because I was broke, I said, "Let's check it out. If it gets sketchy, we'll turn around and head back to San Antonio." At the time, had I known my grandfather was murdered in Killeen by the KKK, I probably would've sided with Jonesy.

We spent the night in a small one-star motel right off the expressway. Besides the slightly suspicious lady working the front desk, whose concerns were quickly allayed when we provided our military IDs, there were no incidents. The next morning, we packed our shit before the sun came up and were back on the road, this time to Corpus Christi. Monty was especially excited to head to the Gulf Coast. He was from rural Wisconsin, and until he joined the military, he'd never left home. He'd never seen the ocean before.

After the four-hour drive to the coast, the only thing we found was disappointment. The beach was rocky and the water was a dark, uninviting brown color. We grabbed sandwiches, filled the gas tank, and made our way back to San Antonio.

For the following week, whenever I bumped into Lacey during training, we'd exchange glances and smiles. After hours, we started hanging out in the chow hall or in coed common areas. We crossed the friendship line and graduated to full-on flirting. And although I was technically single, part of me felt guilty for moving on so fast. But whatever fling Lacey and I were about to start felt inevitable.

The next time we had liberty, Lacey and Courtney got a hotel room and invited Monty and me to spend the weekend with them. Jonesy and Goo Goo got a hotel room next to ours and invited the Goth girls over. After a weekend of drinking and fucking, Lacey and I went our separate ways, and I packed my bags into Jonesy's rental car for the trip back to Lackland.

The two Goth girls asked if they could come back with us. "We just wanna hang out some more. Can we spend the night?"

They wanted to sleep over? On base? A secure military installation? "No chance. First of all, we can't have females in our rooms—especially not civilians," I explained. "Two, we have curfew on Sunday nights, then training bright and early the following morning. And even if we didn't, we don't have visitors' passes for you guys, so we couldn't even get you through the front gate if we wanted."

"We'll give you the best head you've ever gotten in your life." Jonesy's ears perked up and he stood a little taller.

"I mean, it's worth a shot," Jonesy said sheepishly.

He did what any reasonably horny human being would've done and snuck the girls onto the base in the back of the rented Dodge Magnum. Once inside, we snuck them to our respective dorms. The following morning, when they refused to leave, Jonesy called the military police and reported them as trespassers—quite possibly the worst walk of shame in history.

9

YOU CAN CALL ME AL

AFTER NEARLY A year away from my friends and family while at basic and technical school, it was good to be home. Dozens of us shuffled down Campbell Avenue like a lost tribe after the cops had forcefully pulled the plug on a mutual's house party. Black-and-whites were lurking in the shadows on every corner for blocks, waiting to pull over anyone dumb enough to drive home from the aforementioned gathering. After the cops were done checking our IDs and giving tickets to the underaged drinkers, we gathered on the lawn. The party was over but the night wasn't. It was a few hours past midnight and a few years before ride-share companies even existed, so the only obvious move was to walk to the Denny's a few blocks away to get some food and continue the social festivities. There's something about a greasy Grand Slamwich that's great for sobering up.

I walked a little bit taller among my people as we made our way down the sidewalk beneath the underpass toward the bright yellow-and-red sign that beckoned us. While I was in Texas playing G.I. Joe, the rest of the gang were figuring their lives out. Some were making fistfuls of money in tech, with the rising popularity of social media and mobile apps. Others were attending prestigious colleges that would translate into careers in law or medicine or other sectors I knew nothing about. A few were touring the globe with famous musicians or trying their hand in the movie business, and they'd go on to be recognizable names in the entertainment industry.

And then there were the rest of us, the ones who worked low-paying retail jobs or still lived with their parents. The ones who society would consider failures, the ones who knew that life would probably never be better than it was at that moment. I was one of them. The only difference was that my low-paying job came with the prospect of adventure. There was the danger of it all. And while we'd all talked about joining the military at different points during our youth—a common sentiment among poor and middle-class American boys—none of us ever actually considered it.

Until I did.

I just happened to be the only one in our circle who was dumb enough to actually sign on the dotted line and make the commitment. That alone garnered the respect of my peers. Unlike other circles I've been in through the years, there was no jealousy or contempt in this one. We applauded each other's successes. We didn't care about who was making money or who was getting clicks, we cared about each other. And while we all walked together, there was no talk about accolades or achievement. At that moment, none of that mattered because we were all together again, an occurrence that was happening less and less frequently through the years.

When we walked through those heavy green doors, as we'd done a countless number of times before, we were greeted by some familiar faces. This time, our party was four or five times larger than usual. One of the only two waitresses on duty put together three tables for us. There were both close companions and complete strangers in the group, but everyone knew someone. And if you were a friend to one of us, you were a friend to all of us. We ordered a smorgasbord of greasy food and caffeinated drinks. We shouted across the table at each other and laughed over the colorful spread like the Last Supper with a group of drunk apostles. And everything was good.

Until it wasn't.

At the other end of the table, a redhead wearing a cowboy hat and San Jose Sharks jersey, with a sickly pink complexion from hours of drinking, was very audibly dropping the *n*-word. I thought I might've been hearing things, so I stopped and looked at my half-eaten pancakes to listen a little bit harder. He said it again. There was no mistaking it—hard *er* and everything. He was saying it repeatedly and with a casual frequency that others at the table began to hear too. The girl next to him told him to stop. He responded by saying it again and laughing with a mouthful of food.

Uncomfortable glances were exchanged, and all the eyes at the table began finding their way toward me. Rory and I were the only two Black people at the table, and they were expecting a retaliation. This cowboy wanted a reaction. I looked at Rory and shook my head no. We weren't going to give him one. We continued on with our meal and our conversation, but the more we ignored him, the louder he got. *Nigger this, nigger that,* he kept saying.

As the kids say, he'd completely killed the vibe. The once boisterous conversation had all but ended. We sat and ate quietly. I could feel him staring at me in my periphery, and I didn't want my silence to be mistaken for weakness, so I turned and looked Cowboy right in the eyes. We glared at each other for several beats from opposite ends of the tables, like a saloon scene in a spaghetti western. I was about to return my attention back to my scrambled eggs when he pointed at me.

"What the fuck are you looking at, nigger? You got a problem?"

"Oh, he just fucked up," Adrian said to himself under his breath. There were no places to run and hide, so the rest of the townspeople witnessing this showdown waited with bated breath for my response. I looked around the table. *Who the fuck invited this guy?* I could tell my calm demeanor was alarming to those who knew me, because the younger version of myself relished confrontation. The younger version of myself would've jumped across the table and put his hands around that racist fuck's throat without hesitation. Brian and Adrian looked at me with concern. Rory was ready to follow my lead.

"What is your fucking deal, man?" I responded. I was genuinely curious what his endgame was. "We're just trying to have a good time, and you're ruining that for everyone. For what?"

"I'm having a good time," he said.

"Look at everyone else at the table, asshole. Nobody here likes you."

He looked at the girl sitting next to him. She looked away, disgusted. Every eye in the room followed him as he stood and marched his way around the table toward me. He landed right in front of me and hovered over me while I remained seated. My eye line was at his stomach. I made eye contact with each person at the table, then looked up at him. Before I could say a word, he open-hand slapped me across the face as hard as he could.

Admittedly, that was not the response I was expecting, and for a half second I sat there in shock while my ear rang, along with the rest of the patrons of the restaurant. *Did this motherfucker just bitch-slap me?* I was so stunned by the audacity of it all that I had no verbal response.

He brought his hand farther back to slap me again. My sympathetic nervous system shifted into overdrive. It was fight or flight, and I didn't feel like running. The first one was free, a second one would cost him.

Before his hand could connect again, I ducked my head to the side and tackled him from a sitting position into the table. Plates of food and silverware went airborne and jaws fell to the floor. People backed away as I dragged him across the table then dumped him on the floor, where I found myself on top of him in a full mount position, his left arm pinned beneath my knee. I held the wrist of his right arm with my left hand to keep him from blocking the right hooks I threw repeatedly at his face. After he went limp, I let his wrist go and threw lefts and rights until his face was a bloody mess and Adrian pulled me off him.

Rory told me to leave. Someone called the cops and they'd be showing up at any moment. Cowboy stood and stumbled to the nearest table to hold himself up. I'd lost all sense of time, and when I turned around, two police officers were entering the front door. They made a beeline toward me. They looked at Cowboy's destroyed face and my knuckles covered in blood and did the quick math. One officer put his hand on his gun; the other went straight for his cuffs and told me I was under arrest.

Without a fight, I turned and put my hands behind my back. The restaurant manager, who had served me on many occasions, pointed at the Cowboy's bloody face and said, "This asshole was calling him a nigger for no reason, then assaulted him repeatedly. He started it." Then she gestured toward me, "He finished it. But it was in self-defense."

Everyone in the restaurant corroborated this account of the events. The cops loosened my cuffs immediately, then asked if I wanted to press charges. This was considered a hate crime under California law, they advised.

I declined. The way I rearranged his face was more than enough punishment.

It was as if nothing had changed at all. Following basic training and tech school, I went back to my ho-hum civilian life. I was single for a bit and enjoyed the attention I received from joining the military. But despite my mother's repeated attempts to set me up on a blind date with a coworker's daughter, I ended up getting back together with Claire, because she was all I knew. "You should marry a nice Korean girl," my mother would implore me whenever things were rocky between Claire and me. But there was a comfort with Claire, even during the chaos.

I returned to my part-time job at the coffee shop. Andrea was no longer there. She'd transferred to another store. The new manager was in his mid-to-late thirties and had a marked resemblance to the Hamburglar, with his red hair and the two buck teeth that rested on his lower lip, even when he wasn't speaking. Only he didn't pilfer beef patties from Ronald and Grimace, he robbed cradles. He used the little amount of managerial muscle he had to flex on his much younger female coworkers. I wasn't an impressionable teenage coed and had no problem telling him when he was crossing the line, and because of this I began to find my name on the schedule less and less, until I was working less than one shift a week.

When I could, I picked up graveyard shifts at FedEx with Brian, where we loaded a never-ending line of boxes into trucks for delivery the next day. The pay was decent, but the work was backbreaking. After doing that for months, I became a little more understanding when I received a package from FedEx that was in rough shape, because by the end of my own shifts, I was launching boxes into those trucks with no regard for their well-being.

Because we were an Air National Guard unit, I typically only reported to base one weekend a month for drilling. The unit's budget fluctuated and it didn't have the funds to hire all of us on as full-time employees, so the priority went with seniority. I was on the bottom of the totem pole, but I wouldn't be the newest airman for long. On my second or third drill weekend following my return from technical training, another new airman joined our unit. And from the jump, everyone took a liking to him.

Allen Losh was a tall, handsome, blond-haired, blue-eyed kid from Healdsburg, a quiet town in the wine country of Sonoma County. He came from a long line of firefighters. He was an adept mechanic who wasn't afraid to get his hands dirty. He hiked mountains and camped in the wilderness for fun. He's the type of person people would've called All-American when people were still called All-American. Our age is where our similarities ended.

The first time I bumped into him was in the locker room. I introduced myself and offered up a handshake.

"You Allen? I'm Dylan." He grabbed my hand and shook it.

"You can call me Al," he said with a smile.

"Paul Simon was my dad's favorite. *Graceland* might be on the top-ten album list for me too."

He was excited I understood the reference, and just like that, we were homies.

Allen quickly made a reputation for being squared away. He did everything by the book. I was cutting corners and doing the bare minimum. He volunteered to take on extra work or shifts. I was voluntold to do everything, because I didn't want to do anything. And our senior NCOs and officers noticed. I didn't realize it at the time, but I was quickly playing into the stereotype of the lazy Black man. Allen knew I wasn't lazy, I just wasn't motivated. Allen didn't want me to ruin my career before it'd even truly started, so he begged me to at least fake like I gave a fuck.

Our captain was a former Army Ranger who still wore his Ranger tab and other Army badges on his uniform as a reminder to us that he was the big dog for a reason. At the time, this wasn't regulation, but no one was going to tell him he couldn't wear the insignias he'd worked and bled for. And by the way we trained, it was apparent he missed his old way of life. We worked alongside the special operators and pararescuemen (a.k.a. PJs) who we shared facilities with. On the civilian side of the base, NASA pilots would use our runways for their test flights. Our captain had us training right alongside the PJs and future astronauts, making sure his ragtag unit was fit to fight.

Most of the kids I graduated technical school with went on to active duty stations and would spend a majority of their career writing tickets to people speeding on base, or they'd be charged to watch assets the government deemed important, whether that be a bomber plane, a weapons storage facility, or a fat guy with shiny stars on his collar. For us, it was different. Because we were connected to a special operations wing, we had levels of funding for training and equipment that most Security Forces units didn't see.

Our captain had us traveling to Camp Parks, where we'd train air assault—rappelling out of helicopters—with our Army counterparts. We spent an exceptional amount of time practicing shoot or no-shoot scenarios on a state-of-the-art firearms training simulator that we lovingly referred to as the FATS machine. We practiced clearing houses and hostage negotiations. We went down to the range to become adept with new weapons systems like automatic grenade launchers, light machine guns, and heavy machine guns. And the entire time I asked myself, *What the fuck are we ever going to need to know any of this shit for? We're in the Air Force.*

I didn't have to wait long for an answer. The Army put out an RFF, or request for forces, to supplement and eventually replace a detachment struggling with manpower after being ravaged by injuries during some heavy fighting in Northern Iraq. Our captain volunteered us. Now, this wasn't typical of Air Force units, but we weren't a typical Air Force unit. A good amount of the guys in our shop had combat experience. Most important, we were available when a lot of other Army units were stretched thin from lengthy deployments.

When I broke the news to Claire, she broke down crying, which was to be expected. But she wasn't just heartbroken that I was going to war, she was heartbroken that as a result of my news she'd have to reveal news of her own, news she'd been hoping to surprise me with. She was pregnant.

I told her I supported whatever decision she wanted to make, which was a polite way of saying I wouldn't mind her heading down to Planned Parenthood. But that decision wasn't up to me, and for her, it was completely out of the question. She'd gotten one in high school and refused to relive that emotional and physical trauma. With that option off the table, it didn't take long for me to do the math. If I was to be gone for twelve months and babies take nine months to make, give or take a few days, I was going to miss the birth of my first child—a notion that was somehow more stress-inducing than the prospect of war.

I assured her everything was going to be OK, but I was lying to myself. I had no idea how things would turn out. And for that reason, I took her down to the courthouse to get married. If anything happened to me while I was gone, I wanted her to be taken care of.

Now, the scariest part about being a new husband and expectant father getting ready to ship off to war wasn't the pressure of a lifelong commitment, learning to be a good parent, or the reality that I could die overseas. The scariest part was telling my parents—specifically my mother—that I was a new husband and expectant father getting ready to ship off to war. Fearing the wrath of an Asian mother, I reached out to my brother to act as an intermediary and set up a family dinner at our favorite sushi restaurant, Yuki.

With a belly full of miso soup and sake, I finally found the courage to break the news—all of it. I told my family Claire and I eloped. My mother hated Claire, so she scoffed and quipped that we would be divorced within a year. Following the news of our marriage with the news that Claire was expecting a child kept the maternal train from derailing. My mother's reaction was a bittersweet one. She'd always wanted a grandkid, so she softened her stance ever so slightly. She was trying to process all of the information I'd just given her, but I wasn't finished delivering it yet.

"Um, there's one more thing I need to tell you, Mom." The table stared at me for what seemed like an eternity. "I'm getting deployed to Iraq next month. I'll be gone for a year, so I likely won't be here for the birth either."

My old man stormed out of the restaurant. Rory stared at me in complete disbelief. My mom broke down crying, saying I was going to get myself killed.

The manager overheard that I was shipping off to Iraq and comped the appetizers, so the night wasn't a total disaster.

ACT II

AWAY

———

"A good companion shortens the longest road."
—Kurdish proverb

10

AROUND THE WORLD

THE BRIGHT RED letters on the shrieking woodgrain radio atop the hotel nightstand read 3:00 AM. I slapped the snooze button, then turned over. Claire was still fast asleep.

The night before, Brian threw me a going-away party. All of my closest friends were there. Despite the crowd being older, Rory and his friends were there too. After I said my goodbyes and everyone left, Claire and I decided to spend the night in a hotel down the road from the base for one last staycation before my 5:00 AM flight. There was no room service, fancy hotel bar, or any other amenities for that matter, but I had her, and that was all I needed.

I stared at the water-stained ceiling in the aging hotel room for a bit, feeling sorry for myself. Then I remembered there were hundreds of other men and women who were also waking and getting ready to say their goodbyes to loved ones at that exact moment. I kissed Claire gently on the cheek and told her it was time to get up. She sat up looking disheveled and asked if I wanted one last blowjob for the road. Though I appreciated the offer, I wasn't in the mood. I was exhausted, physically from the year's worth of fucking we tried to get in the day before, and mentally after tossing and turning all night while I thought about all of the horrible things that might happen to me over the next year. It's hard to get yourself in the mood when you're ruminating on your impending doom. The absolute best-case scenario was that I'd see her again in eight to twelve months. The worst case was that I'd never see her again.

After saying some goodbyes, I was on a flight an hour later. We stopped off at Creech Air Force Base to do some last-minute desert-warfare training. Creech was a fitting title because it was a place where life seemed to come to a screeching halt. The barren wasteland was occupied by men getting ready to ship off to kill the inhabitants of another barren wasteland on the other side of the world. (Iraq was a beautiful country before we destroyed it.) The sprawling 3.6-square-mile site in Bumfuck, Nevada, right outside of the storied Area 51 complex, was home to the Silver Flag Alpha Regional Training Center. It also housed the Joint Unmanned Aerial Systems Center of Excellence, a gratuitous title for a place that employs a bunch of zit-faced video gamers turned drone pilots who kill people seventy-three hundred miles away from the comfort of an air-conditioned arcade. The state-of-the-art facilities, combined with the hellish terrain and weather and a brutal training regimen, were perfect for getting us acclimated to the environs we would be spending the better part of the next year in.

At Silver Flag we met the other units from around the country that would make up our detachment for the upcoming deployment. There was a colorful cast of characters from an Air National Guard unit in New York: Hawkes was a red-headed, foul-mouthed Irish kid who came off as an asshole, as New Yorkers often tend to do, but that was a front. Behind the scenes, he was a mild-mannered kid who dreamed of being a chef and running his own Michelin-rated restaurant. I told Hawkes I attended an Irish Catholic high school, so that made me an honorary Irishman. He jokingly referred to me as Black Irish for the rest of the deployment.

Smitty, one of the NCOs (noncommissioned officers) from New York, was generally regarded as everyone's favorite. He was short in stature but was armed with an arsenal of funny impressions that got us through long days of training and even longer days in Iraq. Even the strictest no-nonsense officers couldn't help but to crack a smile around Smitty. And while he could have an entire room in stitches with impressions ranging from George Dubya to Chewbacca, he was also a distributor of sage advice to the younger airmen he was entrusted to lead. The prospects of combat were daunting enough, and Smitty took a lighthearted approach to leadership seldom seen in the Armed Forces.

Along with the New Yorkers, we also teamed up with another Air National Guard unit from Montana. Unlike their East Coast counterparts, for the most part they were unmemorable people. That's not to say they were bad folks. We just didn't have much in common, and they seemed to want to keep it that way. I could never remember any of their names if they weren't wearing their uniforms or if their nametape was covered by their body armor, so I called them all Montana—Big Montana, Young Montana, French Montana, Joe Montana, and Hannah Montana.

We spent the next two weeks practicing convoy maneuvers, getting range time with heavy weapons, and pretending to kill people dressed as Middle Easterners while clearing mock villages. In order to simulate combat, we used conversion kits that transformed our firearms into nonlethal weapons that shot high-powered rounds with paint tips instead of lead. The cadre informed us that the "simunitions" *could* be lethal if struck from a close enough range in places with unprotected vital organs. I'm not sure if that's true or not, but it was a way to ensure we took the training seriously. Nothing remotely meaningful would come from a group of young men running around with fake guns playing cops and robbers. We needed to feel some of that same fear we'd experience overseas.

Toward the end of the training, we were surprised with one last night of liberty. And being that we were only an hour from the Vegas Strip, that felt like the obvious choice. It was a long shot, but I called Adrian and Kyle the night before to let them know I had one more night of freedom before Iraq, and possibly ever. Without hesitation, they both called out of work sick, canceled all their plans for the next two days, and caught a flight to see me off.

Now, the events of that night are a little murky after drinking myself into oblivion. However, I do remember falling asleep on a couch in a hotel room in the Palms Casino Resort as Adrian and Kyle cheered while two strippers named Athena and Hera gave me a lap dance. The next morning, I woke up in a panic to several missed calls and text messages saying that I better have my ass on the flight from the nearby Nellis Air Force Base or the master sergeant would personally see to it that I was stripped of rank. I crawled into their beds and, with teary eyes, hugged Kyle and Adrian and told them I'd see them soon. Still there and still nude, Athena sat up and thanked me for my service.

From Nevada, we made a quick stop in New York to refuel before stopping off to refuel again in Shannon, Ireland. When we landed on the Emerald Isle and entered the terminal, we received a standing ovation not unlike one of those Budweiser commercials that ran in the aftermath of 9/11. Locals offered to buy us drinks, and like children begging their parents for permission, we asked our commanding officer if we could oblige them. Camp Warrior, our final destination, was a dry base. Alcohol and sex, or any amount of fun, really, were completely prohibited. That would be our last chance to let loose for the foreseeable future, so the CO (commanding officer) told us to enjoy ourselves. He followed that up with a stern warning that he would kill us before we got to war if we embarrassed him.

A couple of smiling, fair-skinned lasses ushered Allen and I to the nearest airport bar, where we didn't have to wait long before we were handed pints of Guinness North Star. Allen and I sat on one side of the booth, and the two Irish girls sat on the other. I could hardly understand what the girl sitting across from me was saying, and even less so with each accompanying drink, but I stared into her green eyes as she spoke. With strawberry blonde hair, dimples, and a slightly crooked smile, she reminded me of Claire. I told her I liked her freckles. She asked if I knew where freckles came from, which I thought was an odd question. Admittedly, I'd never given much thought to the origin of the patches of colored pigment often seen on less-melanated faces.

"Long ago, when Ireland was a young and broken country, the old gods feared the cloudy skies would keep our people from finding their way. So they painted a map of the stars on our faces," she said with a warmth I knew I wouldn't feel for a while.

Between my blood alcohol level, her beautiful fable, and the existential crisis I was experiencing, my eyes began to water. She reached across the table, held the side of my face, and ran her thumb across my cheek.

"I hope you find your way."

The bartender asked if we were ready for some shots of Jameson, but it was more of a heads up than a question. He divvied out a round to each of us, on the house, and followed it with a toast.

"May the road rise up to meet you. May the wind be always at your back. May the sun shine on your face, the rains fall soft upon your fields. And until we meet again, may God hold you in the palm of His hand."

We rose our glasses and threw 'em back. We followed that up with another shot. And took another after that for good measure. When our names were called over the intercom to return to the plane, the girls gave us kisses on the cheek and wished us well. Allen and I stumbled through the terminal arm in arm and down the ramp toward our awaiting bird. I turned back to wave, but the girls were already gone.

Our next stop was Germany. Or maybe it was Hungary. Allen and I sat in another airport lounge sick to our stomachs, where we were presented with a plate of strange-looking pasta and gray meatballs. I passed. I was too busy gripping the arms of my seat trying to stop the spinning.

We spent several weeks in Qatar, a small, wealthy peninsular country in the middle of the Persian Gulf known for its futuristic skyscrapers and human rights violations. Like thousands of other US service members who were stationed at Al Udeid, a once-secret air base the United States used to position its aircraft for missions in Afghanistan at the beginning of Operation Enduring Freedom, we were all waiting to catch a flight to our AO (area of operations) in Iraq. We dawdled around in Camp Andy, a massive tent city named after Master Sergeant Evander Andrews, the first casualty of Operation Enduring Freedom. The poor bastard was a civil engineer in the Air Force who was killed in a forklift accident a month after the towers fell.

Before hopping onto my final flight to the AO, I found a pay phone and gave Rory a call. It was before noon local time, meaning it'd be late at night in California. But not too late that Rory wouldn't pick up.

"Hello?!" Rory answered with and amalgamation of loud rap music, laughing, and screaming in the background.

"What's up, dude?"

"Huh? Is this Dylan? I can't hear you. Hold on, one sec. Don't hang up!"

There was a line of troops standing behind me waiting for one of the phones to open up. "I'll be off in one minute," I whispered to buy myself a little time before the groaning and complaining started.

"OK. Can you hear me?" Rory said, out of breath.

"What're you up to?"

"We're just having ourselves a little get-together at Vic's house."

"Doesn't sound little. Vic's parents are cool with that?" I knew Rory's girlfriend's parents, and I knew for a fact they weren't cool with that. It was more of a rhetorical question.

"Oh, they're not in town. We're not getting too crazy. It's all good."

"Well, I hope you're having fun."

"Where you at right now?"

I looked up to see if anyone was listening. Everyone in the proximity of the phones was eavesdropping, and OPSEC (short for "operational security" and a fancy way for saying *loose lips sink ships*) was in full effect. I lowered my voice. "Um, I can't say exactly, but I wanted to let you know I'm on my way to the sandbox. Wanted to hear your voice one last time."

"One last time? Why would you say that?"

I'm not sure why I said it that way. I guess it was a reflexive response indicative of how truly scared I was, and an attempt to allay those fears by resigning myself to a grim future.

"My bad. You know what I meant."

"Please be safe, man." I could hear his voice beginning to crack.

"Chalk Fifty-One is boarding in thirty minutes," a voice squawked through a loudspeaker mounted to the wall right above me.

A group of troops grumbled at me under their breath because they all wanted to use the phone too. Several other phones had been occupied longer than mine, but I made no protests. We were all a little on edge.

"Hey, Ro, that's my cue. I gotta go. But I promise you I'll call or write whenever I can."

"OK . . . I love you," he said.

I couldn't remember the last time I heard my brother say those words to me, if he'd ever said them at all.

"I love you too," I replied before hanging up.

I turned and made my way back to some familiar faces. And as I walked through the TMO (travel management office), I noticed that no one else seemed too excited about catching the four-hour flight from Qatar to Iraq either. There was a very anxious energy.

I was asleep in the belly of the C-130 when it banked hard and startled me awake. The girl next to me screamed and grabbed my forearm as the plane went into a steep dive. I could feel a sinking feeling in my stomach as we fell out of the sky. Confused, I looked to the windows. They were blacked out by smoke. *Fuck.* We were hit, and I was going to die before I even stepped foot on Iraqi dirt. Oddly enough, no one else was panicking. I looked across the aisle, and the smile on Allen's face helped me reassess the situation.

We weren't hit. Our plane was in a steep descent known as a combat landing, standard operating procedure that made it harder to get shot out of the sky in active combat zones. The black smoke shooting past the windows was from the oil rigs in Ramadi. We were flying over the second-largest oil field on the planet into Kirkuk, Iraq.

———————

At Camp Warrior, also known as the Krab but formally known as Kirkuk Regional Air Base, our living quarters, or mods, were giant cargo containers that had been renovated into dormitories. When I walked through the front door for the first time, the stench of dozens of different body odors slapped me across the face. Holes the size of fists, feet, and foreheads punctured the walls. Large stains of unknown origin covered the floor like a modern art canvas. It was as if the earlier occupants had participated in regular battle royales to the death, and the bodies of the losers were dragged along the ground and dumped out back.

Our room had three triple-bunk beds and a small refrigerator. I was going to be sharing a fifteen-foot-by-fifteen-foot space with eight other men for the next year. I dumped my bags on my bunk and went exploring around the base.

There was a small Internet café where service members were allotted fifteen minutes a week to check and send e-mails. About thirteen of those fifteen minutes were usually spent telling the guy in line behind you to fuck off and wait his turn. On the other side of the base was a movie room, a church, a makeshift gym, and a spot people called the Library, which was actually just boxes of books stacked behind the latrines. When the toilet paper ran out, which was fairly often, some of the fellas found that the pages of a trade paperback were the perfect size and made for a suitable substitution.

I wasn't much of a reader or writer before Iraq, but there wasn't much else to do, and it wasn't long before I began to keep a journal and immerse myself in every book I could find. What started as a diversion to pass the time turned into a passion, maybe even a border-line obsession. If I was reading a book, I wasn't thinking about the reality of my own situation. And if I was, I would write it down in a journal as a cathartic exercise. It was my therapy a decade before I would go to therapy for the things I saw in Iraq that year.

The books varied in subject and condition. Some were brand new, straight from the sales rack of a Barnes & Noble, books that had obviously been donated by a patriotic support-the-troops, flag-flying mother somewhere in Middle America. However, a majority looked like casualties of war, with their broken spines and bleeding pages. I wasn't sure what I was looking for the first time I dug through those boxes, but I knew I'd know when I found it. I stumbled across a copy of Khaled Hosseini's *The Kite Runner* that was in near-perfect condition. The artwork on the cover was pleasant enough: it had a banner proclaiming it to be a *New York Times* bestseller, and it was lauded by other seemingly important authors I'd never heard of, exclaiming how beautifully it was written. But more important than anything, all the pages were intact. I grabbed it, took it back to my bunk, and dug in.

The Kite Runner is gorgeously written prose about an Afghan family escaping the clutches of the Taliban and emigrating to America. It felt relevant. In the second act, when the family travels to America, it makes its way to Northern California—the Bay Area, specifically.

Amir, the protagonist, enrolls in college—at San Jose State University. I thought, *What are the chances of that? There are over five thousand colleges and universities in the United States, and the author chose the same obscure commuter school I just dropped out of?* There were also mentions of the same farmers' markets and flea markets where I followed my mother around as a child. Now, I realize that San Jose is one of the largest cities in the country, so it's probably not as serendipitous as I imagined at the time, but that small detail made it personal and kept me engaged—10/10. Would read again.

After running through *The Kite Runner* in a matter of days, I went back to the Latrine Library looking for another fix. On the second run, I landed on a copy of Jack Kerouac's *On the Road*. I'd never read it, but it's a title that's constantly brought up in every English Lit course I've ever taken, so I thought, *Why not?* Initially, the writing felt clunky. It was definitely outdated, but the subject matter was one I could get behind. Good ol' Sal Paradise goes on a cross-country road trip with his friends, living life against a backdrop of drugs, sex, and jazz music. Incredible. If I had read it back in school, I might've had an existential quarter-life crisis and done a bunch of drugs, and I probably wouldn't have made it to Iraq.

Toward the end of the novel, on his return back to San Francisco, Kerouac mentions that Sal stopped off in a little town to find work for some gas money to make it the rest of the way. That small town happened to be Campbell, California—*my* Campbell, California. I was sitting in a war-torn country seventy-three hundred miles away from home reading about my tiny little hometown. It was a strange feeling—one that transformed from wonderment to that of an intense homesickness.

Campbell, California, was my orchard. For the foreseeable future, the sprawling FOB (forward operating base) on the outskirts of Kirkuk would serve as an oasis away from home, away from Rory and Claire, away from everything I'd ever known and in a world I'd never experienced.

INTEL BRIEF - A SERIES OF 4
COORDINATED CAR BOMBINGS TOOK
PLACE IN KIRKUK. 23 DEAD, 60+ WOUNDED

10AM - A SUICIDE BOMBER AT A POLICE
      BUILDING

10:30AM - A SUICIDE BOMBER TARGETED
      AN ORPHANAGE

11:45AM - A CAR BOMB DETONATED
      OUTSIDE A MOSQUE DURING A
      GATHERING FOR NOON PRAYER.

12:30PM - A 4TH CAR BOMB EXPLODED
      ON A BUSY STREET IN THE CENTER
      OF THE CITY.

WHAT KINDA FUCKED UP PLACE
      IS THIS ???

11

ALL ALONG THE WATCHTOWER

CRYSTALLINE CLUMPS OF sandy crust formed in the corner of my eyes while I stared into a dark void for hours, waiting for the boogeymen with black beards to appear. They never did. Instead, I watched with a quiet gratitude as the sky slowly transitioned from pitch black into more pleasant and much less threatening shades of pastel. Seeing the sizzling Iraqi sunrise until it rested on the horizon like a lonely egg yolk in a pink frying pan meant I was alive. And however cliché that may be, it was better than the alternative.

A chain-link fence topped with rusting razor wire and about three hundred meters of dead grass were all that separated me from jihad. Beyond the highway on the other side of the fence, Kirkuk displayed its war-torn exterior like a depressing Monet painting. The dark-gray city skyline, with bombed-out buildings, smokestacks, and soft green lights that shone from the minarets, set a melancholy mood for the cradle of civilization's latest unwelcome guests. The fading echoes of the beautifully haunting dawn prayer, called a Fajr, bounced off the walls of crumbling concrete passageways and dissipated into the heavens as the prayers came to an end. I looked at my dusty Timex wristwatch, which had a Velcro strap that was frayed beyond repair; the time: 0455.

The day was just starting for most in Kirkuk, but I worked the graveyard shift, so mine was nearly over. After spending another night in Tower Twelve, an LP/OP (listening post / observation post) located half a block outside the base's protective wall, I was ready to pack it up and get reacquainted with my bunk. My stomach growled because I refused to eat MREs. And not because I'm some soft city boy who doesn't know how to rough it. I'm a soft city boy with a sensitive stomach who doesn't like to rough it. Those are two different types of people. An unusually strong stench of excrement, gunpowder, and death brought by an arid breeze helped curb my appetite just enough.

I was getting accustomed to the quiet monotony, but youth plus boredom can be a dangerous combination, especially when automatic weapons are added to the equation. Sometimes I'd look through the long-range night-vision scope of my mounted M249 SAW (squad automatic weapon), imagining scenarios where I was the last man alive and I was forced to defend the base from a horde of blood-thirsty terrorists hell-bent on ending Western civilization. Through my binoculars, I watched as men armed with AK-47s loitered on rooftops and in front of buildings, wondering which ones were the good guys and which ones were the ones I could kill. It was nearly impossible to distinguish who was who in this Wild West, or rather, Wild Middle East. It's sick and borderline psychopathic, but I wanted to help make some martyrs because that is what I had been trained to do for the previous year. And more than anything, I just wanted some good war stories to bring home.

I had been at war for nearly a month and hadn't seen any action at all. The only terrorist I was fighting on a daily basis was sleep. At night, my partner and I took turns letting the darkness take hold and jolting ourselves awake like two camouflage bobblehead dolls. Our radio chirped, asking for a sitrep (situation report). After relaying that, I looked up, and my partner was nowhere to be found. He had a penchant for wandering off. Maybe he was taking his morning shit in the field below our tower—a field overlooking one of the mass graves of Saddam Hussein's Kurdish genocide decades earlier. Or, maybe my partner had already voluntarily relieved himself of duty and found his way back to our Humvee to grab some shut-eye, as he was wont to do from time to time. Despite having five thousand armed American service members behind me, it was still hard not to feel completely alone.

My bladder ached the way it does when you've been drinking beer all night. Only there was no beer. And we were fresh out of Rip Its, an eight-ounce energy drink packed with twenty-five grams of sugar and two hundred milligrams of caffeine, designed to keep us ultravigilant—read: cracked out and paranoid. (The consumption of too many Rip Its came with a plethora of unpleasant side effects including migraines, nausea, and explosive diarrhea. But at least you were wide awake while you were shitting your brains out.) There was only metallic-tasting water and local knockoffs of American soda that resembled cough syrup more than any carbonated beverage sold back in the States.

The night before, we were briefed by intelligence that a group of insurgent snipers were surveying our base. But with no partner there to relieve me, I decided to take my chances and took a leak off the side of the tower. I could think of few things more American than dying with my dick in my hands and a rifle slung over my shoulder.

Unbeknownst to me or any of the other Americans working that shift, a small maroon sedan packed with explosives was circling the streets adjacent to the sector I was responsible for. While I sprayed liquid waste into the wind, the VBIED (vehicle-borne improvised explosive device) was watching and waiting for a prime target to lay waste to.

I had committed a cardinal sin as a Security Forces member: I had failed to remain vigilant, and I let my guard down, if only for those few seconds. I had forgotten the first of my three general orders, the commandments that governed my position: "I will take charge of my post and protect all personnel and property for which I am responsible." I had neglected to be the human sensor the US government had trained me to be. At that same moment, an Army convoy that made for a much better mark than a single airman with his pants around his ankles was passing in the opposite direction.

It happened midstream—the car connected with a convoy of Humvees, and a portion of the highway right outside the main gate of the base disappeared into a ball of flames. The force of the blast jarred me; I pissed all over myself and almost went over the banister into a puddle of urine and mud.

I stood there for a second trying to figure out what had just happened. My ears rang with a dizzying intensity while I felt to see if my body was still completely intact. There was no blood, and I was seeing white stars, but I wasn't dead. There were no pearly gates, no virgin angels, only seahorses of nausea bouncing around in my stomach that made me retch.

Holding up my pants with one hand, I grabbed my M4 carbine with the other and ran to the top of the tower. All I could see was a thick plume of smoke that had death draped all over it. In all the chaos, I had forgotten basic standard communication protocol and found myself screaming an amalgamation of incoherent noises into the radio. I was hundreds of yards from the explosion and completely disoriented, so I couldn't imagine how the soldiers in the convoy were faring.

Moments later, the methodical thumps of medical helicopters sprinting over my head drowned out all background noise. Then came the buzz of two other helicopters. They were dark and menacing, and the Red Cross logo of those that preceded them was replaced by large-caliber cannons, rocket launchers, and other weaponry—Apache gunships. They flew low and raced back and forth like large mechanical hornets buzzing around their disturbed hive, Forward Operating Base Warrior.

Control came back over the net, "Tower Twelve, sitrep?"

"So, here's the situation, guys. It's, um, well, it's not looking too great. Over."

This is the CCIR (Commander's Critical Info Report):

ACTION OR INCIDENT RESULTING IN SIGNIFICANT MILITARY OR CIVILIAN CASUALTIES: 07:47, reports of a VBIED detonation in the Kirkuk Province at FOB Warrior, Vic Gate and Grid. In report, a vehicle heading north with 3X PAX slowed down. PAX were observed looking into the gate. A second vehicle, a maroon sedan, was also heading north. The vehicle then turned around and detonated in the medium. 3X US WOUNDED IN ACTION. 4X COALITION WIA. 10X CIVILIAN LN WIA. 1X ENEMY KIA.

The higher-ups didn't want to throw us straight into the fire—there would be plenty of time for that later. For the first few weeks, they had us working the gates exclusively, where we'd spend twelve hours patting down potential suicide bombers before walking them through a pedestrian portal. If you were on someone's shit list, you'd be assigned to work the X-ray scanner that provided shockingly high-definition photos of every nook and cranny on the human body, not unlike the machines TSA uses. It was twelve hours of looking at dicks and buttholes in a warm, poorly ventilated room that smelled like dicks and buttholes.

At the vehicle gates, civilian vehicles were searched before enter-ing and leaving. Before they were allowed on the installation to be searched for contraband, we checked their undercarriages with mir-rors, then sent them through a corridor that x-rayed the contents of their carriages. If you got lucky or some logistics troop called in sick, you'd get mail duty, where you'd have to check packages for bombs and chemical or biological substances.

It didn't matter if we were checking cars, packages, or buttholes for bombs, our job was like a sick Iraqi roulette we didn't want to win. And over the course of that deployment, a handful of guys had their number called, spun the wheel, and found themselves in the wrong place at the wrong time.

Every once in a while, we were assigned to escort the local nation-als who worked on the base, usually in some custodial capacity. They cleaned our barracks, scrubbed our shit-caked toilets, served as our barbers, and worked at the various fast-food stands we had on base. The locals and service members who worked alongside them were put on rotating shifts so that individuals never spent too much time working with the same people, which was seen as a potential security threat. Even though the Iraqis were vetted, they didn't want us getting too cozy with "the help." Complacency leads to dead bodies, as my drill instructor used to say.

To help us get a lay of the land, we shadowed teams from the US Army's Tenth Mountain Division, the Twenty-Fifth Infantry Division, and some sloppy and seemingly ill-equipped National Guard units while they patrolled the perimeter of the forward operating base or pulled guard duty at one of the installation's many entrances. Naturally, they gave us a hard time for being an Air Force unit, but we were doing the same job they were, and our presence meant they finally got to go home. Some of those guys had been in Iraq for fifteen months; I hadn't been there a month, and I already missed home. I missed Claire and my unborn child. I missed Rory. I missed my friends. And

I missed my parents, despite the falling out before my departure. I didn't know how I was going to make it another six to twelve months.

While I was pulling guard duty at one of the gates, a group of inquisitive Iraqi kids looking like Peter Pan's Middle Eastern Lost Boys, ranging in age from early adolescence to teenagers, approached Allen and me. They seemed harmless enough, but Allen kept his hand on his sidearm just in case. We'd heard enough of the "unsuspecting American GI gets killed by a child suicide bomber" horror stories during the predeployment training leading up to our trip. The urban legends were propaganda to dehumanize local nationals. I remember an NCO saying, "Most of these people aren't our enemies, but you have to treat them like they are if you want to stay alive." (The aforementioned NCO is a state trooper in New Jersey, so he's probably well-versed in terrorizing people of color.) In my heart, I knew these kids weren't terrorists—they were just trying to make the best out of a fucked-up situation. Which is something I could relate to.

But for every suicide bomber or enemy insurgent, there were ten thousand friendly faces in Kirkuk. One of those friendly faces that showed up to the gate that day was a Kurdish teenager named Brahim. I recognized him as one of the locals I escorted around the FOB while he worked as a custodian. He had a goofy bowl cut and was wearing the same counterfeit Puma soccer pants with brown, tattered, prison-style chanklas he wore every time I saw him. Per policy, we kept the small talk to a minimum on base, so I didn't actually know much about him. My familiar face was enough to get a smile and a handshake.

He touched his chest. "Ibrahim."

"Nice to meet you, Ibrahim. I'm Dylan."

"Dylan," he repeated back to himself.

"You're not working today?" I asked.

"No, no. I only work when they need of me."

"Wanna trade places?" I unstrapped my helmet and placed it on his head.

His friends laughed. The kids giggled, passing it around to take turns trying it on. Allen thought it was funny too, but reminded me if I was caught working without my lid, I was looking at an Article 15. I wasn't too worried about any of that, but I motioned for Brahim to hand it back over for Allen's peace of mind.

Brahim was among the oldest in the group and was one of the few teenagers who worked on base. He also spoke the best English of all of them, so naturally he became an unofficial interpreter for both parties. Seeing these children running around in a combat zone in the middle of the day—on weekdays no less—was slightly unusual. While Brahim was working as a janitor on a military installation in an active war zone, Rory, who was the same age, was back at home living a privileged life. He was doing things like applying to colleges he knew he would never attend, going to prom, skipping school on weekdays, and hanging out at the mall with his friends on the weekends.

I asked Brahim why they weren't in school, and he said they didn't have a school to go to because Americans destroyed it. *Well, that was a dumb question, Dylan.* Foot, meet mouth.

The charred skeleton of a schoolhouse that had been leveled was only a few blocks outside the base's perimeter. As a show of good faith, American engineers struck up a deal with the local government to help rebuild it. Every other week for months, we'd either volunteer or be voluntold to provide security while the new school was under construction. The day the school reopened, children showed up in droves, eager to resume their education and add some normalcy back to their lives. A few days after that, the laughing and squeals on the soccer pitch and playground turned to screams, crying, and then silence when another suicide bomber detonated a truck full of explosives in front of a building next door, killing a dozen children and teachers.

That's the type of place these kids were growing up in, and some-how, despite experiencing horrors and hardships most Americans couldn't even begin to fathom, they (mostly) managed to maintain a positive outlook.

Iraqi teenagers with a less-than-positive outlook for their country's future were often recruited, sometimes by force, into signing on with rebel factions to fight the occupying infidels. And could I really blame them? After some assholes flew a couple of planes into the World Trade Center towers, I signed up to fight for my own country. Only, I wasn't in Afghanistan or Pakistan or Saudi Arabia, helping hunt down the assholes who killed three thousand innocent Americans. For some inexplicable reason, I was fighting for an oil field in a foreign country that had absolutely nothing to do with the dead Americans back home.

Brahim had other plans, however. He was biding his time to become an interpreter for the US military. That's where the real money was, he said. Interpreters could earn *$250 a week*. That amount would qualify as destitute poverty in America, but in Iraq, it was a life-changing amount for a teenager.

The US government had an agreement with Iraqis that if they worked a certain number of years as a translator, they'd be issued a special immigrant visa to come to the United States once their contract was up. And there were plenty of opportunities available, provided they could pass a background check. The high turnover rate of con-tracted translators was due to targeted assassinations. At one point, we were losing an average of one interpreter a day.

Local terror groups would execute anyone they even suspected of working with Westerners, leaving their bodies hanging from underpasses or piled up in mass graves to be found all over the city. Sometimes they'd murder the families and friends of anyone they deemed a traitor to drive the point home. On one occasion, an Army patrol reported coming across decapitated heads on spikes on the side of the road.

Brahim said he understood the risks, but he was willing to do whatever it took to feed his family and help end the war in Iraq.

12

THE KIDS ARE NOT ALRIGHT

WHILE WORKING QRFS (quick reaction forces, or patrols that remained on standby to assist other units), most of our nights were spent sitting in a Humvee, listening to the eerie howl of the wind whipping sand off the side of our truck and the constant radio chatter calling out potential threats. The frequent gunshots and explosions in the near distance kept us on edge. Outside the wire, everyone had their own method to cool their nerves and remain present. Some of the fellas chain-smoked cigarettes; others were constantly spitting the excess runoff of their chewing tobacco into repurposed water bottles. Sunflower seeds and a Brisk Iced Tea were my comfort routines while on duty. There's something about the methodical chewing of seeds that keeps your mind subconsciously active. But mostly it just smelled better than cigarettes and seemed a million times more sanitary than carrying around a bottle full of saliva.

The thing about a bottle full of regurgitated chewing tobacco and a bottle of iced tea is that they look remarkably similar—especially in low-light conditions. And I discovered that the hard way. Getting a mouthful of another man's spit when you're expecting a refreshing drink of sugary tea might be on the top-ten list of the most traumatic things I experienced during my time in Iraq. And as I was hunched over vomiting, I had a realization that my first war wasn't going how I envisioned it would.

Sitting, waiting, wishing is what we did most days. It wasn't the shoot-'em-up, bang-bang adventure I spent the better part of a year training and mentally preparing myself for. My war was nothing like the ones I watched on TV and in the movie theaters. I was reading *My War: Killing Time in Iraq*, a memoir by Colby Buzzell, another half-Korean American service member hailing from the Bay Area. Buzzell is credited as being one of the first—if not *the* first—soldier to have an online blog about his experiences during the invasion of Iraq, in real time. Colby's public journal went viral because it was new and it was an honest look at the conflict Americans saw in the media every day.

My war was nothing like his war either. Frankly, I was bored out of my fucking mind most days. My war was 90 percent masturbation and 10 percent sheer terror. And sometimes it was being terrified while masturbating. On a separate but related note, there's something about jerking off with night vision goggles on while your life is in imminent danger that really takes the experience to another level. The Zero Dark Dirty, we called it.

Sure, there were the occasional moments of excitement. A rocket would fall here, a mortar would land there. There was sporadic small arms fire when we cruised the perimeter of the base, but a large majority of the firefights we'd gotten into were on *Call of Duty 3*. The Internet was unreliable on the FOB, making most online matches nearly impossible to win if we could even play at all. But that didn't stop us from trying, because there wasn't shit else to do on base. Online video game arenas are some of the most toxic forums, and shit-talking in multiplayer games is to be expected. It's no different than an overly serious asshole chirping at you during a game of pickup basketball at the local YMCA. But when it happens, it's never really a surprise.

On one occasion, I was in the midst of another long *Call of Duty* losing streak, and a teenager with a thick accent screamed obscenities at me through my headphones. I didn't even hit the mute button. I barely understood what he was saying, but I understood *exactly* what he was getting at. I told him he didn't know who the fuck he was talking to—*I* was currently in Iraq fighting. So while he was busy playing video games in his mother's basement, I was living the real thing. To which he responded in broken English, "I hope you're better at shooting guns in real life, because at this rate you might not be coming home, you pig."

There wasn't much coming back from that. I didn't touch a video game controller for the rest of the deployment. I later learned Treyarch, *Call of Duty*'s developer, sets matches geographically to offset lag. There was a very distinct possibility we were playing video games with people who were trying to kill us in real life as well.

After being in Kirkuk long enough, shifts eventually transformed from twelve-hour, anxiety-inducing workdays into a grass-growing, paint-drying monotony. To combat that, I quietly brought unauthorized items to work with me, like my first-generation Apple iPod Shuffle—a small MP3 player that held only a few hundred songs and resembled a USB flash drive more than any music player. Ironically, it was loaded with Rage Against the Machine, Jimi Hendrix, Creedence Clearwater Revival, Black Sabbath, U2, and other musicians known for their anti-war stances. But it provided just enough entertainment for me to get through my days. I'd wear one earbud like a secret service agent and kept the volume low so I could still do my job without compromising my safety.

On one of my shifts, Brahim and the neighborhood kids showed up to the gate I was working. He noticed the earbud and pointed to it.

"Music?" he asked.

"Sure is," I nodded.

"What do you listen to?"

I listened to everything from my namesake, Bob Dylan, to death metal. But 50 Cent's "In Da Club" was the song currently playing. I pulled the earbud out, yanked the wire that was hidden behind my armor plates, and took the MP3 player out of my pocket. I plugged the headphones back in, hit the rewind button so he could listen from the beginning, because the intro is the best part of the song, then leaned over the slide arm separating us and handed it to him.

After a few seconds, the beat sank in, Brahim's eyes went wide, and his hips swayed back and forth. His friends grabbed the other earbud and they listened together. Shoulder to shoulder and holding hands, they danced in unison, singing, "Go shorty, it's your birthday," to which I would respond, "We're gonna party like it's your birthday." They kicked their legs out in concert like the Radio City Music Hall Rockettes and twirled imaginary scarves in the air above their head. They yelled "Dylan!" while Allen and I laughed and clapped. I later learned that they weren't yelling my name in excitement. The name of the Kurdish dance is *Dilan*.

Alongside other neighborhood children, Brahim regularly showed up to our front gates or followed us while we were on patrol, asking for American candy and soda. They became obsessed with American pop culture, and we'd talk about movies and music for hours on end. When given the opportunity, I would collect discarded magazines to gift to Brahim and his friends. In exchange for year-old *Maxim* and *GQ* issues—there was always some sort of deal being made—they would bring me Cuban cigars, burner phones, alcohol, and bootleg DVDs of movies that were still in theaters back home in the States. I'm not sure where they got them, because as far as I was aware, there were no movie theaters in Iraq showing Western films in English, but how they were made was obvious from the quality of the films. The movies were all recorded on camcorders in actual theaters. You could hear the audience members laughing or screaming, and occasionally one or two would walk in front of the camera, blocking the screen. Bootleg or not, they were still better than the alternative, which was watching *Star Wars: Episode III—Revenge of the Sith* for the fifteenth time in the movie room surrounded by other soldiers with questionable hygiene.

Brahim brought me a copy of the recently released *Borat! Cultural Learnings of America for Make Benefit Glorious Nation of Kazakhstan.* When I watched it, I laughed so hard I cried. Then I cried thinking about Rory, because that was the type of movie we would've seen together. Borat was the type of character Rory would do impressions of until everyone around him got sick of it. The more I was around Brahim, the more he began to remind me of my younger brother.

For one, they were both extremely mature for their age, which wasn't a surprise. Brahim grew up in a war zone, so conflict was all he knew, and it gave him a steely resolve not seen in most people, let alone in sixteen-year-olds. Over the course of my year in Iraq, we had some very deep and philosophical conversations about life and death and religion and politics—discourse not typically held with a teenager.

Rory fought his own wars when he was young. He had several health scares as a child and was in and out of the hospital repeatedly for surgeries to remove growths in his head, neck, and arms, leaving him scarred. Even as a kid, I could see that the constant uncertainty took a toll on Rory, and he began to lash out. By the time he made it to high school, which seemed like a miracle in itself, he had already attended four different schools for all the trouble he'd gotten in. Then, sometime in junior high, Rory revealed that he was molested as a child at the same private Catholic school my parents put us in to keep us out of the streets. He was attending therapy years before I even really understood what therapy was.

All the trauma Rory experienced, visible or not, helped shape his sense of humor. And, like me, he used it as a shield. As a kid, he followed me and my friends around and developed an adult vernacular by listening to all the jokes we told. As long as he didn't tell on us, we let him watch all the R-rated movies we weren't allowed to watch. Rory was four years younger than I was but spoke with a level of maturity that confused a lot of people. Because of our differing ages, we each had our own circle of friends, but we still tried to do everything together, and over time we became inseparable. My time in Iraq was the longest we'd been apart since the day Rory was born.

On the last day of summer, the thermometer in the truck was still hovering around three digits. I was told my body would eventually acclimate to the weather, but there was no getting used to something like that. I was sitting in the turret behind an M240 Bravo machine gun that couldn't be touched without gloves because it'd been baking in the sun for hours alongside me. When I drank water, loose drops would dot the weapon's receiver assembly and hiss like a frying pan.

Our convoy moved slowly, almost aimlessly, while we patrolled the sector surrounding the base, as we did most days. Being in the turret meant I was the eyes and ears of our vehicle, so I kept my head on a nervous swivel. In the distance, two black specks stood out against a backdrop of tan. I turned the turret and strained my eyes. Wild dogs maybe?

"Yo, pass me the binos," I screamed down to Big Montana. There was no response. I looked down and Big Montana was looking straight ahead. I nudged him with my foot. "Are your comms broken?"

Big Montana checked. He pressed the receiver to talk. Nothing.

"I can't hear shit."

"Hand me the binos!" I said a little louder this time.

Big Montana rummaged around looking through the equipment bag. He crawled onto the center console to ask the navigator. The navigator shrugged. He tapped me on the leg.

"I can't find 'em!"

By now we were running nearly parallel with the two figures in question. I looked a little harder. Two small bodies lay in the no-man's-land between the base and the highway that led into the city. Dead bodies in the streets weren't as common as one would expect in a war zone, but they weren't shocking to see either. Bodies this close to the FOB were. As our small patrol drew closer to the two dark silhouettes, I noticed they were children. And they weren't moving.

I whistled as loud as I could. One of the bodies stirred. It sat up slowly. I made direct eye contact with the child. His black, listless eyes followed us as we drove by, and I knew something was off. The figure next to him didn't move and remained curled up in a ball. When I alerted the CO, he instructed us to keep moving. "Babysitting hajis isn't our mission," he replied without the slightest hesitation or forethought.

Against his orders, I yelled at my driver to slow down, then jumped out of the turret of the Humvee.

"What the fuck are you doing, Park?" Big Montana asked. He was more afraid of the consequences for disobeying orders than the consequences I might face by wandering off on my own.

"Tell the CO we're having engine problems. Just watch my six. I'll be back in a second." I knew I didn't have much time so I jogged toward the children. The little boy was around six years old, and the little girl who I presume was his sister must've been four, maybe five. As I got closer, I noticed they were caught between two razor wire dividers.

The little boy was frightened as I walked toward him, so I slung my rifle over my back out of view, and I removed my helmet and dark glasses so he could see my eyes. Dry tear trails lined his cheeks, and his chapped bottom lip quivered uncontrollably.

"As-salamu alaykum," I said as I approached.

Prior to our deployment, we were taught five lines of Arabic, and four of those were some version of "Stop or I'll kill you." Another was

"Hello." Not exactly a way to win over the people of the country we were occupying, but compassion is a universal language, so I knelt down and held the boy's hand. I could feel him trembling through my glove.

I wasn't sure how long they'd been out there, but from the looks of it, long enough that they had heat stroke and weren't too far from succumbing to the elements. I gave the boy some water from my canteen. After taking a long pull, he pointed at the little girl on the ground. Her leg was tangled in the razor wire. I followed the dry trail of blood and sharp barbs down to a compound fracture in her lower leg. *Fuck.* I rubbed her back gently. Her breathing was slow and shallow, but she stirred and turned her head just enough to look at me and let me know that she was alive. She was too weak to hold the canteen, so I held it for her while she took a sip.

After returning the injured children back to the base for medical care, I was written up and reprimanded by our chief master sergeant for disobeying a direct order and was given an Article 15 with the choice of time in the stockade or docked pay. I chose to forfeit a few weeks of pay because it's not like I was making shit anyway. A short while later, the base commander learned of my disobedience and to my great surprise rescinded my punishment, gave me a letter of commendation, and used the event as an opportunity to gather some good PR in a war that was losing its favor with the American public.

Hearts and minds, or something like that.

ANOTHER SQUAD WAS UNDERMANNED, SO
ALLEN AND I VOLUNTEERED TO WORK AN
EXTRA QRF SHIFT IN A NEW SECTOR.
I WAS IN THE TURRET DOING A CHECK ON
MY 240 WHILE AN ARMY PATROL WAS
QUEING UP TO LEAVE. I LOOKED UP JUST
IN TIME TO SEE THE FLASH. HAD THE WIND
KNOCKED OUT OF ME. COULDN'T SEE SHIT.
EARS WERE RINGING. WHEN I CAME TO
I DISMOUNTED TO PROVIDE AIDE. ALL OF
OUR BOYS WERE WHOLE. ALIVE AND WELL.
ALL PRESENT AND ACOUNTED FOR. THE
ONLY ONE KIA WAS THE ASSHOLE IN THE
CAR PACKED w/ EXPLOSIVES. DIDN'T
KNOW WHAT ELSE TO DO, SO I SNAPPED
SOME PICS OF THE AFTERMATH. AN
EAR AND A FINGER HERE. PART OF A
SKULL AND BRAINS THERE. GNARLY
SHIT. POSTED THE PICS ON MYSPACE
AND WAS REPRIMANDED.

13

HOME FOR CHRISTMAS

BEFORE HOPPING ON a war bird, we were handed a stack of documentation to read, fill out, sign, initial, whatever. One of those forms was for receiving an updated military identification card and new dog tags. Last name, first name, social security number, and blood type—all the information that would be needed if I drove over an IED or met some other gruesome fate leaving my body unidentifiable. The final line of the questionnaire was my religious preference.

Being the son of a Southern Baptist father and Buddhist mother, the husband of a white girl with a Wiccan mother, and a captive to the Catholic school system for nearly a decade during my youth had me stretched thin, theologically speaking. I dabbled here and there when required, but my faith wasn't something I felt too strongly about. So, as a joke, I checked the "other" box and wrote in Scientology. The following day, I was called into the chief master sergeant's office and berated for the better part of an hour for failing to take "warfighting" seriously.

Chief explained that if I died, I would be given funeral rights according to the customs of the religion I had marked on my paperwork. For the Church of Scientology, that entails a minister speaking over my coffin to pronounce my "thetan"—more commonly known as a soul in most religions—released into the heavens. I would then be reincarnated with a new body and life in the latest chapter of a cycle that I've unknowingly been a participant of for billions of years. As far as dying goes, that sounded pretty decent to me. It most definitely beats spending an eternity in the depths of hell, which is certainly where I'd be headed if a Christian hell does exist.

I changed the religion on my dog tags to agnostic.

The next form in my deployment packet, the DD Form 93, is a document troops used to designate who Uncle Sam should notify in case of an emergency or death. While each branch has its own way of doing things, they each require the person on the form be notified before the news of any tragedy is made public. I could only imagine how terrible it would be to learn of a loved one's death overseas from a Fox News chyron right before cutting away from Bill O'Reilly to a Flex Seal infomercial.

The advent of the Internet and social media made keeping a service member's death private before their next of kin could be identified much more complicated. In order to put an end to unauthorized communication following a fatality, installations and surrounding areas of operation were put on reduced communications lockdowns, commonly referred to as "River City."

With daily attacks on both civilians and soldiers, the violence in Iraq reached a boiling point, and communication lockdowns were becoming more and more commonplace. And, like some kind of sadistic cosmic force, River City always seemed to occur at the most inopportune times, like holidays or other special occasions when we needed to call home. But it's hard to complain about not being able to call home during the holidays, when folks back home were being notified by two soldiers on their doorstep that their children wouldn't be coming home.

Holidays and religion are often intertwined. As with my faith, I'd never been a very festive person either. Sure, I used the days off work and the three-day weekends as another excuse to binge drink, like most of the other twentysomethings I knew, but that was the extent of my holiday cheer. I rarely ever celebrated the essence of those "special" days marked on the calendar. Fuck Christopher Columbus, the dead presidents, or Old Saint Nick, I was a Grinch year-round.

Now, one would think being in a war zone would only amplify the bah humbugs—and they'd be dead wrong. My mindset completely changed overseas. I looked at every holiday as a milestone. With each one that passed, I was that much closer to being home, and that was always something to celebrate. And I know most of the other fellas felt the same way.

There was something especially patriotic about traveling overseas in service of our country during the Fourth of July. I'm not exactly sure what a gallantly streaming rampart is, but we had a quick introduction to the rockets' red glare and bombs bursting in air soon after landing in country.

Labor Day was spent laboring. Nine-to-five workweeks don't exist in combat zones. Our shifts were twelve to sixteen hours, sometimes longer, and we were scheduled to work six days a week. And, more often than not, our off days were spent sheltering in place from mortar and rocket attacks. Sometimes we'd get called to assist the doctors and medics with incoming casualties. There was no overtime for this employee of the month.

At the end of September, we were briefed that sometime during the month of Ramadan the Shiites were planning to engage in more acts of violence against US and coalition troops to "demonstrate their strength" and eventually purge the Sunni population in Iraq. The intel group told us the locals wanted to end their holy holiday with a bang—causing as much damage as possible through a brazen show of force. Now, most of our intelligence briefings were pretty ho-hum, but I always paid close attention. The details could mean the difference between life and death. I took this new hysteria with a grain of salt, because of the constant stream of racist rhetoric from the top down. Dehumanizing the enemy to make killing them more acceptable has been a staple of war fighting since the beginning of war fighting. And there were only so many times I could hear another American refer to the locals as camel jockeys, hajis, sand niggers, dune coons, etc. before I realized a lot of the noise was an extension of that dehumanization.

Sometime in mid-October, our detachment was given a brief about a group who called themselves the Mujahideen Shura Council, which partnered with six Sunni tribes to form the Mutayibeen Coalition. The terrorist organization pledged "to rid Sunnis from the oppression of the rejectionists [Shiite Muslims] and the crusader occupiers [us] . . . and to restore the glory of Islam." Hours later, the same group declared the caliphate under the banner of the Islamic State of Iraq. It was hard to keep track. The threat level on our installation was raised, but that was a common occurrence. If somebody sneezed too loud, we were put on high alert.

The constant threats of violence didn't stop troops working the night shift from telling each other ghost stories on Halloween on open radio lines. Iraq was scary enough without a bunch of immature assholes whispering creepy things to each other over the comms, and all the aspiring M. Night Shyamalans were given extra duty until Thanksgiving.

For Thanksgiving, command flew in a team of chefs from Michelin-rated restaurants in Europe to serve us up one of the best meals I've ever eaten. For one night, we gathered around into the mess hall and were mostly able to forget about the stressors that awaited us the next day as we stuffed our faces. A few days before, we received word Saddam Hussein was sentenced to death by a tribunal. Good food and dead bad guys felt like something to be thankful for.

A few days after Thanksgiving, I celebrated—well, maybe *celebrated* isn't the right word—I *had* my twenty-second birthday. Kirkuk isn't exactly a Dave & Buster's. And there were no funfetti cakes or candles. The tracer rounds streaking across the night sky and distant explosions were a terrible substitute for fireworks. It felt like any another day, which is why I was surprised when a large package was placed on my bunk. For whatever reason, Adrian decided he'd ship me a pair of Air Jordans. It was an odd gift to send someone at war. But I understood the sentiment. I was a sneakerhead, and a fresh pair of Js with the tags on them was a morale booster.

The next time I had a chance, I called Adrian to thank him. He asked if I was enjoying them. Enjoying them? They were sitting on my shelf for obvious reasons. And even if I could wear them, which I couldn't, I wouldn't because I didn't want to scuff them. He told me to go back and check the packaging. He'd smuggled me contraband. I discovered a false floor in the bottom of the box and a hidden compartment stashed with porn DVDs. And although Adrian and I don't have the same taste in women—he likes thin pale chicks with tattoos and piercings, I'm more of a curvy-woman guy myself—those DVDs would absolutely come in handy. Pun intended.

When December rolled around, Christmas lights were put up, a Christmas tree was erected in a common area, and we even had a giant Santa inflatable installed in front of the armory. Noise and light discipline mandates saw that all the festive lights were turned off at sundown. I'm not sure if Iraq is a no-fly zone for Old Saint Nick, but if the bright lights were not hung with care, they could be used by spotters to drop mortars on us.

On Eid al-Adha, the Muslim Holiday of Sacrifice and the night before New Year's Eve, Saddam's execution was announced to cheers all over the installation. Intelligence reports had some of the country's officials and local nationals decrying Saddam's hanging on a holy day. In passing, I told Brahim the news. His response was one of disappointment, which confused me.

"Isn't this what you wanted?"

"Yes. Of course. But I wanted this for *my* people. This was a show for *your* people."

"They said he was found guilty for war crimes and crimes against humanity."

"Not our humanity. Many Iraqis don't even see us Kurds as humans. This is our home, and yet we are homeless. We can't claim it."

"Saddam's fucking dead, B. You should be celebrating."

"Iraq killed him before Kurds could put him on trial. They continue to spit in our faces and refuse to acknowledge our pain. That dog left us without looking into the eyes of all the families he massacred. I'm not celebrating this."

There were large swaths of Iraqis from all over the country who weren't celebrating either, and we were told to stay vigilant, as more violence was expected. New Year's Eve was spent on a perimeter patrol. Things were quiet. And when things were too quiet for too long, that typically meant shit was going down in the very near future. Fortunately, we rung in the New Year drinking Martinelli's sparkling apple cider and shooting off illumination flares in relative peace.

At the end of January, I received a letter from the Red Cross to notify me that there were "complications" during Claire's pregnancy and she was scheduled to be induced, but there were no other details. The violence in Iraq was at an all-time high, and not being able to check my e-mail, Myspace messages, and sports scores was a minor inconvenience; not being able to contact my pregnant wife was a helpless and hopeless feeling. I hadn't been out of country long enough to request R&R, but figured under these circumstances I could ask for emergency leave to see my family and be there for the birth of my first child. My request was immediately denied because one of the guys in our detachment broke his arm while joyriding around the base on an ATV, and another accidentally shot himself while cleaning his weapon. We were already down two bodies and couldn't afford to lose another, regardless of the reason.

I hadn't been in touch with Claire or anyone else for weeks. I wrote a letter home, and I don't remember exactly what it said, but for the sake of storytelling I'll pretend like it was some distinguished old-timey Civil War correspondence:

> *My Dearest Claire,*
> *Though we have not spoken in a fortnight, my love for you is timeless and knows no bounds. When I look up at the white moon at night, I think of you. And when I see the whites of the enemy's eyes, I know he is a fearsome foe, but not enough to keep me from you. In safeguarding operational security, I am unable to tell you my exact whereabouts, but indications are strong that we shall move to take back Mosul in the very near future. Shall I fall, know that I fell with you in my heart.*
> *Forever Yours,*
> *Senior Airman Park-Pettiford*

I never got a response, so I assumed my letter was lost in the mail during its voyage halfway across the world. In the back of my head, something much, much worse had happened. I put in another formal request to take leave and was denied again.

The more I pined to be home, the worse the bloodshed in Iraq became. Between 2006 and 2007, the fighting in Kirkuk was the worst it had been since the start of the war. The mortar and rocket attacks increased in numbers and severity. They went from once every few weeks to every other day. Scarier still, with every mortar that fell and every rocket that flew into the base's perimeter, impact points came closer and closer to living quarters and to buildings that were always heavily populated, like the chow hall. We knew that a handful of local nationals who had access to the base were acting as spotters and providing information to those on the outside attacking us. However, finding the spies would be almost impossible, as we were already undermanned to begin with. The nationals we allowed access to the base provided us with valuable information and also served as the cooks, cleaners, and laborers of the installation. Some of the locals, like Brahim, believed in our mission, but most truly just wanted a steady source of income.

Outside the wire, coalition troops were dying daily. It became a regularity to see convoys with damaged vehicles entering the base's gates. Part of me was relieved that our detachment had been retasked from combat patrols to perimeter security for the next few months; part of me felt guilty. Soldiers who usually smiled, waved, threw up peace signs, and high-fived as they came through the gates now looked distant behind the shattered armored glass. Some looked at their feet, some stared at the bloodstained seat in front of them, and others sat there with their eyes closed with a salty mixture of tears and sweat running down their cheeks. Large armored tow trucks that went out with convoys as an insurance policy for disabled and broken-down vehicles now seemed to travel with convoys out of a grim necessity.

The hulls of destroyed vehicles were dumped in a section we called Area 51. I'm not sure who came up with the name, but it stuck because the area looked like a field of fallen stars and UFOs. After a few months, Area 51 was starting to become a crowded graveyard. On some nights the lonely subdivision of the base would fall in my mobile patrol sector, and my partners and I would watch as vehicles were dropped off and left to rot. They were generally sprayed down because oftentimes the blood of troops killed in the field was left in the blackened hulls as a grim reminder for the rest of us. Sometimes no powerwashing was necessary because the vehicles were destroyed beyond recognition.

At the end of our workweeks, morbidly known as "Funeral Fridays," we stood in formation to pay respects to the men and women who had paid the ultimate sacrifice while their flag-draped coffins were loaded onto cargo planes. From there they'd stop in Germany, where their bodies would be prepared for a return to the States. I was grateful not to be in one of those boxes, but there was still plenty of time for that to change.

I woke up on Valentine's Day not feeling particularly romantic. I gathered my things, then went down to the armory to load up some ammo before our next patrol. I was pulled aside by an NCO and handed a letter with the Red Cross emblem on it. My heart sank. I took the letter, found a quiet corner, and sat down to brace myself.

I ripped it open slowly, took a deep breath. It read, *Congratulations, Dad! Brody Brandon Park-Pettiford. 2/13/07.* Attached to the note was a baseball card–sized photo of a child who was several shades too light for my comfort. The guys gave me a hard time about that, but I knew he was mine by his facial features and the smug little grin he was wearing. Brody was the best Valentine's Day present I've ever received.

The next day, Brahim gifted me with a thirty-minute prepaid card for the burner phone to call home and hear Claire's voice.

WOKE UP IN THE MASH. I'M NOT DEAD.
AT LEAST I DON'T THINK I AM.
LAST NIGHT ON PATROL, A POTENTAL
IED WAS CALLED OUT ON OUR ROUTE.
SECONDS LATER, A HELO OVERHEAD
DEPLOYED COUNTER MEASURES RIGHT
ABOVE US. ENTIRE SKY WAS LIT UP.
THE DRIVER GOT SPOOKED, YANKED THE
STEERING WHEEL, CRASHED THE HUMVEE
INTO A BERM, AND EJECTED MY ASS
FROM THE TURRET. DON'T REALLY
REMEMBER THE LAST PART, BUT HERE
I AM. DOC SAID THE KEVLAR PLATE ON
MY BACK SAVED ME FROM BEING A
CRIPPLE. I HAVE A FRACTURED COCCYX (SP?)
WHICH IS A NICE WAY OF SAYING "BROKEN
ASSHOLE." AT LEAST I'LL HAVE A FEW
WEEKS OFF. (THE NURSE WHO GAVE
ME A SHOT OF TORADOL IN MY ASS IS
A TOTAL SMOKESHOW.)

14

THUNDERSTRUCK

AFTER PACKING UP all my gear, I limped along in the pitch-black dark from my living quarters to the armory. Only a few days removed from my Humvee accident, Master Sergeant overrode the doctor's orders for two weeks of bed rest. He said he knew I was faking my injuries and ordered me back out into the field, threatening me with dereliction of duty if I refused.

When I arrived at the wall with the posting roster, I ran my glove-covered hand down the list of names. Master Sergeant had me working the Suicide Gate—again. *Fuck.* Between a few days in the hospital and disobeying a direct order a few weeks earlier when I dismounted my vehicle to help two dying children, the Master Sergeant was going to make my life miserable. I understood making an example of troops who didn't fall in line, but to hold a grudge for a lifesaving act of kindness that in no way jeopardized our mission (whatever the fuck that was) felt strange to me.

Even worse, I was working the Suicide Gate with Romero. I always had a strange, almost uneasy feeling about the kid even though he was from my home unit. I call him a kid, but he was at least ten years my senior. There was just something about his long face, droopy eyes, and slowed monotone drawl that made him seem simple.

His mood was always unpredictable; sometimes we couldn't get him to say a word, and sometimes we couldn't get him to shut the fuck up. But when he did talk, he would always tell me stories about being a Marine before he joined the Air Force. He would look past me with his glossy eyes and proudly tell me how he used to work on amphibious landing craft.

"Well, I didn't really work on them. Like, I wasn't a wrench monkey. I worked *on* them. I watched 'em and stuff. Made sure nobody messed with 'em. And sometimes, sometimes they would let me park 'em—like a valet," he would brag with as much youthful exuberance as a thirty-seven-year-old could have.

Over the next few months that exuberance would become more withdrawn. When we went to go eat as a group in the chow hall, he would take his food to go and eat by himself in his room. If we had movie or game night, he would never show up. I didn't press him much, because I figured it was just his way of coping with the stress of being away from home for so long. Plus, I knew him the least out of anyone in our unit. When I expressed concern, Sergeant Stokes pulled me aside.

"Hey, leave him be—he's always been kinda weird like that. Leave him be."

So I did. But I know I couldn't have been the only one who noticed Romero's once-athletic frame getting thinner under his now baggy uniform.

I figured that since we would be working with each other for the next day, maybe I would have a heart-to-heart with him. I wanted to try to keep his spirits up since I would need his best effort and full focus working; he would be the only person who would watch my back for the night. After reading the posting, I found Romero standing outside the armory alone and told him that we would be partners tonight in Gator Sector, and probably for the next week. He nodded without making eye contact.

To those that had been on Warrior long enough, the Gator Sector entrance was called the Suicide Gate, and rightly so. Every month or so a car packed with explosives or a person sporting a suicide vest would try to breach the entrance, detonate himself, and kill the poor bastards who drew the short straw for gate duty on that shift.

The gate was set up like a funnel—a narrow corridor surrounded by ten-foot-high walls. It was only wide enough for two cars or a handful of people to enter at a time, to minimize any potential threats. At each end of the fifty-yard corridor was a thick metal gate that could stop anything short of an M1 Abrams tank in its tracks. One steel roadblock was adequate, but two would ensure that we could halt anyone who was trying to get on or off base. At one point, both gates were remotely controlled, so the personnel on duty could open and close them from a safe location in an overwatch position encased in bulletproof glass and walls made out of three inches of solid steel.

Unfortunately for me, Romero, and anyone else now manning this post, these gates no longer worked remotely and now had to be manually opened, thanks to all the bombings and firefights that had happened at the entrance in recent months. So anytime a pedestrian or vehicle approached, I would have to leave the safety of the control room, walk the hundred yards in full battle rattle, visually inspect the vehicle or pat down any person, and then pull back a three-hundred-pound solid-steel gate with nothing but the strength the good Lord had given me.

After letting the guests into the corridor, making ourselves even more vulnerable to attack, I'd direct them to go through the same process with my partner down at the next gate. If by some chance they were indeed a threat and managed to get through both barricades and by both men working the post, there was a guard tower overlooking the area armed with a 240 Bravo automatic machine gun that would absolutely decimate anything it reached out to touch. As a very last resort, the tower also had a Mk-19 automatic grenade launcher that could destroy the entire entrance and everyone in it.

If the gate was breached, the operator simply had to get on the radio and repeat the word *lightning* three times, and that was the prompt for the overwatch to eliminate the next vehicle or person to come through the gate, no questions asked.

Just a few weeks prior to this shift, a suicide bomber had attacked the gate. The marks from the explosion were still fresh, and debris from the car still littered the passageway. Someone looking closely could even spot remnants of human remains—part of an ear here, the tip of a finger there. Everywhere you walked there were thousands of spent shell casings strewn about like the lifeless bodies of metallic locusts. They were indeed a plague on New Mesopotamia that took the lives of many of the country's first-born children. They filled the streets and rivers with blood, but they weren't sent from God—they were sent from the barrels of American machine guns.

During our preshift intelligence briefing, we were shown the security footage from the attack. We watched the grainy footage on the projection screen—a lonely soldier checking IDs through car windows as his partner looked on from the far side of the entrance. He pauses at one car, then a fraction of a second later the sector is engulfed in a fireball. I stared in horror and replayed the scene over and over in my head, even as the projection lamp went off and we stood in the dark.

"That is why you must remain vigilant at all times!" Master Sergeant McGill shouted.

Bullshit, I thought to myself. There's no way anyone could've done anything about that. If they want you dead, you were going to die. It only took the wink of an eye and the press of a button to send your ass to heaven. It was the luck of the draw, a sick lottery you didn't want to win.

Tonight Romero and I drew the short straw. Well, we were given the short straw. We checked our M4 carbines, M9 pistols, and a canister of frag and signal grenades out of the armory and loaded up our Humvee with the rest of our gear and food that we'd need to sustain us for the night.

On the short drive down to the gate to relieve the Army MPs on post, all I could think about was being the next pair of poor bastards to get ambushed at the gate, so I tried to break the awkward silence.

"How's it going tonight, man?" I asked.

Romero only replied with a grumble. It was going to be a long night.

I pulled up to the gate's control room and flashed my lights to signal to the other guards we were coming. Two sleepy-eyed Army privates slowly exited their shelter and waved back to acknowledge.

I hopped out of the truck. "You guys have a sitrep for me?"

"Sure, man. Everything was pretty quiet today. All the traffic coming in and out was NATO. Should be an easy night. There's your sitrep. We good to go now? 'Cause we want to get the fuck outta here." The second private nodded in agreement.

"Yeah, no problem. Have a good one, fellas."

As I walked from the Humvee toward the control room, the brass shell casings of spent rounds rolled and crunched under my weathered tan boots. I stepped up into the dark room and felt my hand along the wall to find the light switch. Light discipline was still standard protocol, but I always did a quick visual inspection before entering a dark room, just in case.

When I flipped on the light, a rat scurried by my foot and cockroaches raced from the walls into crevices, hidden away from human eyes. I immediately turned the lights back off, but the dark didn't make me any more comfortable. I knew all the creatures of the night were still watching me from the shadows, similar to the way Romero was still sitting completely motionless in the Humvee, watching me through its dirt-streaked windows. I could feel his eyes following my every action.

The bullet scars on the glass windows were jagged mementos that we were working the night shift in the most dangerous sector on base. I took my night-vision goggles from my bag and attached them to my helmet. If we were going to get into a firefight, I would need these, because all the city lights were off and there wasn't a star in the black Iraqi sky. The city was completely dark, save one softly glowing green light on a mosque's tower in the distance. All the lights were off because of a mandatory curfew. If a civilian was caught out after 9:00 PM, they were subject to search and arrest.

Unfortunately, this same curfew made it easier for insurgents to stalk us. They knew that they could send someone out at night and that we would try and stop them, making us idle targets. The same rules applied for base entrance and egress. Any non-NATO vehicle that tried to enter the base at night was automatically approached as hostile.

I took a seat on the cold metal bench and waited for my first visitor. To keep myself alert, I would chew a bag of sunflower seeds and drink several bottles of Gatorade. Only an hour went by before I saw the first headlights through the glass. I looked at the list of "approved civilian vehicles," which had been provided to us to identify undercover Special Forces operatives without impeding their access onto the base.

The approaching white Toyota Hilux pickup truck didn't have any of the correct markings or identifiers of those on my list. I signaled to Romero, who still hadn't moved from the passenger seat of the truck, with my flashlight. We had unexpected company.

I left the safety of the control room, charged my M4, and unhooked my M9 from the side holster on my leg. I wasn't going to be caught off guard. I walked down the right side of the road as close to the dirt wall as possible, with both hands on my rifle. As I approached,

I motioned for the driver to turn his headlights off. It was still too dark to see, but with their headlights off I could get a better idea of how many passengers there were.

When I reached the far gate, I did a quick visual inspection of the vehicle. There were no loose wires, the suspension wasn't lowered, and there weren't any new or repaired panels on the car, all tell-tale signs of a VBIED.

I glanced back at Romero to make sure he was watching. He wasn't. I lowered my rifle to pull back on the enormously heavy gate. I had to rock it back and forth for a bit to get some momentum, much in the same way that a Viking would've struggled to pull back on the oars of a longship as it sailed through a storm in the North Atlantic.

Once I finally got the gate open, I signaled for the vehicle to pull in and roll down their window. I approached the truck the way a highway patrol officer would. The driver and passenger were both Caucasian, but it wasn't readily obvious due to their dark tans and shaggy beards. The passengers in the backseat both had thick burlap sacks over their heads.

After scanning the interior, I noticed that between the driver's seat and center console, a compact MP5 submachine gun was tucked away. I also noticed that the front windshield was about two inches thick, bulletproof.

"Who are you gentlemen with?" I asked. The driver grinned.

"Your Majesty's SAS. We've got a couple of presents for you." He motioned toward the captives in the back seat.

"Not my Majesty, buddy. But I do like gifts. I just need to see your access card, and I'll let you boys be on your way."

The driver showed me the proper identification, and I motioned for him to go down to the next gate. I looked back, and Romero was nowhere to be found. I followed the pickup and opened the next gate myself. After they drove off, I went into the control room, where Romero was sitting in the dark, silently.

Over the next few hours, we had a few more vehicles trying to get on base. I would repeat the same process over and over: walk up, inspect the vehicle, struggle to get the gate open, close it, then walk all the way back and do the same at the second gate, all without the support of my partner. As the night wore on, so did my patience. I understood that something was amiss, but while we were on the job, I expected Romero to put his problems to the side to watch my back like I did his.

Frustrated, I marched toward the guard shack. "Hey man, what the fuck is your problem?" I yelled. "You're just gonna let me do this alone all night?" Again, there was no response.

"Fuck you," I added.

I tossed my helmet down to wipe the sweat from my brow, sat down across from Romero, and popped open my canteen to get a swig of lukewarm water. I looked up, and he just sat there staring directly at me. He still hadn't said a word.

"What the fuck are you looking at? Quit sulking." At that point, I wasn't even pretending to give a fuck about his worries.

We locked eyes like two wild animals do before they try to tear each other to bloody ribbons. Neither of us blinked. Then, before I could react, he lunged at me. Chairs and equipment went crashing everywhere. He had me pressed up against the back wall with his hands around my throat.

Romero stood almost a foot taller than me. I stared up into his sunken black eyes and watched as the dark bags underneath them flexed as he increased the pressure around my throat. I threw a left jab to his body, but he barely flinched. When he saw that I wasn't losing consciousness, he let his right hand go and balled it into a fist and repeatedly struck me in the face as hard as he could, until I didn't have any fight left in me.

"I'm sick of this shithole!" he screamed with tears streaming down his cheeks. "I'm sick of you, McGill, everyone! I'm fucking done!"

I could already feel my eyes swelling shut and taste the metallic bitterness of blood in my mouth. I was defeated physically, but he hadn't cut out my tongue.

"You're a bitch. No wonder you couldn't hack it in the Marines. You're a worthless piece of shit," I croaked.

"What did you say?"

"You heard me, you pussy. Fuck you."

His grip loosened, and with one hand he took his M4 and pressed the cold metal barrel right up against my left cheekbone until I could feel it fracturing under the force. I closed my eyes and tried not to wince from the pressure of the barrel digging into my face. He charged the weapon, and I could feel his finger on the trigger.

At the very same moment, I slowly unlatched my sidearm. I was getting myself ready to kill this man. We had practiced for different hand-to-hand scenarios endlessly in technical school and deployment training, but none like this. My M9 came out methodically and efficiently. I didn't waste any movements. I had it aimed directly at the soft spot between the plates in his body armor, but before I could talk myself into pulling the trigger, he struck me across the face with the butt of his shortened rifle, freeing his grip on me.

I staggered out of the room hunched over, pistol in hand, and blood flowing from my broken face. I stumbled toward the guard tower signaling for help. They didn't see me.

Still reeling and in complete shock from what had just taken place, I turned back just in time to see a muzzle flash illuminate the tinted windows of the guard shack.

15

DON'T START 'TIL YOU GET ENOUGH

ON ONE OF our rare days off together, Allen and I planned to meet up at the base's ice cream stand to catch up. It wasn't Baskin-Robbins, but their bootleg rainbow sherbet was better than nothing. I didn't see Allen anywhere, so I took a seat in the dining facility, or DFAC. Half of the chow hall was cordoned off while it was undergoing repairs after the building was struck during another rocket attack a few days prior. I don't think it killed anyone (that time), but it left a hole in both the roof and our psyches.

The dangers of living and working in a place like Iraq became readily apparent the day I watched an American convoy get ambushed from my vantage point in one of the base's guard towers early on in the deployment. But that was from a distance. It was almost like watching a snuff film. Now the violence was beginning to hit closer to home. On casualty rosters, I was starting to see the names of people I knew.

By now, I had been to several funeral formations for fellow service members whose bodies were being shipped home. Whether it was from firsthand experience or from hearing it from the guy who bunked down the hallway from you, you knew about every grisly story that happened outside (and sometimes inside) the wire. The ultraviolence was inescapable. My skin had developed a thickness. Nothing came as a surprise anymore. In fact, several of my peers lauded my newfound ability to remain calm and collected even under the worst circumstances.

But after a few months at Forward Operating Base Warrior, I began to wonder about my chances of becoming another flag-draped statistic. What were the mathematical probabilities that I could become the 2,717th American fatality? (By the end of Operation Iraqi Freedom, 4,493 American troops would die.)

When Allen finally showed up, he ordered a double scoop of rocky road in a waffle cone. Risky, considering the heat. When it came to eating ice cream, our politics were opposite. I was more moderate, rarely ordering fancy flavors with toppings, but always playing it safe and getting my order in a cup. Couldn't chance getting it all over one of the few uniforms we were issued. Laundry day was always a pain in the ass.

Instead of staying and enjoying our frozen treats at the picnic tables located in the eating area, we made our way back toward our living quarters and climbed onto one of the roofs for a decent view of the Kirkuk skyline. There weren't any mandates forbidding us from being up on the roof as far as I was aware, but no one ever went up there because of the threat of enemy snipers. Allen and I didn't care. *Whatever happens, happens*, as he would say. He wasn't being careless, he just wasn't going to let fear dictate any of his actions anymore.

"We could die tomorrow, so we might as well [activity that was frowned upon]," he'd say.

He uttered those words so casually and with such frequency that they almost became a throwaway line. He always had a positive outlook on things. Unfortunately, he was always right too. Neither of us knew it then, but soon after returning home from his second deployment to Iraq, he would fall ill. The day his daughter was born, he was diagnosed with a rare late-stage stomach cancer due to his exposure to the burn pits where he constantly volunteered to work. He would be dead less than a year after that.

I asked Allen how things were going in his assigned sector. I was out of the loop after I was transferred to another unit. The morning after the incident with Romero, I was pulled into an office by MPs and questioned about the incident. I told them everything—well, almost everything. I stopped just short of admitting we basically drew firearms on each other in a room the size of a phone booth. They pulled up security camera footage of me staggering out of the guard shack holding my bloodied face. Slightly embarrassing, to be sure, but it also corroborated my explanation of being assaulted by a soldier who was having a mental breakdown.

Following an investigation, Master Sergeant McGill had me transferred to another unit for the remainder of the deployment. Romero's weapon was taken from him for "negligently discharging" his firearm, and he was placed on a psych hold.

Allen said things had been quiet since I was moved and everyone else noticed. "We never get any action. I need to request a transfer to your squad. They're calling you the Black Cloud . . . and a few other choice names."

He was right about that too. I was developing a strange, almost mythical reputation with my peers. Things always seemed to go sideways when I was working. Some guys relished the action and volunteered to ride in my Humvee. But most tried to stay the hell away from me, just in case the curse was real.

"What happened with Romero? Everyone's talking about it," Allen asked.

"I'm under strict orders to keep my mouth shut until the investigation is over."

"Yeah, I get it." Allen didn't want me to say something we would probably regret later.

I looked into my melted ice cream. It was now just pink soup with orange swirls in it, almost identical to the setting sun in the background. I ditched my spoon in the trash pit and drank the rest like soup. It wasn't bad because it reminded me of eating ice cream as a kid at the park with my little brother.

The awkward soup and silence were interrupted when Allen noticed dozens of armed men gathering on rooftops directly across from us. On an adjacent roof, more armed men appeared. Allen and I perked up in unison. We didn't understand what we were about to witness.

The buildings were about twenty-five yards apart, and the mobs continued to grow larger on Kirkuk's skyline. We could see them on the edges of the rooftops, screaming and waving at each other. They were too far away to hear, but the animosity was readily apparent. I felt like I was watching some twisted adaptation of the Broadway musical *West Side Story*. Instead of the Jets and the Sharks, it was the Sunnis and the Shiites. Or maybe the Kurds were fed up again—and rightfully so. We were sitting on top of a Kurdish graveyard: specifically, the mass graves of Kurds that Saddam Hussein murdered during the Anfal Campaign, a "counterinsurgency operation" carried out to rid the area of Kurds, ending their bid for a free and sovereign Kurdistan. The narratives and rivalries were always changing, and sometimes it was hard to keep up with what was what.

But these folks weren't sporting switchblades and Chuck Taylors while getting ready to dance some musical number; they were armed with AK-47s and hand grenades. We weren't exactly sure what was occurring; we just knew it wasn't good. We could see the small silhouettes posturing, and they were pointing their weapons at each other.

Seconds later, the repeated cracks of gunfire echoed in our direction. Bodies on both sides began to fall. Whether they were ducking or dying remained to be seen. The action was a little too close for our command's comfort. Minutes later, a pair of F-16 fighter jets were screaming over the rooftops in a show of force. Only instead of dropping munitions, they showered the combatants in flares, scaring the shit out of the combatants and sending them scattering.

When we weren't pulling sentry duty, running patrols, or escorting officers and politicians around for their wartime photo shoots, we were often tasked with additional duty, like setting up razor wire around the perimeter or working the burn pits. Lugging razor wire around was difficult and slightly dangerous, but spending hours dumping trash and human waste into a burning hole in the ground was worse than war itself. If anyone ever volunteered for that shit, they rarely volunteered to do it more than once. But Allen, like the good troop he was, routinely accepted this duty and all the extra duties he could. He volunteered for custodial duties. He volunteered for optional training classes. He even volunteered to go back to Iraq months after we returned home.

On the nights after he worked the burn pits, he'd return to the barracks covered in soot, smelling like shit. In those vulnerable moments he was an easy target for jokes, but no one ever gave Allen a hard time. Why would we? There was a quiet gratitude every time he took one for the team.

After he hit the showers, he'd retire to his bunk. His conversation was cursory. He only really spoke when spoken to, keeping his answers short and emotionless. There was a night when I saw the frustration on his face that he sought to hide from others.

"This shit is hard enough. We get one day off a week if we're lucky. Why are you running yourself ragged and volunteering for all this extra bullshit?"

"Because it's better than listening to everyone else bitch and moan about it." Allen wasn't just a team player, he was a leader in every sense of the word, often putting our morale and well-being before his own. From that moment, I refused to let him go it alone and routinely volunteered for additional duties alongside him.

On occasion we were assigned to assist our Army counterparts with training Iraqi police and military recruits. If the United States was to fulfill its stated mission of outing a violent dictator and reconstructing a truly democratic Iraq (I'm doing a jerk-off motion with my hand right now, you just can't see it), we'd have to arm the Iraqis with updated defense technology (read: weapons and equipment from American manufacturers) and retrain them in modern military tactics before eventually turning the country back over to them. We wouldn't be there forever—Western oil companies that had all been shut out of Iraq's oil market prior to the invasion were "awarded" bids and installed all over the country—and the newly installed Iraqi government needed to become proficient in defending itself against factions, some of which were being funded by the CIA, which wanted to retake control of the vulnerable country while there was still a vacuum of power.

During a daily brief before meeting up with our Iraqi trainees, we were informed that training would be canceled for the foreseeable future. After receiving some intel from an inside source, an Army patrol had discovered an IED and suicide vest–making workshop in the basement of a local home. Evidence pointed to the manufacture of at least a half-dozen completed suicide vests, most of which were already "out in the wild."

A few days after that, a group of naked Iraqi men showed up to one of the gates in a sector where Allen was working. They were Iraqi police, and their station had been overrun by armed men who stole their uniforms and weapons. The obvious irony here is that we'd given them uniforms and weapons to combat these insurgents.

Increasingly, bases and outposts in both Iraq and Afghanistan had been targeted by suicide bombers dressed as the local police or military allies. Next to IEDs, "green-on-blue" attacks were becoming our biggest nightmare. Through closed channels, our CO notified all the Iraqi police stations in the area to give their men orders to stay home from work for the foreseeable future. Any Iraqi seen wearing a uniform would be challenged by coalition forces and treated as a threat. I contemplated asking Brahim to report any men he saw wearing or carrying Iraqi uniforms, but I thought better of it. I didn't want to put his life in more jeopardy than it already was.

Boiling sweat dropped from my brow like a faucet in the bathroom of a gas station somewhere in Middle America. No matter how much attention I gave it, no matter how many times I wiped my forehead with the back of my camo-covered forearm, the sweat kept coming, and it kept stinging my already bloodshot eyes. Some of the salty drops stuck in the sandpaper-rough stubble above my upper lip, while others ran down the side of my face, where they came loose only to evaporate before hitting the ground.

My sunglasses fogged a little more with every breath that I took, but I didn't bother with wiping them because they were already scratched beyond repair. Whether I was looking through my government-issued Oakleys, peering through the window of a Humvee, or just daydreaming, I always seemed to be staring through fractured glass.

Traffic had been nearly nonexistent that morning, so when a little tan hatchback turned a corner approaching the base, it immediately caught my attention. From a distance it was hard to tell how fast it was traveling. The heat caused a ripple effect along the pavement, and the car appeared to float across a perpetual oil slick. As it drew closer, it became obvious that it was moving much faster than the posted speed limits.

I watched as the driver accelerated toward my position with remarkable speed. My trigger finger twitched repeatedly, not because I was ready to use it, but because the faux leather on my glove was splitting, causing a pesky abrasion on the back of my pointer finger. The car kept coming.

It blew by signs that read STOP, 5 MPH, and USE OF DEADLY FORCE IS AUTHORIZED! My eyes narrowed, but I didn't flinch. I figured the car would slow down at the next set of signs and roadblocks. Cars always did.

But this one didn't. The car kept coming.

It was a city block away and picking up speed. I straightened up, took a few steps back, and braced myself for the worst. I looked up at the heavy gunner in the Humvee to see if he was paying attention. He wasn't.

"Hey, Montana. Heads up!" I chirped to get his attention. The car kept coming.

It swerved around barriers, effortlessly ripping through plastic fences the way an X-Acto knife runs through tape on a cardboard box. I charged my weapon and raised the sight to my eye. I was ten seconds away from having an early-'90s Toyota Tercel sitting in my lap. I'd never shot at anyone in my life, and it was obvious the zit-faced kid from Montana who sat in the gun turret hadn't either. The car kept coming.

"What do I do?! This ain't right. Should I light him up?"

I knew what we were supposed to do, but I couldn't verbalize a command. I radioed the overwatch tower.

"Park! Do I shoot him?" he asked again with even more nervous urgency.

"Wait! Hold your fire! Don't fire! Don't fire the .50!" I screamed.

I zeroed my sight on the driver. My trigger finger pulsed. It was now or never. I glanced through my optic and was just about to squeeze off a three-round burst when the passenger-side windshield exploded and the car swerved ninety degrees to the left. That was the warning shot from the tower.

The screeching wheels locked up and tattooed black streaks across the asphalt as the car teetered, nearly flipping onto its side. When it hit a barrier, it came to an immediate and violent halt. A short, balding Caucasian man fell out of the car screaming and writhing in pain. I could see blood pouring from his forehead as he crawled around on all fours. *Holy shit. Did I just watch this guy get murdered?*

A responding QRF (Quick Reaction Force) rushed toward the individual with weapons drawn. By the time they arrived at his location to challenge him, he had his hands raised and was completely compliant. He was a journalist who was new to the country, was separated from his host, and had gotten lost in the wrong part of town.

Montana asked if I needed medical attention. I didn't understand. Then I tasted the blood pouring from my mouth. I had bitten a hole in my lip. The thought of taking someone's life put a lead weight in my throat that would make its way down through my heart and into my stomach. I didn't want to have to do that ever, but this was my reality.

And the cars would keep coming.

16

ROCK THE CASBAH

I **WAS GOING STIR-CRAZY.** Or maybe I was just going crazy-crazy. I missed socializing. I missed the normalcy of home. Sure, war has been a constant since the beginning of human civilization, but nothing about war is rational. I needed a break from whatever it was we were trying to rationalize. There were no weapons of mass destruction. Saddam Hussein was captured three years earlier and would be hanging from the gallows shortly after my boots first touched Iraqi soil. So what the fuck were we even doing there?

However, if I had to be there, I didn't feel it unreasonable to want to learn a little something about the place where I was probably going to die. I'd only seen Iraq from the sky, through binoculars at the top of a watchtower or from behind a turret-mounted machine gun. I wanted a more intimate look at the country I was fighting in. So I did what anyone else would've done . . . and snuck off base. (Disclaimer: This was years before the Bowe Bergdahl incident in Afghanistan, I was off duty, and I had no plans of abandoning my post or going AWOL.) And of course, I recruited Brahim to be my tour guide and partner in crime.

Because FOB Warrior was divided in two halves—one where Air Force personnel stayed and another where Army personnel bunked—slipping off the installation proved much easier than it should've been. Security protocols were more concerned with unauthorized guests entering than they were with the base's occupants leaving. I took the shuttle that ran parallel with the flight line until I reached the farthest sector on the base. I had Brahim approach the gate and tell the guards he was an informant waiting for his escort. I showed up in civilian clothes making sure my DoD identification was clearly visible. Beneath my jacket, I wore a shoulder holster meant for a sidearm. Most of the time, Air Force personnel left their weapons in the armory and only carried while on duty, so the holster was actually empty. I was wearing it for the outline—method acting. I had a black-and-white kaffiyeh wrapped around my neck, as it was a common accessory for service members in more clandestine positions. It also covered a portion of my baby face and my lack of facial hair. My biracial ambiguity gave me a complexion light enough to look like an American, but I was just dark enough to pass as a Middle Easterner walking around the streets of Kirkuk.

When Brahim approached the gate, I instructed him to lift his shirt to show me his stomach, then to put his arms out to the side and to spread his legs so I could give him a quick pat down in front of the MPs posted at the gate, as was standard operating procedure. I thanked them, then told them I would be back at the end of the day. I told the guard that my name likely wouldn't be on his control list because the gate I was supposed to use was shut down, and had him add it so I could return with no problems later. I asked if he wanted to contact my CO to confirm. He didn't care, jotted my name down, and waved me through.

Brahim and I walked along the side of the highway for a bit, and when we were far enough away from the base in a business district, we hailed a taxi. If we'd done it too close to the FOB, we might've been seen as informants working for Western forces. Which I guess we were, technically.

Located in the heart of the birthplace of civilization, Kirkuk is a region steeped in history. The remnants of Neanderthals were found in caves on the outskirts of the city. It served as the capital of Akkad, the first empire of Mesopotamia. In the center of the city, an ancient fortress known as the Citadel rests atop a manmade hill on the skyline, watching over Kirkuk's residents. Being a short fifteen-minute drive from the FOB, I decided we should make that our first stop.

The Iron Age casbah was a marvel that was hard to miss and was at the top of the list of my Middle Eastern tourist destinations. Brahim didn't make the greatest tour guide because he didn't actually know much about the Kirkuk Citadel, but it was hard to blame him when studied historians don't either. Some believe it was constructed by nomadic Sumerians three thousand years ago. Others posit that the castle was built by the Assyrian king Ashurnasirpal II eight hundred and something years before the birth of Christ. Centuries later, the castle was given a medieval HGTV renovation by Alexander the Great's successor, Seleucus I Nicator, while he waged war in the area. It's also said to be an ancient Airbnb used by one of the conquerors who followed in the footsteps of Genghis Khan: Timur, a man responsible for killing seventeen million people—5 percent of the world's population at the time—during his reign over an area that spanned from Turkey to India.

Within the Citadel's walls, the city's oldest graveyard is preserved in the Red Church, a pre-Islamic place of worship. The building, clad with a fusion of arches, pillars, domes, and minarets all from different cultures and time periods, had seen empires rise and fall over the centuries. At one point, the structure was a Jewish synagogue, belonging to one of the hundreds of Jewish settlements in Kurdistan around the twelfth century. It then alternated between a mosque and Christian church, depending on who was winning whatever war was being waged in the area at the time, before finally settling as a *masjid* toward the end of the Mongolian reign.

Located within the Red Church is a tomb attributed as the resting place of the prophet Daniel, the one from the Bible who was thrown in the lions' den. And while five other cities in the Middle East claim to hold the remnants of Ol' Danny Boy, for the purposes of this story, Kirkuk is the undisputed home of the Tomb of Daniel. And, like the Red Church and the Citadel around it, Daniel can be found in venerated texts of Judaism, Christianity, and Islam. I was surrounded by walls that had not fallen during the best and worst of humanity's offerings. And while I didn't know much about the place I had been living in for months, it seemed to hold on to the best and worst of humanity.

Just being there, walking in the same dirt and touching the same bricks that had been there in antiquity, was remarkable. I'm from a country with strip malls and condominium complexes on every other corner, that teaches its children and brainwashes its elders to believe that the most atrocious acts witnessed in its young history—the enslavement of Black people, the displacement of the Natives, and the genocide of Jews—are acts of ancient history not worth remembering. It was difficult for me to truly fathom history like this.

I could tell how proud Brahim was of his culture. I couldn't blame him either; the history there was awe-inspiring. Brahim asked if there was anything notable or interesting about my hometown. He was probably expecting me to expound on the glories of America—the pop music, the cars, the celebrity culture. It's not all rock 'n' roll and supermodels where I'm from, I confessed. I told him the town I grew up in was famous for inventing the fruit cup. He didn't even know what a fruit cup was, which hurt my feelings a little bit.

We walked through an outdoor marketplace and stopped for kabobs, fresh-baked bread, and tea. While we ate, a series of large explosions could be heard in the distance. We'd both become so accustomed to those that neither of us looked up from our plates. The food was too good to let something like a li'l ol' IED spoil it. I don't know if I'm romanticizing that meal in my head—maybe I'd built up a ravenous appetite from all the exploring—but I still think that might've been one of the best meals I've ever eaten. I asked Brahim how they made their bread so good. He looked at me, rolled his eyes, and said, "Because we invented bread."

I hadn't thought about it like that. It was a fair point.

Brahim asked if I wanted to visit Baba Gurgur—the "Father of Fire"—a literal field of fire that has been burning since the dawn of humanity, fueled by oil deposits beneath Northern Iraq. Just two hours north of Kirkuk, it's another Biblical site, the place where King Nebuchadnezzar threw the companions of the aforementioned prophet Daniel, three Jews—Hananiah, Mishael, and Azariah—into a fiery furnace for refusing to kneel to his golden statue. The story goes that after the three were thrown into the pit of fire, they emerged hours later alongside Daniel, completely unharmed. This left such an impression on Big Nebby that he promoted Hananiah, Mishael, and Azariah to high government offices and wrote a decree that anyone who blasphemed their Jewish god would be executed.

In his second-century manuscript, *Lives*, the philosopher and historian Plutarch recounts Alexander the Great standing over the field of Baba Gurgur in wonderment as "fire [rose] in a continuous stream, like a spring of water, out of a cleft in the earth." Naturally, that's a place I needed to see, so we caught another taxi toward Baba Gurgur in the ancient city of Arrapha, which was now just northern Kirkuk. During our long drive, I looked out the window to take in the sights and sounds of lovely Kirkuk, not unlike a backseat passenger might while traveling America's Route 66.

Then I remembered the IEDS planted all along those highways. The wonderment was quickly replaced with a sense of uneasiness. I found myself closing my eyes and holding my breath going over potholes. Brahim would pat me on the leg.

"We're safer in this taxi than you are in your big tanks. Those bombs are made for Americans," he whispered. *I am an American*, I thought, but I understood what he meant.

Up ahead, a black plume of smoke hung in the air, likely from the explosion we heard while we were eating in the bazaar. As we drew closer, the traffic slowed until it came to a complete stop. American soldiers and Iraqi police had a defensive perimeter set up as another truck attempted to pull the burned skeleton of a Humvee off the road.

I told Brahim we needed to turn around. He told me it'd probably only take a few more minutes before we were on our way.

"We need to go. *Now*."

He chalked this up as me being an impatient Westerner. In reality, I knew this is how insurgents liked to ambush Americans. It was a simple practice that they'd perfected. Step One: kill Americans with an IED. Step Two: wait until more Americans show up to save their dying buddies. Step Three: kill more Americans. I told Brahim to ask the driver to take the next exit and turn around.

We drove around aimlessly with no real destination. I asked Brahim if I could stop by his house but realized that him being seen with an American could get him and his family killed, so I immediately recanted. With only an hour or so until sunset, I wasn't ready to end my little Arabian adventure. I asked Brahim about the nightlife in Kirkuk. I wanted to know what they did for fun. Surely there were ways to escape the stressors of living in an occupied country, if even for an hour or so at a time.

Brahim reminded me that because of the 9:00 PM curfew implemented by coalition forces, there wasn't a "nightlife" in Kirkuk. If the local nationals were caught outside after dark, they were subject to arrest. And that was if the occupying forces were in a good mood. Trigger-happy GIs could lay waste to civilians and then claim they were afraid for their lives, not unlike how American police officers continually get away with state-sponsored executions back at home.

However, he *did* mention that there were hookah spots, and he knew of a dance club that was open until thirty minutes before curfew. The last time I went dancing at 7:00 PM was probably my eighth-grade Winter Ball, but I was game.

Outside a bullet-riddled building, armed men with AK-47s stood watch while the muffled bass from the music inside clashed with the beat of sporadic gunfire in the distance. Because of my golden-brown complexion, I didn't really stand out, though I might expose myself as an infidel if I wasn't able to respond in Arabic. But I was eager to get drunk and let loose, so I gave Brahim a few American dollar bills to slip to the guard. After a quick but aggressively thorough pat-down, they let us in.

Being an ignorant Westerner, I failed to realize how different our cultures were. To my dismay, they didn't serve alcohol (because Islam), and women were not permitted to enter (also because Islam). It was what an American frat boy might refer to as a sausage fest. For a society that still persecuted gay people, seeing a bunch of men holding hands and dancing together was a bit odd.

Brahim explained that women and entertainment were not synonymous; they were merely for procreation and keeping house. I'd seen the misogyny in practice while working the front gates of FOB Warrior. We routinely let women on the base first, and that always upset quite a few men. To me, there were so many things wrong with that ideology, but I wasn't about to cause a scene and shut the club down over it.

Brahim asked if I wanted to dance. *Fuck it, why not? When in Rome, right?*

While we danced with a group of other young men, two men held hands, pressed their bodies together, and swayed to the beat. I quipped that this would be considered homoerotic in practically any other country in any other place on the planet. One of the men asked Brahim what I said, and he translated—reluctantly. The response was complete disgust bordering on imminent violence. I told Brahim to tell them I meant no disrespect. My transgressions were not salvageable, and moments later, another gentleman pulled Brahim aside. Brahim turned to me and said we were asked to leave. The party was over and we were escorted out.

17

TEAM SLEEP

SLEEP WAS FLEETING. My desperation for just one good night's rest was almost fiendish. Entire days were spent just going through the motions physically while I was absent mentally.

On a particular night when the noise on base was unbearable, I grabbed my woobie, a multipurpose blanket-like poncho, and a pillow, and wandered outside to the farthest edge of the base, which was off-limits to most personnel. I knew the place would be deathly quiet—a local graveyard. I realize sleeping in any graveyard could be considered taboo. I just figured this small act was probably toward the bottom of the list of disrespectful things the infidels had done to this beautiful country. What I didn't realize was that this place, the Sultan Saqi Shrine, wasn't any other cemetery. It was an especially holy site in a country full of the holiest sites. Sultan Saqi and his sister, Sultana, were grandchildren of Jafar al-Tayar, a cousin of the Prophet Muhammad. And there I was, another dumbass American, shitting all over venerated heritage. Lesser transgressions have been punished by death.

That night I lay between two graves and slept like the dead who surrounded me. The next morning, I was awakened by the caretaker of the graveyard. He screamed at me and poked me with a wooden staff. While I didn't speak Arabic, I knew exactly what he was saying, and he wasn't wrong. I apologized profusely, packed my shit, and made the walk of shame back to my barracks.

My bunk was right outside the Dust-Off helipad, where medical helicopters delivered patients in need of critical care. Wounded soldiers, civilians, and enemy combatants were dropped off at all hours of the day. Periodically, an alarm would sound, asking for all available hands on deck. If we weren't working, we were required to stop whatever we were doing to report to med station. This usually meant assisting flight medics, nurses, and doctors with transporting the wounded. It also meant getting zero sleep.

The moment I got settled, the alarms went off, and I made my way back to the mobile Army surgical hospital (MASH) to help move a man, who'd lost an arm and leg in an IED blast, from the gurney onto a bed. Afterward, I took a seat in the hall and stared at the blood covering my hands. I was waiting for the commotion to die down so I could use their sink to clean up when the same nurse who administered my shots of Toradol following my Humvee accident burst through the doors. When she saw me, she stopped and asked if I was there for another shot. I raised my hands.

"Caught me red-handed," I said sarcastically.

"How you holding up?"

"The painkillers are keeping me upright, but I—"

"Haven't been sleeping." She could see the dark bags under my eyes and the mix of helplessness and hopelessness on my face.

"I haven't gotten a decent night's sleep in months. I camped out in the graveyard last night for a little peace and quiet."

"Excuse me?"

"I know, but it's the quietest place on base. Look, is there any way you could get the doc to prescribe me something to knock me out for a day or two?"

"You know I can't do that."

"If I knew you couldn't, I wouldn't have asked. Thanks anyway." I stood and made my way toward the exit. "I'm gonna be back for another one of those shots this week."

"Wait. Hold on a sec," she said. She knew I was in dire straits. She exited briefly and, when she returned, took my hand and put a packet of pills in it. "Under no circumstances do you take these while you're on shift."

"What are these?" I asked.

"No-gos."

"Nose-goes?" I pointed to my nose like the childhood game.

"No-gos. Temazepam. We give 'em to pilots and flight crews to put 'em to sleep after they've been hopped up on stimulants."

"Got it."

"These will put you out cold for twelve hours, so you'll only take 'em on your day off. Understand?"

"Yes, ma'am."

Still groggy from the unauthorized pharmaceuticals I'd taken the night before, I almost missed Brahim as I walked sleepy-eyed to the PX (post exchange). Under the supervision of armed guards, he was carrying cleaning supplies and headed toward the latrines to scrub some more shit-caked toilets. I shook his hand and was staggered by his body odor.

"You doing all right, Bee?"

"Yes. I'm fine."

He wasn't. The truth was another series of bombings in the city had left hundreds dead and had crippled portions of the city's infrastructure. Rolling brownouts and inadequate plumbing made the simplest things like basic hygiene a near impossibility. And I felt partially responsible for that because, after all, I was a cog in the war machine that had destroyed this kid's home country. His chaperones looked impatient, so I kept things brief and let Brahim go on his way.

While at the PX, I grabbed several bars of soap, some shampoo, deodorant, toothpaste, and a couple bottles of water. I asked the cashier for an empty cardboard box, threw the toiletries in there, and went to track down Brahim. At the latrine, I pulled the guard aside to ask if Brahim could take an early break. When he walked out slightly confused, I handed him the box. He put it on the ground and rummaged through the contents with the same excitement as a kid opening presents on Christmas morning. Then, he abruptly stopped and closed the box.

"This is too much," he said without looking up at me.

"It's fine, you don't have to pay me back or anything."

Dark dots began to appear on the cardboard box and dirt around it. I realized how embarrassing this probably was for him and took a step back to give him some space. Though this offering came with good intentions, I was shining a light on his insecurities, and I was only a few years removed from being an insecure teenager myself. I knew exactly what this felt like. Hell, I was still an insecure adult. After wiping the tears from his cheeks, Brahim stood and grabbed my arm. With red eyes he thanked me, saying this was the kindest thing anyone had ever done for him, and that he owed me his life—his *life*.

He hugged me.

"OK, but I'm not kidding. You really need to take a shower," I said, pulling away and pretending to catch my breath. He pushed me away and we both laughed.

The sleep I'd been looking for came like a quiet storm after that. One morning, we were being mortared heavily, and when Allen didn't see me in the bunker, he returned to the CHUs (contained housing units) to find me sound asleep. As explosions shook the barracks and shrapnel rained down on the FOB, he pulled me from my bed. I thought I was dreaming.

EYELIDS ARE HEAVY. GO FROM
DAY-TO-DAY IN A FOGGY HAZE
WONDERING HOW ANY OF THIS IS
REAL. I'VE BEEN SLEEPWALKING
THROUGH EVERY SHIFT. JUST STUMBLING
AROUND A FOREIGN COUNTRY WHERE
PEOPLE WANT TO KILL ME. I WANT
TO BELIEVE ALL OF THIS HATE IS
A FIGMENT OF MY DELIRIUM.

I WANT TO BELIEVE THIS IS ONE LONG
NIGHTMARE. BUT EVERY FRIDAY WHEN
WE PUT THE FALLEN ON PLANES AND
SEE THEM OFF, I WAKE UP JUST
LONG ENOUGH TO PAY MY RESPECTS
AND I KNOW ALL OF THIS IS REAL.

IS IT BETTER TO BE NUMB TO ALL OF
THIS OR TO HOLD ONTO MY HUMANITY
AND FEEL THIS HURT?

18

HOLD ON, WE'RE GOING HOME

———

SPRING CAME, AND so did the monsoons. Staying dry was next to impossible. Allen and I stood shoulder to shoulder to share what little body heat we had left. Our heads were down, the hoods of our field jackets pulled up, and our Kevlar helmets low to help keep the water out of our eyes. Even under the cover at the front gate, we were soaking wet from a rain blowing horizontally from the strong winds.

I hadn't packed for cold weather because I didn't realize how cold and wet it could get in Iraq and wanted to keep my bags lighter. The discomfort was tolerable only because we were on standby, waiting for an itinerary for a flight home that could come at any moment.

With us were two new airmen who'd just landed in country days earlier. Their uniforms were bright and freshly creased. Allen's and mine were faded and stained. The looks on their faces were reminiscent of the one I'd had when I first landed in Iraq. We didn't call them "nervous in the service" when they kept their heads low and darted from cover to cover apprehensively, as the troops who we'd relieved had called us earlier that year.

Their anxiety was warranted. We were in a war zone where anything could happen. Days earlier, while some of the newer troops were shadowing us on patrol, a rocket was shot in our direction. It struck a mud puddle just yards from us, failing to detonate. The EOD (explosive ordnance disposal) member tasked with disarming the rocket told us to go home and play the lottery.

For weeks, the new airmen picked our brains, asking the same questions we'd asked when we were the new meat. We answered them as honestly as we could. They asked about the locals and the lore. They asked us about all the rumors and urban legends they'd heard. They asked about the danger. Were there snipers? Sure, but the odds of being hit by one were slim, we answered, clarifying that the chances weren't zero. Two airmen in our sister detachment were both hit by sniper fire weeks into our deployment.

While telling them about the suicide bombers and attackers who were thwarted from sneaking onto the base, a cloaked figure appeared in the distance. The two airmen behind us brought their weapons to a low, ready stance. Allen and I waited until the figure got closer. I couldn't see his face through the rain, but I could tell by his pants, shoes, and gait in his walk that it was Brahim coming to socialize with us.

He greeted Allen and me with a smile and handshake as he'd done dozens, maybe hundreds of times before. I told the airmen we were with to relax—Brahim was one of ours.

That spring, after putting in countless hours of scrubbing toilets, mopping floors, doing laundry, and patiently biding his time, Brahim was given the opportunity he'd been waiting for. He had been approved to work as an interpreter for a company contracted by the Department of Defense. It was a bittersweet feeling for me. On the one hand, he now had the means to take care of his family, at least financially. On the other, I knew that he'd just signed his own death warrant, like so many of the interpreters before him. The chances of him living through his contract were slim to none, and I felt obligated to tell him that.

He said that as long as I was around, he wasn't worried about his safety. We were brothers and we'd take care of each other. It was flawed thinking, as I could hardly take care of myself, let alone guarantee the safety of anyone else. More than that, I was weeks, maybe even days from being relieved of duty. I wasn't going to be in country for much longer and definitely not long enough to see to it that Brahim would stay safe.

On my last night in country, I tracked Brahim down to say good-bye one last time. I bought both of us ice cream, and we sat on the roof looking out on Kirkuk as tracer rounds reached out into the sky in the distance; it was almost romantic if you didn't know what the flashing lights were from and what they aimed to do.

He was excited for things to change for the better in Iraq. He knew things would be back to normal soon. He said the past few years had been difficult but Iraq would be better for it. And so would his people when Kurdistan was a recognized state. He was naive, but sometimes that's better than being hopeless.

We climbed down off the roof, and I gave him a hug and joked the Old Spice smelled good on him. He'd soon be issued a uniform and body armor like the other terps. I told him to follow me back to my CHU. I gave him a pair of new boots I hadn't worn. Then I gave him the Timex watch with the fraying band from my wrist. He told me to find him when I came back, and I said I would. But I knew I was lying. In my heart I knew I would never be back and that I'd never see him again.

I shook his hand, and the next day I was on a bird back home, where both my old life and a new one awaited.

We hopped and skipped west back through Europe and back over the Atlantic, eventually finding ourselves in Baltimore, where we transferred from a military aircraft to a civilian airliner. I, along with hundreds of other troops, was in full uniform.

I was stopped by a TSA agent going through security while the rest of my unit headed for our gate. I was regularly stopped by TSA as a civilian—one of the byproducts of being a brown guy with a Middle Eastern middle name—but to be stopped in full uniform by airport security after spending the better part of a year in Iraq was absurd to me. Allen shook his head in disgust as he continued on past me.

I watched as the man dumped the contents of my bag onto a metal table and rifled through them. "Can I ask what's going on here?" I was genuinely confused.

"I'm just doing my job."

"You're not doing it well," I responded, losing patience as he unzipped more pockets and rifled through them. "You know what my job is? I was just in Iraq getting fucking shot at for the past year. You think I'm wearing this fucking uniform for fun, homie?"

"Lower your voice, sir."

"Put all the shit back in my bag. *Now.*"

Allen dropped one of his bags and stepped up beside me.

"What are you doing?" Allen asked.

"I'm not in the mood for this shit, Al. I don't need you patronizing me too. I—"

"No. I'm talking to him." Allen turned back to the TSA agent. "I asked what you're doing, man."

The TSA agent was speechless.

"Look, bud. We're tired. We've been traveling for days after months of getting shot at in the sandbox. We just want to get on our next flight as soon as possible, so we can get home. I don't know if you're bored or you think you're some hotshot Ricky Rescue, but you look like an idiot for harassing someone in uniform. You understand what I'm saying?"

The TSA agent's manager joined the conversation, asking if everything was OK. The agent tried to justify the shakedown by saying the names on my ID and uniform didn't match exactly. One was hyphenated, the other wasn't. The manager rolled his eyes at this half-assed excuse to harass me. We didn't need to explain anything else, and the agent was instructed to pack my belongings up, before the manager thanked me for my service.

"Unbelievable, man. I'm sorry you have to go through shit like that," Allen said contritely.

On the plane back to Nellis, I was offered a seat in first class by a fellow traveler who was feeling patriotic. Master Sergeant McGill told me to stop fucking around and take my ass to the back like the rest of them. When we landed in Nevada, several of our weapons crates were missing, and we weren't able to make our connecting flight.

I called Claire to let her know I wouldn't be back until the following day. She was disappointed, naturally. After we hung up, she told all the people who had gathered at the apartment to surprise me to go home.

Post Deployment Letter of Evaluation:

Superb Gate 3 sentry! Controlled access of 250-plus personnel and 50-plus vehicles daily with zero unauthorized entries. Constant vigilance—Up-channeled 100-plus SALUTE reports of possible enemy activity, paralyzing hostile intents. Facilitated in the aid and medical treatment of two injured LN [local national] children, solidifying LN and Coalition relations! Diligently scrutinized Gate 2 entry/exit procedures—accredited the success of 1300-plus coalition mission sorties. Fortified perimeter security for two clandestine ESU and Army sorties—contributing to 100% survivability rate. Provided perimeter security for Major General Holland and Major General Baldwin—coined for his excellence!

Demonstrated blatant lack of respect toward numerous NCO's and SNCO's—received UIF [unfavorable information file] form 506 ESFS/CC. Exhibited lapse in judgement in respect of orders of leadership. . . .

ACT III

SOMEWHERE IN BETWEEN

"For your service to our great nation, we're offering a free Bloomin'
Onion and any Coca-Cola beverage (with the purchase of an entree)
for all military veterans, active service members and their spouses on
Veteran's Day. Welcome home."
—Outback Steakhouse

19

WELCOME HOME

I **STARED UP AT** the ceiling, which was covered in hanging bras and one-dollar bills with names or funny notes scribbled on them. Between my alcohol intake that evening and my refusal to get prescription glasses, my eyesight was failing me. I squinted and craned my neck to read all of the new messages that were added in the year I'd been gone. A lot of the notes scribbled on the dollar bills were pop culture quotes: HEY DIRTAY, BABY I GOT YOUR MONEY. LOVE & HAPPINESS. TRICK LOVES THE KIDS. KEEP THE CHANGE, YA FILTHY ANIMALS. Some of the messages were the drunken ramblings of frat-bro philosophers attempting to be poignant. YOU ONLY LIVE ONCE. IF YOU LOVE HER LET HER KNOW. And others were from drunken frat bros writing out the things drunken frat bros say: IF U SHOW US YOUR TITS U CAN HAVE THIS and FUCK YOU, PAY ME. Most of the messages, like the one I'd written and stamped on the ceiling years ago, were there to cement our place in our favorite dive bar: DYLAN WAS HERE. Not exactly Caesar's *Veni, vidi, vici,* but it got the point across.

My eyes trailed down from the ceiling to the sea of familiar faces. I was feeling loved from the never-ending stream of free drinks, warm

185

embraces, and exchanged pleasantries. I was glad to be home but quickly tired of all the interaction.

The first thing folks do when they find out you're a combat veteran is thank you for your service. And until this day I'm still not quite sure how to respond to that. I usually just counter with some awkward version of "I appreciate that, but you don't have to thank me," which is seen as a form of humility. Then they'll say something like, "Of course I have to thank you. What you did was heroic, and I could never do something like that. Veterans don't get the respect they deserve." Meanwhile, in my head I'm thinking they definitely don't have to thank me for participating in an illegal war. Their idea of freedom was actually just an invasion and occupation one degree away from turning into the genocide of the Iraqi people.

The second thing people want to know is if you got hurt or if you're OK—questions generally asked with good intentions. I usually leave out the part where I broke my ass. Then finally, they ask how many people you killed or what the worst thing you saw overseas was—a question meant to quench their thirst for the gory details. The worst parts of a veteran's life are entertainment for others. And I was tired of entertaining that evening. It was all a bit overwhelming, so I took a seat at the crowded bar, making myself less accessible.

Sitting next to me was a face I thought I'd recognized, a face I felt I might've known in another life. We made eye contact, and he did a double take as well, then stared back at me with equally bloodshot eyes. He pointed at me, snapping his fingers, trying to jog his memory.

"Oh, shit. How you been, man?" he yelled over the music. I still couldn't place him. I was slightly embarrassed. "Sean Boyton? St. Lawrence?"

Although I hadn't seen him since our eighth-grade graduation, my mother still has a photo of Sean and me on her refrigerator that she'd taken during one of our school field trips in the third or fourth grade. In the picture, Sean and I are arm in arm, wearing bright neon jackets, as was the style in the '90s, and even brighter smiles. With the ocean as a backdrop, he's striking a pose while I'm giggling and giving him the bunny ears behind his head. It's a photo I see every time I visit, and one I'd never really thought about until I was staring adult Sean in the face. The joy captured in the photo was long gone.

During our accidental reunion, we discovered we'd both served and we had both recently returned home from overseas. In our adolescence, Sean and I gave the nuns and priests at St. Lawrence a fair share of headaches. As adults we'd spend the next hour giving ourselves headaches by trading shots of whiskey and war stories.

Admittedly, our experiences weren't comparable. Sean was an Army Ranger who had seen the worst of the worst. He'd been in hard combat. I'm pretty sure one of the guys in his battalion received the Medal of Honor, and a disproportionate number of men in his unit were KIA or WIA. I was nothing more than a glorified security guard driving laps around the base, opening doors, and babysitting generals who wanted to see "the shit" to slap more colorful ribbons on their chest so that people would call them heroes when they got home. He had just spent fifteen months in Afghanistan. I was in Iraq for a soft eight.

I don't remember much of the conversation Sean and I had, but I remember it was nice knowing I wasn't completely alone in my journey back. We came from a place where people didn't often join the military. We exchanged e-mails, but I've only spoken with Sean once since that night. St. Lawrence had recently announced it'd be closing its doors for good after nearly fifty years. A classmate of ours put together a reunion for everyone who attended the small private elementary school, middle school, or high school at some point. I e-mailed Sean to ask if he was going. He replied nearly a month later. "I will not be attending. All the best." I didn't attend either.

After Sean killed his drink and left, Brian took the empty seat next to me while I stared into another empty glass.

"You need another drink?"

"Nah, I think I'm done for the night."

Brian put his arm around me. "I'm glad you're home, man. I missed you."

"I missed you too, brother. This almost doesn't feel real."

"Well, it is. It's very real. How does it feel to be a father? You getting any sleep?" My eyes went wide. I've never sobered up faster in my life.

Just two days earlier, and minutes after my sand-covered boots touched the tarmac at Norman Y. Mineta San Jose International Airport, I was handed a sleeping fourteen-pound, three-month-old baby boy. Less than forty-eight hours before that, I was coddling a twenty-two-pound squad automatic weapon. For weeks Claire joked that I carried Brody around like he was a machine gun. I went from "This is my rifle, this is my gun" to "This is my baby, this is my son."

Just two days after my arrival, Claire left town on a business trip. While I was in Iraq, she'd been passed over for a promotion because she couldn't attend the mandatory managerial training conference her company required. She'd already dropped out of college, which had always been a quiet point of contention, so it wasn't fair for her to also set aside her professional goals for me. Plus, we needed her to get that promotion. The little amount of money I'd saved while in Iraq was only going to last us a few more months. She was going to be the breadwinner until I found myself another job.

I'm sure she expected some pushback. She thought I'd be hurt if she left right after I got home. And that might've been true of the previous version of myself. I probably would've called her selfish, maybe worse. The younger me, just to start a fight, might've asked if she was going to see her ex–fuck buddy who now lived in Houston.

But I didn't. She'd been waiting for me for nearly a year. She'd gone through the hardships of pregnancy and given birth without me. The truth is, she was the real hero in our little family. So, after a short conversation, we agreed she should make the trip to Texas. In return, she gave me one assignment: keep our son alive for the next two weeks. And I was already failing.

Brian saw the look of horror on my face as I stood from the bar. "What's the problem, dude? Where you going?"

The problem was that while I was getting hammered at the bar, my infant son was home alone in his crib. Walking to our favorite dive bar on a Friday night was muscle memory. I'd done it a thousand times before and a thousand times since. I had quite literally forgotten I was a father. I threw a twenty-dollar bill on the counter, then levitated for two city blocks to our apartment complex, up a flight of stairs, and into Brody's room, where he was still sound asleep.

The fear I felt the night I left Brody by himself changed something in me. The world no longer revolved around me. The father switch turned from off to on. And just like my rifle, I would never lose track of that child again.

———————

What's that saying about it taking a village to raise a child? Well, that village saved my life. Kyle, Brandon, and Brian did their best to help with my crash course in parenting. Remember that movie *Three Men and a Baby*? It was like that but not nearly as funny.

Knowing I had daddy-day-care duty and couldn't leave the house, my friends began to drop by in the evenings after work. I'd put Brody to sleep, we'd all crack open some beers, I'd tell war stories over dinner, then we'd settle down and watch a movie. After lots of trial and error, we eventually developed a system to socialize while staying quiet enough so we didn't wake the baby.

After school, Rory would come over with his girlfriend, and they'd watch Brody while I made dinner, ran errands, or just took a break. Both Claire's parents and mine had been babysitting Brody for months before I arrived home, as well. It was a little strange that everyone had a more personal connection with my own child than I did. Whenever Brody cried in my arms, my mother would take him, and he would stop. And while she was only trying to help, I would be lying if I said my feelings weren't hurt when that happened.

When Claire returned from Texas, my friends—the support system I had been leaning on—were no longer allowed to come over to the apartment. Claire's reasoning was that she worked early every morning and didn't want people in the house keeping her up. It was a fair request. When they offered to leave at a decent hour—say, 9:00 PM at the latest—she still declined. Claire wasn't particularly fond of my brother either, so she stopped allowing him to come over on weekdays as well. I had little say about anything. Following a year of violent conflict, I wanted as little confrontation in my own home as possible. I just wanted to keep the peace. Plus, Claire was the breadwinner, and she reminded me of that every chance she got.

I was reduced to being a stay-at-home father in complete isolation. I ended up having to see my own brother outside the house. I don't know what she had against him, but Rory always made me proud. Bucking convention and safety, Rory dropped out of community college and decided that his time would be better spent starting his own business. He was apprenticing with a local jeweler and wanted to start his own line. Rory was incredibly ambitious, an entrepreneur in every sense. The word *dream* wasn't a part of his vocabulary; if he wanted to accomplish something, he laid the groundwork to do so, no matter how far-fetched it seemed to the rest of us.

When he wasn't hustling and I wasn't parenting, we would drive up to Oakland whenever possible to catch a Warriors game like we did in the good ol' days. We were both incredibly busy with our new lives, and it was a way to spend some quality time together. But because of Claire, even those moments were becoming fewer and farther between.

20

THE NEW NATIONAL ANTHEM

THE GREEN METAL slats of the park bench were uncomfortable, yet somehow sitting on that park bench was one of the most comforting things I knew. It was that same park bench hidden under the shadow of a large oak tree I'd sat on countless times during my youth.

When I was in sixth grade, I tried to impress some friends by doing a trick off that very bench on my skateboard. I ended up breaking both of my middle fingers. With my digits locked in metal splints, I was stuck flipping double birds for nearly eight weeks. In the tenth grade, I got into a physical confrontation with my father and "ran away." Like most fourteen-year-olds, I didn't have my escape plan thought out before muttering under my breath, "Yeah, well, you'll never see me again," and walking out the door with a packed duffel bag. I soon figured out I had nowhere to go, but my pride kept me warm while I slept on that very bench for a single night before I went back home the following day with my tail between my legs.

It was the same park bench where I had my first kiss, and it's where I went to cry after my first breakup. I had plenty of other awkward quasi-sexual encounters in the middle of the night there too. There was the overzealous hand job from Katie that left both of us washing our shirts in the water fountain. There was the night the cops threatened to arrest me and Jessica as they shined their lights into our wide eyes while I scrambled to pull up my pants. I was sitting on that park bench when Vanessa told me she thought she was pregnant a few weeks after I'd lost my virginity to her. I left a trail of nervous vomit from that bench back to my parents' front door. Vanessa wasn't pregnant—she just didn't want me to break up with her. I still did.

Like a real-life version of Shel Silverstein's *The Giving Tree*, that park bench had witnessed my growing pains, countless failures, and rare triumphs during my formative years, but this time, the bench felt different. Holding little Brody in my arms felt like an accomplishment. His big brown eyes gazed back at me with no judgment, only wonderment. Soft fuzz grew on his cheeks, and tiny fingers reflexively curled around my thumb. Every time he smiled, I was glad I made it home to him. Just weeks prior, I was dodging falling mortars; now the only thing I wanted to dodge was diaper duty.

Brody and I sat quietly and watched other children entertaining themselves on the playground. They squealed in delight as they clung on to and jumped off an assortment of plastic and wooden play struc-tures. The other parents sat on other benches circling the playground while micromanaging their children's play. Billy needed to be more careful while climbing. Olivia was ordered to stop putting things in her mouth. Jonathan was being interrogated about the location of his missing shoe.

The sun bounced off the brim of my Oakland A's cap, and I did my best to shield Brody's sensitive eyes from the light. We'd been walking around the park for the better part of the afternoon. It was time to go home. Brody locked eyes with me and spit his pacifier onto the concrete. I picked it up off the ground, dusted it off on my jeans, and put it in my pocket. It was hard to tell what Brody was thinking, but I couldn't help but feel contrite. The idea of missing his birth was upsetting. It was something I'd never get back. I felt like I really let my wife down. Thinking about her being pregnant for nine months and fending for herself pained me. But I wasn't the only one. Dozens of others in my detachment had left pregnant wives or young children at home. Even worse, some parents never came home to their families at all.

I would've apologized to him for missing his debut. I would've told him I'd be there for him until my last breath. But I didn't because he had no idea what I was saying. Instead, I smiled at him, gave him Eskimo kisses, blew raspberries on his belly, and pretended to eat his little foot while he giggled.

I packed up, put Brody in the stroller, and wrestled with the tangled cord of my headphones. We took a long concrete trail that cut through a grass field and through the shadows of towering redwoods that lined the park. Across the field, on the horizon, sat an elementary school with multicolored buildings that looked like giant building blocks. It was the same school Claire went to as a child.

The sun was eerily reminiscent of the one that had been torment-ing me for the previous year in the desert of Iraq. Instead of sporadic gunfire and the occasional explosion in the distance, the air was filled with the shrieks of laughing children and the periodic pings of base-balls connecting with metal bats at the baseball field that centered the park. There was no radio chatter in my ears calling out IEDs and potential hostiles; instead, a familiar voice crooned through my earbuds. My close friends Eric, Adrian, Hrag, and Ryan had released their second album, *Strata Presents the End of the World*, while I was in Iraq. I was finally getting a chance to listen to their new single, aptly titled "The New National Anthem."

Ryan's soft guitar riffs were perfectly in unison with the geometric patterns of the birds flying in the sky. "O say, can you see? By the dawn's early light. We get 'em young, give 'em guns, and ship 'em off to fight. While the rocket's red glare is keeping everyone scared, they say, 'Just relax, put your trust in me, and you can sit back and watch the war on your screen.'"

Hrag's bass thudded along with my footsteps on the cracked sidewalk. "The country's run by lunatics, they're picking up their pens, writing themselves into Revelation, 'This is how it's gonna end!' Well, I tried hard to bite my tongue, like a good American, but they recruited my little brother, and they're shipping off my friends."

Adrian's drum beats matched the rhythm in my chest. "Broad stripes and bright stars through the perilous fight; you know those who stand to gain are not the ones who sacrifice. Watching bombs burst in air from a comfortable chair, they just say, 'In God we trust, and God trusts in greed,' yeah, as long as they never show real blood on TV."

The anger in Eric's voice was palpable. "I'm not sorry if this makes you mad; in fact, I hope this wakes you up, 'cause you'll never see what's going on with your eyes so tightly shut. There are too many unanswered questions, from the towers in New York to the lies leading up to another corporate-sponsored war. Well, I'll support the troops by asking what they're really fighting for, and I think that's more patriotic than flying a flag from my front porch. Come on, let's go out and start a fight! 'Cause you know two wrongs always make a right."

The message was obviously political. Eric was standing up for me like a protective older brother. He hated that I'd joined, partially because he disagreed with the war and partially because he didn't want me to get hurt. He couldn't physically fight for me, so he'd do it the best way he knew how, and that was by screaming fuck-yous into a microphone to the type of people who would never listen to the type of music he made. At the time of its release, I didn't need to ask because I knew. Years later Eric confirmed that the song was written for me.

The tranquility was interrupted abruptly when one of the wheels on the stroller snagged on something and locked up while we attempted to cross the street. As I was bent over trying to locate the source of the problem, a lifted silver truck came flying around the corner and slammed on its brakes. We were closer to the sidewalk, so I yanked the stroller back and without looking up gave the driver a wave. He could have easily gone around with minimal delay, but instead, he decided to lay on his horn. Terrified, Brody burst into tears.

The driver pulled up alongside me and rolled down the passenger-side window. I braced myself.

"Hey faggot, get outta the street before you get run over."

I looked up at him and shrugged, as if to say, *What do you want from me, man?* As he sped away, I caught a glimpse of an American-flag sticker and a faded yellow ribbon magnet: SUPPORT THE TROOPS.

After Brody and I returned home, I put him in his crib and hopped on my aging Dell laptop. My inbox was saturated with job listings from all the résumés I'd sent out while canvassing LinkedIn, Monster.com, Jobing.com for hours on end every day. Outside of the police academy or being a private security guard, being a grunt in the military hardly translates into any civilian-sector gigs. I was having a difficult time finding meaningful work in an ever-expanding tech landscape where employers looked for college graduates with skills in software development, software engineering, data analytics, programming, people management, technical writing, network maintenance, business analysis, and a bunch of other bullshit I didn't understand. I was adept at getting shot at.

After deleting e-mail after e-mail of job listings that either I was not qualified for or were out of state, I landed on an e-mail with the subject line INFO RECRUTEMENT LÉGION ÉTRANGÈRE. The translation is "Foreign Legion Recruitment Info."

I hated myself for leaving Claire alone during her pregnancy, and I hated myself for missing Brody's birth, but I hated being useless even more. I was unemployed and idling. I was an extra mouth to feed. Would it be better for me to be gone and sending money home than being at home with no money?

A few nights earlier, while scouring the internet for work at 2:00 AM, I stumbled across listings from both the French Foreign Legion and the Australian Defence Force. They were looking to recruit American veterans with combat experience. Without giving it much thought, I submitted my contact info. So I'm not sure why I was surprised that I was actually being contacted. But I was.

There was something exciting about the mystery of the French Foreign Legion. When I was a child, my old man would watch Jackie Chan or Jean-Claude Van Damme movies every weekend. The *Legionnaire* VHS was in regular rotation on our television.

Without Claire's knowledge, I began the enlistment process by sending them my military records. A few days later, I received an e-mail saying I could skip the "pre-selection" in Paris and was given instructions with directions to report to the French Foreign Legion Selection Center in Aubagne, France. I would have to buy a one-way plane ticket on my own dime, but they made it clear I would be provided with free food, free accommodation, and free clothing for as long as I was in the service or until I was kicked out. I responded to the e-mail asking if I could speak with an English-speaking recruiter on the phone.

At 5:00 AM the next day, I received a call from France. I slipped out of bed as quietly as possible and took the call on the front patio. The man on the other end of the phone spoke with a comically disarming French accent, like a talking candlestick from a Disney movie.

"Why are you interested in joining the Legion?"

"I got home from Iraq a while ago, and I'm feeling a little . . . misplaced in the world, I guess," I told him.

I explained that I'd enlisted as a bright-eyed teenager eager to do my part to bring justice to a man who killed thousands of innocent Americans. Instead, I found myself in *another* Middle Eastern country shooting at windmills like Don Quixote. The Legion had been in Afghanistan since the start of the war. The attacks on the Twin Towers triggered Article 5 of the NATO Treaty—an attack on one member state is regarded as an attack on every member state. France immediately volunteered its Foreign Legion. If I wanted to go back to Afghanistan, he said, the Legion could make that happen.

"Any other histories you carry?"

I thought it a strange way to frame a question but chalked it up to context lost in translation. "I'm not in trouble with the law or anything," I clarified.

He explained that contrary to popular belief, the Legion doesn't just accept anyone into its ranks. That's not to say they don't take individuals with checkered pasts, but the ultra-lax recruiting guidelines corresponded with the need for capable bodies while the entire world was at war fifty years earlier. Still, those who do join the Foreign Legion are required to change their identities. In doing so, recruits declare their loyalty to France, the country giving them a second chance, and the playing field is leveled for all, questionable pasts or not. After six months to a year, legionnaires may apply to reclaim their old name under a process called regularization of military situation.

"Are you married? Do you have children?"

"I am. I have a young son."

"Are you prepared to leave them?"

"I mean, I guess." I looked up, and Claire was in the kitchen preparing a bottle for Brody. I waved and gestured to her as if to say *One second.*

"When you join the Foreign Legion, we become your family. You are no longer married. You do not have children. *Legio patria nostra.* The Legion is our fatherland."

"So what does that mean? I have to abandon them?"

"You will always have your family, but for the first year you will not contact them. Then you travel only where we say you can travel. If, after that, you have proven yourself, we will allow you to marry."

"But I'm already married."

"You will be married with the *fraternité*. You are a new man. After three years of service, if you have proven yourself, you will receive permit for residence and French citizenship. If you give your blood for France, we'll send you to spend the rest of your days in the south of France in Montagne Sainte-Victoire."

Through the window, I watched Claire feed Brody his bottle, and I hung up.

21

HELLO, GOODBYE

―――――

I KNEW EXACTLY WHAT time Claire was going to be home. She was home at the same time—give or take a few minutes—every single day. And I also knew it took me about ninety minutes or so to get the house in order before she got home. If she came home to a clean house, it wouldn't look like I was sitting around in my underwear all day playing video games, watching porn, and catching up on all the movies I'd missed the previous year. I'd sent my résumé out to dozens, maybe even hundreds, of companies and was waiting for calls that would never come.

I was in the middle of loading the dishwasher when I heard the recognizable footsteps on the stairs leading up to our front door, followed by the door unlocking. She was home exceptionally early.

"Hey babe, you're home ea—"

"We should move."

"What? Why?"

She looked panicked, the kind of look someone has when they're trying to hide the fact that they are panicking. Like she was running from something—or someone.

"I've been thinking we need a fresh start," she said.

I was confused, partly because she wasn't pissed the house was a mess, but mostly because I thought *this* was our fresh start.

"We don't have the money," I stated, which was a weird thing for me to say, because Claire had always been the fiscally responsible one.

"We live in the most expensive city in the country. *That's* why we don't have the money. We'd be totally fine anywhere else," she countered.

"Not in New York."

"I'm not talking about moving to New York, Dylan. Can you just pretend to be serious for once in your fucking life?"

"OK. . . . Then where? Everything we love and everyone we know are here. We don't have a support system anywhere else."

"We can be our own support system."

We'd never lived under the same roof before my return from Iraq. We'd skipped the engagement. There was no trial run or feeling-out process. We went straight from senior prom to marriage and a family. While I was away, Claire learned how to be the mother of a newborn on her own. She employed a strict routine. It kept her grounded when she was feeling overwhelmed. She rarely deviated, and she'd found comfort in that. Claire had been like that since she was a child.

Her mother, Jenny, was a free spirit who upped and left when Claire was young. That's not to say that Jenny was an absentee parent, because she wasn't, technically. She kept in constant communication and flew Claire out to Breckenridge, Colorado, or Austin, Texas, or wherever her latest muse had taken her. Jenny was a young mother, but she had other priorities—most notably drugs and partying. The free love mentality and counterculture stance Jenny adopted as a teenager in the '70s never left her. She never outgrew it. And as folks often do, she held on tightly to the things she loved during what she considered the best years of her life.

The first time I met Jenny, I was confused. She was Claire's opposite. They had almost nothing in common—emotionally or physically.

There was something about the clashing floral patterns, dreadlocks, missing teeth, and stench of bad weed, patchouli, and body odor that I found repulsive. But Claire absolutely loved her and refused to be embarrassed by her mother. Which I admired.

I got a glimpse of Claire's obsessive-compulsive behavior the first time I walked her to her locker after class. Her locker was always organized; her folders and schoolwork were always labeled and arranged. She meal-prepped and made her lunches for the week before meal-prepping was a fad. Ironically enough, Claire would've made a great soldier.

I was struggling to cope with the things I'd just experienced while I was learning how to be a father and husband on the fly. And now she wanted to abandon the comfort of home? Maybe she was right. I wasn't totally convinced this was the move, but I could be persuaded.

Claire began watching HGTV religiously. "Finding a fixer-upper and restoring it could be fun," she'd say.

We began to research other parts of the country, and after doing some math, we landed on Phoenix, Arizona. The combination of proximity to California, affordable housing, and year-round sunshine made it attractive. But most important for me, I'd still be able to see my Golden State Warriors play in person several times a year.

I'd saved around $30,000 from the year I spent in Iraq. Part of that went to the purchase of a used SUV, and the other half would go to the down payment on our home. Neither of us had ever been to Phoenix, but we began scouring Zillow for homes in the desert. A local real estate agent saw our inquiries and reached out to us. He sent us a list of palatial homes for a fraction of what it would cost in the Bay Area.

I enlisted Kyle to fly out to Arizona with me. The real estate agent drove us around all over the valley. And while I thought it a good idea to buy in a more urban area, or somewhere near the university, the agent convinced me to buy a home in a gated community in Laveen, a neighborhood twenty miles to the west of downtown Phoenix. It was a fairly new residential development, and every house was painted a shade of tan and looked the same as the house next door. However, we could get almost twice the house for the same amount as a home in Scottsdale or Tempe, and it was hard to argue with that.

When I returned home from my scouting trip, we looked at our finances. The pet store Claire managed was a national chain, so she could put in for a transfer. The house I'd toured and wanted to buy was off the market two days later, but there was another available house with the exact same layout two homes down on the same street.

"It's a great deal. You should move on it before someone else does," the real estate agent warned.

Not wanting to lose out, we put in an offer, sight unseen. It was immediately accepted. Something felt odd about a bank giving me, an adult-child without a job, hundreds of thousands of dollars to purchase a home. It was even stranger that we could buy a house like we did for the price we paid, when similar homes in the Bay Area were selling for five or six times more. The mortgage in Arizona for that two-story, two-thousand-square-foot house off of Baseline and Ninety-First was less than the rent for our seven-hundred-square-foot apartment in San Jose.

Less than two months after closing, we were packed and moved to Arizona. Once again, I'd upped and left without giving my family a proper heads-up. I'd run away from home and slept on a park bench as a child, I'd run away to the military as a teenager, and now I was running away as an adult.

Since I paid the down payment on our new home, Claire and I agreed I would take some time to finish college, which would inevitably help my job prospects. When I finished, Claire would go back to school to finish her degree. We knew it would be a struggle for a while, but it was an investment that would pay dividends in the future.

Moving to Laveen felt like a mistake almost immediately. Maybe it was the inconvenient thirty-mile commute to just about anything that wasn't a Walmart or Applebee's. It could've been the dirty looks we got from our neighbors. Seeing grown men open-carrying six-shooters, treating the local Safeway supermarket like the OK Corral, was a bit jarring. There was something menacing about the fields of cotton that surrounded us and the frequently flown Confederate flags that made the small rural town feel more like the Antebellum South than the Southwest. All that confirmed moving to Laveen was a mistake. I just wouldn't admit it to myself, and I definitely wouldn't admit that to Claire.

After being accepted by the illustrious Arizona State University, a rigorously selective academic institution not at all known for its partying (sarcasm) and commonly referred to as Harvard of the Southwest (a flat-out lie), I looked for work to save some money and pass the time until the new semester started. Eventually I landed a gig as an intern for the Phoenix Suns and was offered a job on a new public relations team for the Arizona Diamondbacks, as both franchises were under the same ownership group.

After accepting the position, I quickly discovered "public relations" was a professional euphemism for cheerleading. I found myself jumping around on the dugout with Baxter the Bobcat, alongside attractive college coeds; shooting T-shirts into the stands; and yelling at the crowd to get louder. Despite how absurd it was, I didn't mind. It was a job as far away from Iraq and the military as I could get. It wasn't a lot of money, but I was being paid to smile and watch baseball with a bunch of babes. Like most of the jobs I'd held over the years, this one didn't last too long either. The entire public relations team was disbanded when it was discovered that a staff member had been throwing parties, getting my underaged coworkers intoxicated, and sleeping with them.

The following day, I had a mandatory meeting with my new college counselor before the semester started. We developed an academic game plan that would have me graduating in three years instead of four. Despite being unsure of the poli-sci major with a minor in history that I'd picked—I'd convinced myself that I wanted to be a political pundit who moonlighted as a high school history teacher—I felt good about the general direction I was heading in. I had my fingertips on the normalcy I'd been searching for.

On the way home from campus, I picked up Brody from day care, then stopped by the Sonic drive-through for a celebratory burger and milkshake. At home, sitting on the couch and unwrapping my burger on the coffee table in front of me, I turned on the TV. During a break between my curly fries and shake, I looked up at the screen. The local news anchor was sporting a serious expression, as they always do. However, in the insert above his right shoulder was a photo of my street, followed by the mugshot of a serial killer named Mark Goudeau.

Between 2005 and late 2006, Goudeau, known as the Baseline Killer, had killed nine people in the surrounding area and sexually assaulted dozens of others. I looked around at my new digs—the vaulted ceilings, the massive staircase, the crown-molding-lined walls, the travertine tile floors, the marble countertops, and all the other things we shouldn't have been able to afford—and I knew exactly why the home we were living in was so cheap. We were living in a neighborhood that was the hunting ground for a notorious mass murderer just months earlier, and the property values had still not recovered.

When Claire returned home that evening, I was prepared to tell her about what I'd just seen on the news. Instead, she surprised me with some news of her own. She was pregnant again.

Hendrix Park-Pettiford came to us at the end of our first sweltering summer in Arizona. For me, his birth was a reprieve. He was another chance. Hendrix would teach me how to love the little things in life again. For a while, anyway.

22

SUN DEVIL

FROM THE BACK row of a dark auditorium, I stared at a map, with countries highlighted in a dark shade of red, projected onto a screen in the front of the classroom. One of the underscored countries was a place in the Middle East I'd just returned home from a year earlier. The words "America's Foreign Policy" were scribbled on the white board next to the screen.

My better judgment told me to stand up and walk out. I didn't. I couldn't drop the class because we were too deep into the semester. And I couldn't afford to take a hit to my GPA either. Falling below a certain grade point average would disqualify me from my GI Bill. My educational benefits were connected to a federal work-study program that, by rule, could be my only form of income while using the GI Bill. It paid me $730—a month.

My eyes shifted to the clock on the wall. I was early, embarrassingly early. In the military we had a saying: if you're not fifteen minutes early, you're late. Punctuality was just another of the habits I'd picked up during my time in the service. But at least this was one of the good habits. Slowly but surely, other students began to file in. The only familiar face in the room, Max, a flamboyant eighteen-year-old who

I shared an anthropology class with, took a seat next to me. He had a pleasant disposition, so I enjoyed his company. Still, it was strange being four or five years older than Max and everyone else in the room.

When everyone was mostly settled, the professor jumped right into a lecture about the same topic presented on the board, but not before schooling us on how America has financed nearly every geopolitical opponent the country has ever had. In 1940, America gave aid to China and implemented an embargo on Japan. That pissed Japan off; they attacked Pearl Harbor and dragged the United States into World War II. Just years earlier, members of the American and British governments showered Hitler and Mussolini with praise—and money. By the end of the war, America was funding the Chinese and Russians to fight alongside them in the Pacific theater. Less than ten years later, America was fighting both the Russians and Chinese during the Korean War.

"You starting to see a pattern here?" the professor asked.

During World War II, the OSS—predecessor to the CIA—gave a Vietnamese dude by the name of Ho Chi Minh truckloads of money to fight the Japanese. A couple decades later, Ho Chi Minh's boys were kicking our asses in rice paddies in 'Nam. In the '50s, America financed the coup to overthrow Iran's prime minister. Then, under the Atoms for Peace program, the US gave Iran a nuclear reactor and weapons-grade plutonium. A couple of decades later, Iraq invaded Iran. The United States supported the leader of secular Iraq—some guy by the name of Saddam Hussein—with money, training, and weapons.

"Guess who America went to war with just a few years later? You guessed it. Iraq." Slowly, hands began to raise, but the professor continued. "Just around the corner in Afghanistan, the US was also funneling money to the mujahideen to fight the Russians. It gets slightly convoluted, but in the interest of time, we'll skip a few steps to the part where the mujahideen essentially rebranded themselves as Al Qaeda. And I think some of you might know what happened next."

It was rhetorical commentary, but that didn't stop students from beginning to raise their hands. The professor called on a kid in a polo shirt.

"But can we really blame America's past mistakes on the current administration?"

"America's previous policy often dictates its future policy. And war will always be big business," the professor countered. "The same people America armed turned around and killed three thousand innocent Americans, dragging us into another war which would eventually lead us back to Iraq. Call me unpatriotic, but the war in Iraq was based on false pretenses to make some old rich white men a lot of money through weapons sales and the acquisition of oil. There was no link between Saddam and Osama. And there were no weapons of mass destruction."

This bristled some feathers. A genuine wave of disgust ran through a good portion of the class. After all, this was Arizona State University, a public college in a largely conservative state. The class began to take sides. On one side were the straitlaced, boat-shoe-wearing teens who would eventually grow up to be the staunch MAGA hat–wearing Republicans we see today. On the other were the ultraliberal, pseudo-intellectual kids who can be found on most public college campuses. In the middle was me. I sat quietly and watched the debate unfold.

"We saved those people from Saddam. And now we're saving those people from themselves," another student chimed in.

"That's reductive logic at best and another racist white savior trope at worst." By the looks on a lot of their faces, they'd never had a white person talking to them like this. "I'd wager you'd get a different response from a lot of the men and women who actually served in Iraq and Afghanistan."

I made myself as small as possible, sitting lower in my seat and putting my head down, just as I had done many times in Kirkuk. Max raised his hand, then pointed to me when called on.

"Dylan served. Ask him."

Fuck me, man. Why would you say that?

Everyone turned and looked. I was now planted firmly into a foreign policy debate, because I was the only one in the room with any foreign policy experience. The professor asked if I had anything to add. I did, but I didn't want to, so I attempted to take the easy way out by saying things were complicated. War is never good, but sometimes war is necessary. We did some bad things, but we also did some good things. Yada yada. No one was buying it—including myself.

Some of the liberal kids got ballsy and labeled me an imperialist pawn (not completely inaccurate) and insinuated I was a baby killer (by proxy maybe), with a whole host of other post-Vietnam clichés. And, the funny thing is, I actually didn't disagree with them. I deserved everything they said.

It was strange having a bunch of Republicans who I shared almost nothing in common with, and actually despised most days, coming to my defense. When the class ended, Max apologized for putting me on the spot. I told him it wasn't a big deal. What this did was give me the clarity to realize I was wasting my time with a poli-sci major. I didn't want to be a politician or some pundit for a news outlet.

At the end of class, another student, named Jonam, approached me. He wore a striped polo with a popped collar, and I pegged him as another frat boy who I'd want nothing to do with. But Jonam was actually a member of ASU's Army ROTC program and wanted to pick my brain about my experiences overseas. I obliged, and eventually we became drinking buddies. I prefaced all of the war stories—both good and bad—by saying that I left the military as an E-5 and that I wasn't a particularly good warfighter. The second he graduated he'd be an officer with a completely different set of responsibilities than I ever had. However, I was able to offer him some advice from the perspective of a junior NCO. I told Jonam that the fastest way to lose the respect of his men was breaking their balls for no reason. When given any amount of power, a good number of men will look to abuse it. There are times when leaders need to be hard on their men, but a sincere camaraderie that didn't cross the line of fraternization would be the best way to win them over. For as long as I knew Jonam after that, he always bought my first round.

I enjoyed the professor and some of my classmates, so I didn't drop the course. But as soon as the semester was over, I paid a visit to my guidance counselor and requested a change of majors. She asked what I was thinking. I went in with the intention to change my major to history, but then I thought, *What the fuck would I do with a history degree?* The entire point of attending college was to get a degree that would land me a job with the security to provide for my family. That is exactly why I chose to enroll in Arizona State's new . . . Film and Media Studies program. Nothing says job security like a film degree.

A few days later, while watching a young Black senator from Illinois who would later go on to be the president of the United States speak to a group of students on campus, I bumped into one of the kids who in class called me a baby killer. I pulled him aside and told him he had every right to say what he said, and that I didn't even necessarily disagree with him, which I think caught him off guard.

I told him I regretted being a member of the American war machine that had a hand in what amounted to a genocide in the Middle East, and I was going to spend the rest of my life trying to make up for it. But, because I'm me, I ended the conversation by saying if he ever tried to embarrass me in front of our peers again, I would graduate from baby killer to college underclassman killer. I was joking, obviously, but he didn't seem to get that. He apologized, shook my hand, and disappeared into the crowd as fast as he could.

A day later, I was summoned into the counselor's office with a police officer present to explain the situation. I wasn't angry about it; I actually appreciated that they were taking threats of violence on campus seriously. I assured them it was all a misunderstanding and that I was a pacifist, a new member of the Veterans for Peace even. They didn't have to worry about me shooting the school up, because I'm not an angry white kid. Again, a joke—mostly. They didn't seem to appreciate my sense of humor either.

———————

While sitting in a lecture scrolling the Internet instead of paying attention, an e-mail popped up on my screen from Mitch Renner, a name I vaguely recognized only because he was a friend of one of Claire's friends in San Jose. *Odd.*

I'd met Mitch briefly at a few outings—dinners, birthday parties, and whatnot—but outside of a few exchanged pleasantries, he was essentially a stranger. An e-mail from him was completely out of the ordinary. My initial thought was that he'd been hacked and his account was spamming all of his contacts, and I almost deleted it.

I wish I had. Had I ignored that e-mail, my life could very well be completely different from the one I've led in the decade-plus since. I didn't ignore it because the subject line was "Claire."

> Hi, I'm not really sure how to go about writing this email, but it's one that I felt I had to send. My name is Mitch and I worked with your wife. I don't know how to say this delicately, so I'll just say it: I was sleeping with Claire. The thing is, I didn't know she had a husband, and I definitely did not know that he was fighting overseas. I knew she was a couple months pregnant. She said that the father was a deadbeat. We were in a relationship for a few months, but once I found out about you, I cut it off. She threw a tantrum and tried to get me fired from work for sexual harassment. I'm sorry. This is so shitty. I just thought you have the right to know the truth. If there's anything I can do, please don't hesitate to reach out.

Without a hint of irony, he said he felt terrible because of all the things I'd gone through overseas. Veterans deserve better, he said. He also spilled the beans on Claire's previous business trips. The trip to Houston right after I returned home? As it turns out, those trips weren't solely for business; there was a little pleasure mixed in. She'd been having an affair with a former high school classmate of mine. Mitch finished the e-mail by thanking me for my service.

Instead of confronting Claire, I withdrew from the world. I'd effectively ended things without even telling her I ended things. When I wasn't watching the children, I was locked up in the office doing homework, interacting with old high school classmates on Facebook, or sleeping away the depression on an unforgiving futon.

On campus, I walked around in a stupor for weeks. That is, until a fairly involved midterm assignment in my English class and the girl I was partnered up with who required my attention.

Allison needed me to pull my weight so I didn't tank her grade on the project we were working on together. Her annoyance with my lack of enthusiasm for academia slowly transformed into genuine curiosity when I began to open up about my life and my experiences. Slowly, my sense of humor returned to me and the nineteen-year-old girl who was brought up in a wealthy conservative family in the nearby enclave of Chandler, Arizona, became enamored with me as a person. We became fast friends.

I was only twenty-two at the time, but Allison's wonderment about my travels, the deference she showed me for my military service, and the gushing she did over photos of my children made me feel like a relic. "You look too young to have kids," she'd say.

I *was* too young to have kids. She often joked that I was a DILF. That kind of attention was something I hadn't felt since Claire and I began dating half a decade earlier. Eventually, our late-night study sessions turned into movie dates, and eventually those movie dates turned into something more romantic.

I spent the weekdays at home with Claire and the kids, but we were essentially roommates, and she treated me like a glorified babysitter. The days Claire was home from work, I spent on campus or in Chandler with Allison.

Allison's parents owned a massive ranch home that was so expansive I could spend the night there and they wouldn't even know. And while they didn't know I had been dating their daughter for a few months, Claire figured it out sooner, and she wasn't thrilled about it.

23

IF YOU GOTTA GO, GO NOW

THE FREEZING WATER felt good on my broken back and achy joints. My latest VA doctor in the constantly rotating carousel of VA doctors said something about cold water breaking up lactic acid in muscles, which helps alleviate pain. I didn't understand the science behind it, I just knew I didn't want to take any more prescription drugs. I was already prescribed to a half-dozen scheduled narcotics for all my other ailments, none of which I was sure were actually working. So weekly physical therapy and nightly ice baths or ending my showers with two minutes of ice-cold water—something that can be bearable only in a climate like Arizona—became a nightly ritual. It wasn't a cure, but it did bring some relief.

It was the evening of New Year's Day, and I was planning on hanging out with Allison. So I wanted to freshen up after spending the day recovering from the hangover from drinking the night before. But this shower didn't finish with me standing under a stream of cold water to ease the chronic pain in my joints; it would end with the door getting kicked in and me being dragged out of the bathroom by three Phoenix police officers.

I'm not proud of the sound that left my mouth when uniformed officers burst in, startling me. It can only be described as a yelp several octaves higher than my regular voice as they bum-rushed me, followed by a high-pitched squeal as they wrestled me to the ground. Other than the soap suds covering my body and the shampoo that had not yet been washed out of my hair, I was completely naked.

I might not have been embarrassed, but between the shrinkage and the handcuffs, I was feeling pretty powerless. More than anything, I was confused. I asked what I was being arrested for. Assault and battery, the officer said.

"Where is my wife?" I asked. "Is she OK?"

"Why don't you tell us, asshole," one responded.

"What the fuck is going on? Seriously."

I asked if I could at least put some clothes on before they took me away. What were they planning on doing? Putting me in the back of the squad car completely naked? The cops looked to each other for answers. I had a valid point. The officer asked where my clothes were. Because I had my hands behind my back and couldn't point, I nodded to the dresser across the room. The other officer pulled all the drawers out and dumped the contents all over the floor.

"Was that necessary?"

"It's for our safety," he replied.

"But you didn't need to throw my things all over the place and make a mess."

"That should be the least of your worries right now. Everything in your pathetic life's about to get a whole lot messier."

"Yeah? OK, well which one of you pigs is putting my underwear on for me?"

They eyeballed each other. No one volunteered. Before the officer took my cuffs off, he warned me not to make any sudden movements.

I grabbed the first shirt I could find, a wrinkled one with the word CHOCOLATE on the front, followed by a pair of bright-red American Apparel boxer briefs and some ill-fitting jeans. Before I put on my shoes, an officer took the soles out, checked the heels, then pulled the laces out before handing them back to me. I asked if they'd at least have the decency of taking my cell phone and wallet for me, and I was met with no objections.

Minutes later, I was in the back of a black-and-white, taking in a views of Phoenix at night between the metal bars that covered the glass. I began to plead my case. The officer ignored me. I realized he probably heard excuses, lies, and alibis that sounded just like mine all day, every day, so I stopped.

The lack of blood flow from the sitting position and the overtightened cuffs made my hands go numb. My body and scalp were itchy from the dry soap, so I attempted to scratch that itch by rubbing my back along the plastic bench seat, not unlike a bear would do against a tree in the woods. The most uncomfortable part about all of this was the uncertainty of why I was even under arrest in the first place. This was certainly a new low point for me. And yet somehow, I was still able to find the basement below rock bottom.

After taking mugshots, being fingerprinted, and receiving a squat-and-cough cavity search, I was transferred from one holding cell to another, until I was finally placed in a twenty-foot-by-twenty-foot cement square. In the center of the room was a steel toilet that was currently occupied. Concrete benches with metal bars lined three of the walls. Along one wall were the Aryans and Peckerwoods, the type to call themselves the master race, despite their receding hairlines, bad teeth, and crusty skin covered in tattoos that Popeye the Sailor might wear if he were a member of the SS. The Mexicans sat against the wall in the center. They sized me up the moment I stepped foot in the room. With self-preservation in mind, I thought it better not to hold eye contact with another man who had face tattoos. Occupying the bench on the third wall were the Blacks and Samoans. They didn't know what to make of me. Was I Black? Was I Asian or an Islander? The tattoos of California and Hawaii on my arm suggested I could be both.

There was nowhere to sit, so for those of us who weren't affiliated in any gangs, for those of us like the pink-polo-wearing frat boy who was standing next to me trembling, it was standing room only. If we stood too close to someone seated on one of the benches, we were threatened with violence. This is one of the few places I didn't think I could talk myself out of an ass-kicking or verbally clown someone into submission, and I had almost zero chance of winning a fist fight. So, with no other choice, I decided to mind my own business. I looked at my feet or the wall or the ceiling while the man taking a shit just a few feet from me grunted during what sounded like a particularly difficult bowel movement.

I found it heartbreaking that all of these people were reduced to caricatures you might see on *Saturday Night Live*. They were once human beings with hopes and dreams. And now they were wasting away in an irresolution with little to no prospects for anything but tragedy.

In the corner was a pay phone that had been occupied for a majority of the night. When it freed up, I stepped forward to use it. The first call I made was to Claire. It went unanswered. The only other phone number I knew by heart was my parents' landline. I called and my father, who had very obviously been fast asleep, answered, disgruntled.

"Dad?"

"What is it, son?" he replied.

"Um, so, I'm in jail."

"I know. I accepted the collect call, didn't I?"

I tried to explain that I had no idea why I was actually in jail. Understandably, my old man was skeptical.

"Where's Claire?" he asked.

"I don't know. She didn't pick up my phone call. I need you to bail me out. If I don't get out tomorrow, I'll be spending the weekend in—"

The alcohol-covered halitosis of a belligerently drunk Mexican man, who had just entered too far into my personal space, slapped me across the face. His nose was inches from my cheek.

"Hey man, can you back up?" I asked, as politely but as firmly as one can. My father heard this too.

"Dylan, don't be starting shit in there. That's not a private school playground. Those boys are looking for any excuse to put hands on you," he warned.

"I'm not doing anything. This dude is in my face and I—"

"*Amor eterno e inolvidable, tarde o temprano estaré contigo, para seguirrrr . . . amándonossss,*" the drunkard crooned in my ear.

I held the phone to my chest and turned to him. "Yo, man. Back *the fuck* up." All of my cellmates were watching now. Even the man on the toilet paused his wiping and turned to get a glimpse of the action. "I'm not going to ask you again," I warned.

My father could hear the frustration in my voice. "Lower your tone. Don't be stupid."

Swaying back and forth, the drunkard continued his singing inches from my face. "*Yo, he sufrido mucho por tu ausencia . . .*" Before he could finish the next verse of Juan Gabriel's love ballad, he paused, looked at me with glassy eyes and a blank stare, and projectile vomited directly onto my neck and chest.

A string of sounds and an amalgamation of obscenities poured from my mouth. Reflexively, I pushed him then tried to strike him with the phone receiver in my hand, but he stumbled backward out of distance of my improvised club. I could hear my father pleading for me to stop before I got myself killed.

I spent the evening huddled up in a corner on the concrete floor, wearing nothing but those red American Apparel boxer briefs. I didn't sleep out of paranoia. I'd seen enough movies to know what goes on behind bars. And I likely would've been a nice little target if I wasn't covered in another man's bile. War was punishing, but it was a cakewalk compared to the hard twenty (hours) I served in Maricopa.

Following my release the next morning, I hopped on a bus. The closest stop was miles from my home, which was still in a developing unincorporated community. I had no choice but to walk the rest of the way. Covered in dry puke, I shuffled along the dirt sidewalks that crisscrossed through West Phoenix, my laceless shoes flopping the entire way. By the time I reached my front door, the skin had been rubbed raw off my heels. I looked like Curt Schilling without the World Series rings and collection of Nazi memorabilia.

The locks on the door had already been changed, and Claire had filed a restraining order against me. Both my debit cards and credit cards had been locked, so I was starting over with the clothes on my back, twenty-eight dollars in cash, and the keys to a Chevrolet Aveo with a quarter tank of gas. With no other options, I slept in the back of my car for a few weeks and showered at the gym in the school's rec center.

Friends and family called to check up on me periodically. I pretended life was great. They didn't know Claire and I were separated, and they had no idea I was homeless. A mutual friend called to ask me why Claire was telling everyone I beat the shit out of her. This was news to me. When Claire's father called me, threatening to kill me if he ever saw me, I got the sense that this wasn't going to blow over like I'd hoped. I told him I'd never laid a hand on his daughter in my life. He should've known that. He said Claire told him Iraq changed me and that she was afraid of me. That may have been true, but not in the context she was providing.

"Greg, she got caught cheating, so she's fucking embarrassed. And instead of being remorseful, she's throwing me under the bus," I explained.

"I know my daughter. She would never do that."

"No offense, but that's bullshit. And you fucking know it. How's Claire's mother doing? Do you even know? You keep in contact with Jenny after she cheated, then up and left?" I'd probably crossed the line, but I needed to drive the point home. It was pointless. He was never going to find fault with his daughter. He was never going to believe me. I probably wouldn't have believed me either.

My old man advised me to hire a decent attorney for my upcoming court hearing if I didn't want to go to jail for the assault charges I'd been slapped with. I scrolled through the phone book and found a lawyer who advertised himself as being able to beat or match the fees of any other attorneys, so he seemed like the logical choice. Even the cheapest lawyer was still thousands of dollars, so again I was forced to sell my car to foot the bill.

There's that age-old adage—you get what you pay for. The day of the hearing, I was sitting in the hallway waiting for my newly hired representation. He was thirty minutes late and the hearing was about to start, so I moved into the courtroom thinking I'd been scammed. While awaiting the judge to call my name, a man wearing a zoot suit, complete with the black-and-white wingtips and long metal wallet chain, entered. The guy looked like the backup trumpet player in the Brian Setzer Orchestra.

"Is there a Dylan . . ." He looked down at his file again. "Is there a Dylan Park-Pettiford here?"

This is the fucking guy? I thought. An image of the judge smacking down his gavel, yelling "I sentence you to life," flashed through my head. Mighty Mighty Bosstone, Esq., pulled me into the next room, shook my hand, and sat me down. He'd already had a quick powwow with the overworked prosecutor. I'd been offered a deal for the new Veterans Diversion Program. All I had to do was pay a small fine and take anger management classes once a week for six months, and any charges would fall off upon completion of the program.

"*Or* we could risk it and go to trial," he proposed. "I don't *think* we'd lose, but if we *did* . . ." He sucked his teeth. "You could be looking at a year-plus. Probably closer to six months, because you have no priors and I know you'd behave yourself."

I looked at his frosted spiked hair, the rose-colored glasses, and the pinstripes on his suit. Then I looked down at the offenses on the sheet—assault and child endangerment. I imagined Claire on the stand crying her crocodile tears while the jury lapped it up and I looked on helplessly. Who were they going to believe—the cute petite blonde or the disgruntled homeless Black war veteran with PTSD, tattoos, and an unfiltered mouth? I already knew that answer. There was a historic precedent for this kind of thing.

"Let's take the deal," I uttered without hesitation.

"I'm obligated to mention, if you take this deal, and you get in trouble, violate the restraining order, or skip out on any of the classes for any reason, they *will* throw the book at you. And that means the maximums."

I didn't anticipate that being a problem and copped a plea.

The anger management classes weren't too bad. Our counselor had a warm disposition and soothing voice with a calming presence. I actually looked forward to our weekly meetings. I didn't have shit else going on anyway. She became the mother figure to a roomful of troubled men. And like any good mother would, she brought drinks and snacks and handed them out to us like we were children on a Police Athletic League soccer team called the Convicts. She warned us explicitly that it was one snack per each. The county didn't reimburse her for anything, but she thought it important her students be as comfortable as possible, so she paid for them out of pocket. Eventually, she caught me sneaking extra snacks and chided me. I told her I was homeless. I was also flat broke, and my next meal was always something of an uncertainty. The following week she brought me a Subway sandwich, a box of granola bars, and a case of water.

With nowhere to go but the homeless shelters, I took advantage of the school library's twenty-four-hour open-door policy. I slept on the top floor in the back of the room next to a stack of books, where I was out of sight. Ironically, being homeless made me a better college student. I didn't have anything else to do but to focus on schoolwork. However, it wasn't long before the library caught on and changed their policies. They began to close at 11:00 PM, and only students who received passes could stay past closing, so I was back to sleeping on park benches.

With the last money I had, I purchased a prepaid phone card, then knowingly violated my restraining order by reaching out to Claire to reconcile. I prefaced my pitch by saying we didn't need to get back together or anything. I'd sign the house over to her—whatever she wanted. I just needed a roof over my head until I got back on my feet. I'd sleep in the office, and I'd babysit at nights to save her some cash if she wanted to go out with her friends. She wasn't interested in any of that. She was already dating someone else, and he enjoyed movie and dinner nights at the house. My presence would kill the vibes. Claire followed up her rejection by making it clear she was going to ruin my life for embarrassing her.

Claire sent text messages to some friends admitting that she'd given herself a black eye by slamming her face on the kitchen counter, and she was going to use that as evidence: "I gave myself a black eye and sent the pics to the detectives." Most of her friends didn't like me, but for one of them even, that was a line too far, and she texted me to warn me about being railroaded.

Now, one might ask why anyone would admit in a text message to breaking the law. Well, this was early 2008. Touch screen phones were brand new, and the iPhone had just come out months earlier, along with the advent of technology we now take for granted—the screenshot. That is exactly what I took advantage of. I took screenshots of the conversation, then went down to the school library and printed them out.

Just as Claire had hoped, officers from Phoenix PD tracked me down and arrested me again for breaking the conditions of my diversion program. The next morning when I went to face the judge, I presented him with the photos of the text messages I'd exchanged with Claire and her friend. The new charges were dropped, but because I'd technically violated the old orders, I was sentenced to an anger management diversion program. Upon completing a year of night classes that were held in an empty office space behind a Domino's Pizza in Mesa, Arizona, any record of the incident would be erased.

I should've married a nice Korean girl like my mother wanted.

———————

A new veterans center opened on campus, and I applied to join their staff. I was a war vet, and the center's entire mission was to support veterans trying to go back to school. I assumed I was a shoo-in.

During the interview, I mentioned my recent deployment to Iraq and said that although I was no longer a member of the military, I still had a desire to work with other veterans and service members. The interviewer rattled off all the statistics—twenty-two veterans a day commit suicide, veterans make up nearly 20 percent of the homeless population in America, and of those homeless veterans, 56 percent were Black or Latino despite only accounting for 25 percent of the veteran population, blah blah blah. I wasn't fishing for sympathy points, but I mentioned that I was homeless as well.

"Oh, wow. Sorry to hear that. Well, we'll definitely be giving you a call."

I never got a call back. A week later, I returned to the office to inquire about the opening, and the new office manager, an attractive blonde coed, filled me in that she was actually the one who'd filled the position. She wished me luck on my job search. I asked if she was a veteran as well.

"I'm not. But my grandfather fought during WWII."

"So brave. Thank you for your service," I said before exiting.

24

NO PLACE FEELS
LIKE HOME

THE MELANCHOLY OF an indie rock band from the suburbs of
New Jersey drowned out the sounds of the rain and my clumsy
footsteps on the wet concrete.

"Regrets are worthless," Gabe Saporta, the vocalist of a pop punk
band from New Jersey, sang. "As time has passed, no one understands.
And to say the least, the years have been unfair. . . . It's easier when
no place feels like home."

Sure, I had plenty of regrets, but I wasn't patient enough to let
time heal those old wounds. At the moment no place felt like home. I
had nowhere to go and no one to confide in. The torrential downpour
only added to that misery.

Like two sinking vessels in the Atlantic, my worn combat boots
had taken in as much water as they could handle. With every step,
I could feel water secreting from my socks through the sides of my
soles only to reabsorb more dirty water like a sponge when I lifted
my foot. I continued to slosh through the puddles, because by that
point there was no use in trying to avoid them.

Ahead in the distance, the light from a neon sign reached through the cold, gray haze just enough to grab my attention. I squinted and craned my head forward to make out the words HOE TOWN. When I got closer, I noticed the *m* from HOME was missing.

A crusty old lady who smelled like a lifetime's worth of cigarette smoke handed me the key to my room. It wasn't a key card like most hotels use now, but an old brass key on a mangled keyring that looked like I needed a tetanus shot just to handle it.

"End of the hall, take a right. No trouble tonight, 'kay?" she croaked before reaching to light up a shriveled cigarette butt in the ashtray in front of her.

What the fuck was that supposed to mean? I wondered. The offense was quickly displaced after I realized that she could see how drunk I was.

"No, ma'am. Just trying to stay out of the rain tonight. Thank you."

"Ma'am? Do I look that old to you?"

The answer was yes, but I apologized and said it was a habit from my days in the military.

"Well, thank you for your service."

I turned, and a solitary light at the end of the tunnel emitted a sickly green hue onto the checkered floor that stretched out in front of me like some dismal chessboard. As I plodded toward my room, the echoes of my sopping footsteps were eaten by other sounds emanating from the bottom of each door. There was a heated argument happening in room 103. A couple was fucking in 107. The ice machine grumbled angrily, like it was annoyed by how loud the TV in room 110 was.

When I reached the end of the hall and made a right, things quieted, as though I had just stepped onto a platform that led into another world. I put the key in the doorknob and turned the handle. Nothing. The door was stuck. I wiggled it forcefully, but it still didn't budge. Annoyed by the minor inconvenience, I lowered my shoulder and threw all my weight against the door once, twice, three times, until it freed itself from the frame.

The first thing I did when I got into my room was click the power button on the hotel's awkwardly large television remote. It was a curious reflex, considering I had no plans of watching television at all. I was there to do something else.

The patterns on the patchy, worn carpet ran parallel with my thoughts, and just like the red and green floral print of the comforter on the bed, my intentions were ugly. The covers were pulled tight on the bed, just as they had been while I was in basic training. I thought about lying down for a moment, but after pulling back the blankets revealed questionable stains, I decided against it. I looked around for the minibar; there was no minibar. *Fuck.* Of course there wasn't. This wasn't the Marriott in Palm Springs, it was a no-star motel in a rough neighborhood in Phoenix.

I sat down in a chair in the corner, the chair no one ever sits down in when they stay in a hotel. The unyielding cushion underneath was proof of that. I threw my backpack onto the bed, unzipped my duffel bag, then haphazardly dumped out all the contents in front of me. There was a black leather-bound journal, a couple pens, half a dozen shooters of Jameson—most of them empty—three orange bottles of prescription medication, and a handgun, presumably stolen, that I was holding for a Samoan kid in one of my classes.

I had a cocktail of illicit chemicals running through my blood, so logical reasoning was effectively absent. I was determined to find some peace, some understanding. What that meant exactly or how I was going to go about that, I hadn't figured out yet. But I was feeling creative. Continuous cycles of muffled movie trailers played in the background. I added Larry the Cable Guy's new movie to the list of reasons why I should kill myself.

I took a swig of Jameson. The biting sensation of the whiskey reminded me of how much fun I had in Ireland. There weren't any fair-skinned girls with funny accents in this hotel room, though. In between the pulls of Jameson, I threw back a couple tablets of citalopram and sertraline. One of the bottles instructed me to TAKE ONE EVERY 12 HOURS FOR MOOD. So I took two, just in case.

The light in the corner flickered intermittently as I sat there hunched over, scribbling words in the waterlogged journal. Sand and dirt from Iraq trickled from between the pages. These were supposed to be the last words I ever wrote. I explained why I was doing what I was doing. I wrote love notes and fuck-yous while flashing lights from the television screen bounced shadows off the wall in front of me. I was writing confessions and apologies. I was writing about squandering opportunities when I saw something slide across the room out of the corner of my eye.

Someone was in the room with me. I looked toward the front door; it was cracked open. I hadn't fastened the deadbolt. I was so drunk, so consumed with my own pain, that I didn't even notice someone had followed me into the room to rob me—such a stupid mistake to make in a place like this. I was preparing to kill myself, but suddenly self-preservation mattered. I swiped the gun and racked it—muscle memory.

The light in the corner flickered.

I scanned the room quickly and spotted a shadow leaking out onto the floor behind the bathroom door. I crouched down and slowly made my way along the wall toward the bathroom with my weapon trained in front of me. I'd been through this drill a thousand times in training and a couple of times in the real world. This asshole didn't stand a chance, because I wouldn't give him one.

The light in the corner flickered.

I stopped just short of the cracked door. It was dark in the bathroom, so I let my eyes adjust to the dark. I stood there. Watching. Waiting. Breathing. Nothing. Complete silence.

"I know you're in there. If you leave now, I won't call the cops," I pined. I was trying to reason with someone who was probably worse off than I was, because I was afraid of the alternative. I was tired of fighting.

"I really don't have anything to give you. Please, please just come out."

I felt sorry for whoever it was who needed what I had. But I felt sorrier for myself, because I had nothing of any value to give them. Adrenaline-fueled tears of anger began to stream down my face.

The light in the corner flickered.

"Please, man. Please," I pleaded. "We can share this bottle. I don't have much money, but I have drugs. Whatever you want. I don't want to kill you. Please don't make me—"

Before I could finish my sentence, the shower curtain moved.

When I pivoted a half step back, I saw him in the mirror. He had dark eyes. He was wearing a camouflage jacket. He was clutching something. Maybe a knife, maybe a gun. He had ignored my pleas. I wasn't really sure what else to do.

I took a deep breath, committing myself, then I rushed. I kicked the door in with speed and violence just like I'd been trained to do. I swung the pistol and caught him square, but he raised his knife and cut the back of my hand, disarming me. I followed with a devastating left hook and connected, but again he slashed me. I reeled over in pain and fell back into the bathtub. I assumed a defensive position, flailing for my life. But he never came. He was gone. I lay there in the dark, on my back in the bathtub, clutching the loosened shower curtain and rod.

The light in the corner flickered.

When I knew for certain that I was alone, I crawled out of the tub and turned on the light. Blood was everywhere. My hand was cut to the bone. I looked up at the mirror and noticed that it was completely shattered. Glass lay everywhere. I needed to stop the bleeding. I took off my camouflage jacket and wrapped it around my hand. Wait. *My* camouflage jacket? I looked into the shattered mirror and stared back into my own dark lifeless eyes. There wasn't anyone else in the room, and there hadn't been. I was completely alone.

I found my way back to the chair, leaving a trail of blood on the way. I lay back, clutching my hand. The pain sobered me up. And I knew I needed help.

The light in the corner flickered.

Things were not going as planned. I never wanted to be a twenty-something divorcé. Even if I hated my father's tough love as a kid, at least I *had* a father in my life. The court-ordered supervised visitation with my children at a McDonald's PlayPlace every other weekend was cruel and unusual punishment. I didn't feel like I was playing any substantial role in their lives, and it made me feel like a deadbeat parent. The boys were too young to know what was happening, and they loved eating Happy Meals and running around the playground every other Friday and Saturday night. The only person who was hurt by this new arrangement was me.

But then again, not being saddled with the responsibilities of a full-time parent allowed me to finish school and have that raucous college experience I was hoping for when I attended San Jose State half a decade earlier. I procrastinated on homework and essays, I didn't study for my finals, I stressed about not studying for my finals, and I partied on the weekends I didn't have the boys.

Being a slightly older undergrad with "fun" war stories made me popular among my peers. But no matter how much I socialized, no matter how many handles of alcohol I drank or how many women I slept with, there was always an impending sense of doom in the pit of my stomach. I was always tiptoeing on a precipice. My hypervigilance was becoming obvious to everyone around me. I couldn't walk down a street without looking for snipers on rooftops. If I was out eating at a restaurant, I looked at the torso of everyone who walked through the front door to make sure they weren't wearing a suicide vest. In class, I was always wary of abandoned book bags and sat nearest the closest exit.

These were all signs of severe PTSD, but I refused to admit I had it. I didn't want to be one of the caricatures of a troubled veteran you saw on TV shows and in movies. I didn't want to be a trope. I internalized all of it, not telling anyone how I really felt. And that's a hard way to live.

I woke up one morning, and Allison was sitting up next to me, staring at me with a look of concern on her face. I asked if something was wrong. I'd been crying and screaming in my sleep, she said. I had no recollection, but the tear stains on my face and a damp pillow suggested she was being sincere.

I was too embarrassed to tell anyone else, so she drove me across town to the local VA hospital. After reviewing my records and undergoing a physical, it was determined that I qualified for a medical pension. I was then sent to another floor for a psychiatric evaluation. There, I was prescribed a cocktail of drugs—sertraline for depression, bubpropion for mood, prazosin for nightmares, gabapentin for nerve damage, omeprazole for my stomach ulcers, Adderall for impulse control, and trazodone as a sedative.

I had a ton of questions for the doctor but was too overwhelmed to remember most of them. One of the questions I did ask was if there were any adverse side effects. His answer was that medication like sertraline is prescribed as an antidepressant but that one of the common side effects was "suicidal ideation." That seems pretty counterintuitive for a drug people take because they *don't* want to kill themselves, but what do I know? He's the one who did eight years of schooling to take care of college dropouts like myself who were dumb enough to get ourselves into this predicament in the first place. Who was I to question his medical expertise? I thanked the doc and took home a grab bag of controlled substances.

Over the next few months, I degenerated into a shell of my former self. I shuffled to and from class like a zombie. I wasn't interested in anything other than eating and sleeping. I gained a ton of weight, my sex drive was nonexistent, and when I did want to have sex, my equipment didn't always work. This particular detail was a serious point of contention for my girlfriend and me. We went from fucking like rabbits to almost no physical intimacy at all. And for a young woman brought up in a society where she's constantly told her worth is directly related to her looks and by the amount of people who give her attention, that can cause some major insecurities. She let me know several times that there was a roster of men waiting in the wings who would give her the attention she deserved.

Worse than losing those around me, I was losing myself. The doctor had warned me of the side effects of drugs I was taking to keep myself from suck-starting a Glock, but I wasn't a quitter and continued to take the list of meds I was prescribed, thinking I might get over the hump. I was hoping I'd wake up one day and be cured. That the fog would be lifted. I was warned to follow the medication schedule, but the relief never came.

I hated feeling the way I did, so I started experimenting with my own routines, which included discovering my threshold for alcohol consumption while taking a variety of meds. With a little peer-reviewed research, I was able to find the sweet spot—the euphoric combination of uppers and downers and all-arounders.

Warning labels were invented for a reason. And ignoring them caught up with me. One night, hours after taking my prescribed meds, I engaged in heavy drinking with some friends. Keg stands, beer bongs, beer pong—all that sophomoric bullshit that college students do. I fell asleep on the couch, then woke up in the hospital the next day. Some strangers who were at the party said I had a seizure and was choking on my own vomit while convulsing. I'm grateful they called 911 instead of just recording me on their phones and posting the videos online, which seems like the go-to response nowadays.

For the two days I was laid up in a hospital bed, eating shitty hospital food with my ass hanging out in those weird robes they give you, I attempted to explain to the doctors I wasn't trying to take my own life—not that time, anyway. It was just a devastating mistake made by an irresponsible young adult. I wasn't thinking.

They didn't believe me and recommended me for a psych eval and a psychiatric hold. I didn't accept, and when the coast was clear, I checked myself out.

The first thing I did when I got home from the hospital was flush all the pills down the toilet.

25

NOSTALGIA, ULTRA

THE YOUNG BLACK senator from Illinois who I watched speak a couple years earlier returned to Arizona State's campus, this time as the president of the United States. Although I wasn't graduating, I sat in the stands and watched Barack Obama deliver the commencement address to the graduating class. I pretended he was speaking to me. And that was the only commencement address I'd ever witness in the flesh.

The following year, on the morning of my own college graduation, I was too hungover to get out of bed. My parents refused to fly out to Arizona to attend the ceremony—their son receiving a degree in film from a notorious party school wasn't something to be celebrated—and the majority of my closest friends had already dropped out or graduated. Sitting among strangers in the desert sun for hours, draped in polyester, listening to speakers recite platitudes about achievement and changing the world, didn't interest me at all, so I decided to skip. That, in hindsight, is something I very much regret.

After graduating I was offered a low-paying, entry-level gig at the new Google satellite campus in Phoenix. On my second day of work, I was pulled into the HR office, where I was told they had to let me go due to my "violent criminal record." The thing about that is I didn't have a criminal record. Or I shouldn't have, after completing the diversion program.

The HR lady handed me a document from the company contracted to conduct the background check stating that my court case was "pending." I told her I could prove this was a mistake, but she wasn't having it and they let me go. My mom was still working at Intel, and Intel had a new fabrication plant right down the road in Chandler, Arizona. A little nepotism landed me a job I was definitely not qualified for. For the next six months, I worked in an underground facility, surrounded by hundreds of millions of dollars' worth of machinery, where I wore a bunny suit to manufacture chips, wafers, and other doodads.

The plant looked like something out of Kubrick's *2001: A Space Odyssey.* Everything was a sterile white, there were robots everywhere, and equipment with colorful flashing lights lined the walls. There weren't any windows in the massive facility, and under the rare circumstance I did bump into another employee, I couldn't speak with them because of the masks and noise. All communication was done through e-mail and text messages. Monotony mixed with seclusion and a lack of natural light felt like solitary confinement. I worked three twelve-hour days one week and four twelve-hour days the next, which should've been agreeable. During the winter I started at 6:00 AM, when the sun was still down, and by the time I exited the facility around 7:00 PM, it was dark out. I put in my two-week notice when I noticed I was starting to have conversations with myself.

My wait in the unemployment line didn't last too long. Mike Nichols, my old friend from the surf shop, called and asked if I wanted to come work for him to install solar panels in Hawaii. He was having trouble finding folks with experience. Manufacturing chips wasn't the same as installing solar panels, but he was certain that if I was smart enough to work at Intel, I'd be a quick understudy. (I forgot to mention to him that I didn't know what I was doing at Intel either, but those are just details.) The pay was sixty dollars an hour plus overtime. That was four times more than I made working in the fab and a lot more money than I'd ever made in my life. The catch was that I had to be in Maui and ready to work by Monday morning. It was Thursday afternoon.

Even though I knew the answer, I called Rory to see what he would do in my situation. He said he'd move with me if he could, but we agreed that when I settled in, I'd fly him out to visit. The following day I packed my bags, kissed Allison goodbye, and bought a one-way ticket to Maui.

I moved into a condo in Kihei overlooking the Pacific Ocean, and I was clearing $5,000 checks every two weeks working the easiest job I'd ever had. I made more money in three months than I did during my year in Iraq, and I wasn't being shot at. I'd wake up at 6:00 AM, spend a few hours bolting solar panels to roofs, and be off by 2:00 PM, then I'd head to the beach to surf or sunbathe—every single day. It's funny how a little money and some vitamin D can help you forget your trauma.

Life was perfect. Until it wasn't.

———————

On the morning of November 17, 2012, I woke up to dozens of messages and missed phone calls. The sun wasn't up yet, so I figured there was no point in responding. I ignored them and turned on the stereo. Rory had sent me *Nostalgia, Ultra*, a mixtape he'd been begging me to listen to by his favorite up-and-coming artist, Frank Ocean. I'd promised him repeatedly I'd give it a chance. This is the type of music Rory wanted to make. It was fresh and avant-garde, but it sampled the classics. It was rhythm and blues, but it was also hip-hop. It was soulful, but rebellious. It was Rory. I didn't always understand his art, but I understood this. I understood why he wanted to emulate it.

I danced along while getting dressed and making sure all the tools I'd need for the day were accounted for. I hummed along while making my roommates a fresh batch of coffee and eating a bowl of instant oatmeal.

While we waited for my work carpool, I opened up my phone and began going through my messages. There were several panicked voicemails from my mother asking me to contact her as soon as possible. When she answered, there was a tone in her voice I'd never heard before, a fear so palpable that I could feel it from across the Pacific. I asked her what was going on, and she couldn't find the words.

Outside my front door a car honked twice, signaling the arrival of my ride. Again, I asked her to tell me. After what felt like the deepest, darkest silence, she let me know Rory had been shot the night before.

"What hospital is he in?"

"He's not at a hospital."

"OK, well can you tell him to call me?" There was a brief moment of relief.

"He can't call you."

"Why not?"

"He's dead, Dylan."

The trap door opened beneath me.

In the background the *Nostalgia, Ultra* continued to play. "There will be tears, I've no doubt. There may be smiles, but a few," Frank sang. "And when the tears have run out, we'll be numb and blue. I can't be there with you, but I can dream. I can't be there with you, but I can dream. I can't be there with you, but I can dream."

Just a few hours before that phone call, Rory sat in his car, stopped at the light for what seemed to be longer than usual. Reds, yellows, and greens from the stoplights watching over the intersection reflected off the asphalt, made glassy by the recent rain. He was always moving, always on the go with something to do. He maximized every last second of every last minute in the short twenty-four hours a day holds. Something as trivial as being stuck at a red light might've bugged him any other day, but he was flying high.

The BMW Rory drove looked like it had just rolled off the factory floor. The car was actually two years old, but it was new to Rory. He'd just bought it the day before with money he made selling a haul of rare sneakers, jerseys, and jewelry to a private collector. He'd spent the day driving around in his new ride looking at apartments with his girlfriend, Brittany. He hadn't asked her to move in with him. Their relationship hadn't gotten to that point yet. Rory was looking at new digs for himself, but it gave Brittany a glimpse of what their future might've been like together.

With the last of the money he had left from his big sale, he scheduled time at a local studio to finally record some of the music he'd written. It was Friday night, and really the only thing left to do was celebrate all the good things that were happening all around him. Riding shotgun was Rory's closest friend, Ardy, the son of Bosnian immigrants who'd fled violence in their home country.

Rory and Ardy didn't know it at the time, but they were on a collision course with Jonathan Wilbanks and Adonis Muldrow, two armed fugitives who were fleeing from the authorities after robbing a restaurant, gas station, fast-food joint, and spa, with violent carjackings in between.

"You mind if we make a quick pitstop at 7-Eleven to pick up some Swisher Sweets?" Ardy asked.

"Sure, but you can't smoke in this car. I let you do that shit before, and it killed the trade-in value of my E36."

"That piece of shit didn't have any value," Ardy joked, knowing he'd get a rise out of his friend.

"Keep talking and I'm going to make you use your Chevrolegs and walk the rest of the way." Rory unlocked the doors and feigned like he was going to push Ardy out of the car, which wouldn't have been possible if he really wanted to, given Ardy's size.

Minutes later, the cashier at the convenience store eyeballed Rory and Ardy in the reflection of the spherical mirror hanging from the ceiling in the back corner. The two walked down the aisle to the back to grab drinks. There was no dawdling up and down the rows. They didn't buy an assortment of munchies like they'd done a countless number of times after getting high. They knew exactly what they came for, and the transaction was quick.

When they exited the store with a case of beer and a pack of Swisher Sweets in hand, Wilbanks and Muldrow, both wearing ski masks and brandishing firearms, emerged from the shadows. Rory had his back to them and didn't see them coming. With wide eyes and an air of panic, Ardy told Rory to get in the car. Rory turned and stood face-to-face with the man who would end his life. Rory quickly slid into the car and closed the door. Wilbanks put his gun against the glass window separating them.

"C'mon, man. Just go," Ardy pleaded.

"He's pointing a fucking gun at me!" Rory screamed as he fumbled with the push-button ignition, partially because he'd only been driving this car for two days but mostly because he had a gun in his face. Rory started the car and the gunman pulled the trigger almost simultaneously. The bullet struck Rory in the side and he slumped back. He turned to Ardy and whispered, "I'm shot." The gunman pulled the trigger twice more in quick succession, killing Rory as Ardy watched in horror from the passenger seat.

Muldrow looked nearly as surprised as Ardy that his partner had just killed someone in front of him. Sure, they were criminals, but they weren't killers. At least that's what the younger Muldrow thought the agreement was before he agreed to participate. Wilbanks turned and ran. Muldrow stared at Rory slumped over in the driver's seat for a brief second, then followed suit.

I know these details because I watched it happen. I watched the high-definition security camera footage while Jonathan Wilbanks stood trial for his crimes. I watched my brother take his last breath. I watched it over and over and over again. And it's something I can still see every time I close my eyes. I'd been through a lot in Iraq. I survived suicide bombings, sniper attacks, and mortars falling all around me. But Rory's death caught me more off guard than any roadside bomb in Iraq ever could.

Mike told me to take the week off from work, and the next morning I flew home to claim my brother's body and make funeral arrangements.

26

THE FUNERAL

PLEASE WAKE UP. *Please wake up*, I kept telling myself. Rory looked like he was sleeping. I wanted to believe he was. I wanted to believe this was just another one of Rory's elaborate pranks, another one of his sick jokes that left me so embarrassed that we'd be on the verge of a fistfight as had happened so many times before. But when I patted his chest, I could feel how hollow his insides were. His hands were rigid. The mortician did a decent job, but no amount of makeup would hide his gaunt and gray appearance.

The week prior to Rory's death, I'd purchased plane tickets to fly home to spend the holidays with him. I still used those same tickets to fly home. Only now, I was there to bury my brother. Admittedly, this viewing was much more palatable than seeing his bullet-riddled body on a metal table in the morgue days before. I held my crying mother, as she kicked and screamed trying to fight her way into the autopsy room where his body was being held. I knew seeing him like that would destroy her, and I think she knew it too, because the fight didn't last long.

I still remember the look on his lifeless face when I entered to identify his body. I remember being presented with the bill from the funeral home. And I remember trying to figure out how to come up with the money to pay for it. Thankfully, Adrian took the initiative to set up a donation fund for us. He knew we were scattered and wanted to do anything that could relieve the pressure from our reeling family.

With the help of an officer from the San Jose Police Department, and my mother's employer matching all donations, we raised over $40,000. After paying for the funeral, a good portion of the funds went missing. The SJPD liaison who accepted some of the donations on our behalf went on an extended vacation with his new mail-order bride in Miami. When I questioned him about the money, he said the rest was used to pay for the "administrative work" behind the scenes. He blocked me on social media, and I never heard from him again.

Before the memorial service, a crowd dressed in black gathered out-side the small funeral home in the heart of downtown Campbell. It was on the same street my brother and I had biked or skateboarded down countless times as kids. The same street where I worked as a panini-press engineer, the same one I'd shopped on, ate on, and lived on for most of my life until that point. It was on that same street that several hundred mourners turned out, forcing the Campbell Police Department to put up barricades and redirect traffic.

Like the night I returned home from Iraq, a stream of people pushed through a crowd to greet me. Only now, they approached me to offer their condolences with hugs, handshakes, and kisses on the cheek. Some of the faces I'd known all my life, and I still found no comfort in them.

News vans jockeyed for the best parking spots. Cameramen shad-owed reporters desperate for sound bites. They put their microphones in the faces of anyone willing to talk. To my right, a twentysomething woman with pink, blonde, and black hair looked directly into the lens, delivering a tearful soliloquy about growing up with my brother and me. She was an old family friend of ours, she said. I'd never met her in my life.

During the service, my mother and father sat on opposite ends of the room. They had spent the prior week blaming each other for Rory's death and couldn't even bear to look each other in the eyes. When my father took the podium, his eyes were on the congregation, but he was looking through us, as if we were all ghosts.

"This might as well be my funeral too," he said. "A part of me died with my son Rory."

He didn't have to say it, but I knew he wanted to switch places with Rory. He'd now lost both his father and son to violent deaths. Rory Sr. had always been the strongest, most vocal person I'd ever known. He didn't talk too much after my brother's murder.

The rest of the service was more of the same. Friends and family all stood to offer a few words. My cousin, who we lovingly call Little Virgil despite his being six foot six and the better part of 250 pounds, took the microphone and sang an original song he'd penned. Admittedly, he was an exceptional singer and musician. He'd written and composed songs for several famous artists but never had anything to show for it. And his career never took off. So now he was using my brother's funeral to showcase his latest single like we were executives at Def Jam.

"If you liked that, see me after the service. I'm selling CDs, with a portion of the proceeds going back to my family."

Others stood and offered up more clichés and platitudes. He's in a better place now. He's watching down on us from heaven. He wouldn't want us to be sad; he'd want us to celebrate him. *Gimme a fucking break*, I thought. Like Pat Tillman's younger brother a few years earlier, I wanted to take the podium and tell everyone to fuck off. *He's not with God—he's fucking dead. In a few days, he'll be a pile of ash and bone in an ornate vase on my mom's fireplace mantel.*

While I was saying my goodbyes to everyone who attended, I received a Facebook message from a girl named Hannah. She apologized for not being able to make the service and sent me a string of photos and videos. Most of them were ones I'd never seen before. But one particular picture looked familiar. It was only vaguely recognizable because I was in it. I just didn't remember the photo being taken. In this grainy still frame, Rory, Brian, Adrian, Kyle, and I had beers in hand, with our arms locked around each other and smiles on our faces. I stared at it for a second. It was taken at the going-away party Rory and Brian threw me before I left for Iraq. And Hannah had taken it. She was one of the friends Rory brought with him that night.

Young-Ae was always destined to lose one of her sons. She knew in her heart she'd have to bury one of us someday. It was a mother's intuition. However, her premonition was only partially correct. She had been prepared to bury her eldest, the son who had trouble in school and ran away as a child, the one who went away to fight in a war that was sending young men and women home in boxes weekly, the son with substance-abuse problems and mental health issues, the one who had been in trouble with the justice system. So when her first son made it through the gauntlet, she was able to breathe a sigh of relief. She let her guard down.

And maybe that made Rory's death even more unbearable. Rory didn't die doing what he loved. He wasn't being a hero and saving lives. His death wasn't even a freak accident. He was murdered walking out of a convenience store, for no reason. That's it.

The truth is, had Rory not lost his life tragically and senselessly, I likely would've taken my own at some point. I ruminated on that often. I thought about suicide regularly; admittedly, I still do. I've written dozens of goodbye notes only to toss them in the trash and put it off for another day, not because I was scared but because I was insecure in my purpose. No matter how much I didn't want to be around, I was more scared of being forgotten.

In reality, Rory's death saved my life. Every time I truly contemplated ending my own, I thought about the heartache and the suffering it would cause my mother. Relieving my pain wasn't worth the pain it would put her through. So I didn't, and I promised myself I wouldn't.

I returned to Hawaii a few weeks later. Kyle and some old high school friends came to visit. Things didn't feel the same. When my mother asked me to move home, I told her I was already planning on moving back. I loved Maui. I thought it might be the place I'd call home for the rest of my life and where I'd get married and raise my kids. But I knew my parents needed me. The decision to move back to California was an easy one.

But before I moved back, I needed to return to Arizona to get all of the things I'd stored away when I'd left for paradise.

27

BLACK BOX

_____

WITH NO WAY around it, the captain pointed the nose of the plane up, taking us above the storm clouds. It was some of the worst turbulence I'd ever experienced. Not since my first combat landing in a C-130 into Iraq did I think there was an actual possibility of experiencing a plane crash. And while the woman next to me on the flight into Arizona wasn't throwing up in her helmet like my wingman was on the descent into Kirkuk, the other passengers around me were grimacing, groaning, and gripping their armrests. My heart was already in the pit of my stomach, and my head was in a tailspin for different reasons. I was secretly wishing we'd fall out of the sky. It would've been much easier than dealing with reality.

No matter how hard I attempted to control my emotions, I couldn't keep myself from crying periodically throughout the flight. I hated thinking I could be making the passengers around me more uncomfortable. Most of them were probably coming home from happy family vacations. But I couldn't help it. I couldn't stop the tears.

The lady sitting to my left pulled out her iPad and put her headphones in. She was probably sick of my shit too. And I didn't blame her. Out of the corner of my eye I saw her pull up the *San Jose Mercury*

News; she pressed the screen a couple times, and Rory's high school graduation photo appeared.

I buried my face in my hands. *This can't be real life*, I thought. Not in Iraq, during my divorce, or even while I had a gun in my mouth had I ever been this hurt. She eyed me with some concern. She looked back at the news article and quickly did a double take back to me and put the puzzle together.

She took out one of her earbuds and whispered to me, "Do you know him?"

"That's my younger brother."

"Oh, honey. I'm so sorry," she said.

"I'm sorry. I'll stop crying," I apologized.

"Don't be embarrassed." She tapped then squeezed my hand. "Let it all out."

I fell asleep watching *Ice Age*.

A chime and page from the plane's captain woke me from my much-needed sleep. Outside the window, the usual tans and reds of Arizona's landscape were hues of dark gray. I was spinning from the shot of rum and prescription meds I'd taken before the flight.

"We've started our descent into Phoenix. Please make sure your tray tables are forward, your seat is in an upright position, and that your seat belt is securely fastened. We hope you enjoyed your time in the islands. Thanks for flying with us today, and *mahalo*."

After experiencing homelessness, giving up my six-figure salary was difficult—depressing even. But I would've traded everything I had for one more day with Rory. I saved as much as I could, put in my two weeks' notice, and bought a ticket back to Arizona to get my things out of storage, rent a U-Haul, and make my way home. Being closer to my family was the right thing to do, both for them and me.

After the plane came to a sliding stop, I grabbed my rucksack and camouflage backpack from the overhead compartment. A gentleman watched me as I gathered my belongings. "Thanks for your service," he said. I nodded in appreciation. "Hopefully you had some good R and R."

I knew he meant well and I should not have lashed out, but I did anyway. "I'm just here to bury my brother, who was murdered a few weeks ago. I hope you had a good vacation though. Aloha."

The man stood there speechless. I threw the bright green fifty-pound rucksack over my back like a dead body and thanked two flight attendants wearing fake smiles before I disembarked the plane.

Outside the terminal it was pouring, so I pulled the hood of my jacket over my head, partly to keep the water off my face but mostly because I was embarrassed that I'd been crying in public and my eyes were puffy and bloodshot. I squeezed through a group of travelers waiting for their luggage and made my way to the taxi stand. There was a long line, but I was in no rush, so I let the family with two young children go ahead of me.

After an usher directed me toward the next cab, I hopped in the back seat and gave the driver directions. He put them in his GPS, then sped away. With my head pressed against the window, I struggled to keep my eyes open. The taxi's constant hydroplaning and the driver laying on his horn ensured I didn't sleep. The speeding and swerving in and out of traffic in the rain was borderline reckless, but the thought of an accident didn't seem so bad.

Except for the growing skyline of modern buildings that run parallel with State Route 202, the dusty tan landscape crowned with jagged red and brown mountain peaks wasn't too dissimilar from some of the views I'd taken in half a decade earlier in Northern Iraq.

The junkyards in West Phoenix looked like fields of bombed-out vehicles in Mosul. A homeless man sleeping under the shade of a bus stop bench could've been any one of the corpses left on the side of the road to rot in Iraq. A short Mexican woman with a hunchback selling *elote* from a cart reminded me of the young Kurdish boys who sold me cigars and bootleg DVDs. A handcuffed man sitting on the curb while a police officer searched his car was a daily occurrence at every checkpoint in Kirkuk. A backfiring car jarred me from my delirium the same way gunshots would. I sat up straight. This garnered the driver's attention.

In slightly broken English, the driver started up some small talk: "Where you from?" "Why are you in town?" "What do you do?" I didn't want to bring up my brother's murder, so I half lied and told him I had just landed a new job in California and was in Arizona to pack up my apartment.

"What do you do for work?" he asked.

"I work in renewable energy." Trying to keep the conversation to a minimum, I kept my voice low, avoided eye contact, and responded with the shortest answers possible. That didn't deter him.

"Do you travel a lot?"

"I used to. Not so much anymore."

"I like to travel. America is the farthest I've been from home." He was waiting for me to ask him where he was from. I didn't. "I'm from Iraq."

"I've been to Iraq. Beautiful country."

"It was once. The war changed things. Were you military?"

"Yeah. I was in the Air Force and spent some time in Northeast Iraq."

"Where?"

"A little place called Kirkuk."

"I'm from Kirkuk," he said. His demeanor was no longer upbeat and jovial. We exchanged a quick glance in the rearview mirror, then it got quiet. *Real* quiet.

Something was off. I had the same uneasy feeling in my stomach I would get in Iraq. This man probably hated me, and I couldn't really blame him. I was an infidel who played a part in destroying his homeland.

I could feel him staring at me in his mirror, and I looked up just quickly enough to see his furrowed brow and the apprehension in his eyes. I averted my eyes to the window. Each second seemed longer and more drawn out. I noticed he passed our exit.

"Hey, uh, you passed our exit," I cautioned.

He kept driving, passing a couple more, before eventually taking an offramp. Then, without explanation or instruction, he slowly pulled the cab to the side of the road. I gripped my backpack a little bit tighter to my chest with my left hand and grabbed the door handle with my right. I envisioned Rory's lifeless eyes as he sat slumped over in the driver's seat of his car.

"Dude. What the fuck? Why are you stopping?"

He didn't respond. I saw his hands clench the steering wheel tight. The blood drained from his knuckles like he was working up the courage to do something. And I didn't want to be there to find out what that something was. I began to open my door when he turned around.

"Dylan, you remember me? It's me, Brahim."

He sat a foot taller, his English was better, and he no longer had that goofy bowl cut, but it was him. Five years after I left him seventy-five hundred miles away in Iraq and only a few weeks after my younger brother was brutally murdered, Brahim was sitting in front of me once again.

We both got out of the taxi and shared a warm embrace in the rain while we cried tears of joy right there on a bridge, like a scene straight out of *The Notebook*.

I pushed him away to get a look at his face.

"What are you doing in Phoenix, Bee?"

He explained that after I left Iraq, he completed his contract as an interpreter, and, as promised, he was offered a visa to the United States, some cash, and a one-way ticket to anywhere in the States.

"They asked where I wanted to go. I didn't know. I thought maybe California. Maybe I'd find you in Candle."

"Campbell."

"I told them I wanted to be someplace where the weather was like Iraq. They sent me here, to Arizona. It's hotter here."

"But it's a dry heat," I joked. We hugged again.

I'd lost one brother and got another one back.

28

HEY, BROTHER

I **ENTERED THE COURTROOM** with my family, friends, and Hannah, who was now my girlfriend, in tow. We all took our seats in the gallery. Across the aisle, the family and friends of my brother's murderer glared at us. For some reason, they were all wearing gray. I returned their stares with a clenched jaw and a clenched fist.

Only feet away and with his back to me sat Jonathan Wilbanks, the twenty-six-year-old who pulled the trigger that ended my brother's life. One bailiff stood near the judge, one watched over all the other prisoners who were also awaiting their sentencing, and another stood between both families to keep the peace as if we were the Montagues and Capulets.

There was no security between Wilbanks and me. I had a free and clear shot. I thought about grabbing Wilbanks by the back of his throat and choking the life out of him in front of his family. I wanted to. What I didn't want to do was cause my family any more pain, so I sat quietly and eyeballed him.

With my blessings, the state sought the death penalty for Wilbanks, but he took a plea to serve life in prison without the possibility of parole. Before his final sentencing, the judge asked if I had anything to share with the court. I did. I stood, walked down the aisle, and took the podium, facing the court.

I retrieved a piece of paper from my back pocket with words that some of Rory's friends had asked me to share.

"Before I address the court and before I address this piece of shit, I want to read a few quotes from some of Rory's friends."

I was fully expecting the judge to warn me about my language. He didn't.

"Danielle Sitnyakovsky said, 'Rory was an amazing person. He had the biggest heart and cared about everyone. There wasn't a single person who disliked him.' Kevin Shaffner, who is sitting right here in this courtroom, said, 'Rory was my good friend. We shared a lot of good memories. Now he's gone forever and every day that I wake up knowing he's not here, is another day with a broken heart.' Megan Jordan said, 'I can still see his smile in my mind. He was always happy and always making people laugh.' Dave Banuelous said, 'Rory never gave up on anyone and always showed love no matter what he was going through.' Dylan Hansen told me, 'Rory was the first friend I ever made in high school, because he was the only person who would talk to me.'"

My mother was crying.

"The quotes go on and on. I could stand here forever reading all the wonderful things people have to say about Rory, but it feels pretty redundant to talk about what my brother meant to my family. I don't have to stand here and tell everyone what a bright and intelligent young man Rory was. I don't have to remind my friends and family how he made everyone laugh every time he entered a room. I don't have to explain how he touched everyone in his life in a positive way at some time or another. We all know what an amazing human being Rory was. I've been sharing my favorite memories of Rory for the last 384 days. And even though it's been over a year, talking about my brother in past tense still doesn't sit well with me. But I'm standing up here because I feel like I should speak on Rory's behalf to the man—and I use the term 'man' very loosely—who murdered him. I'm here because I want to speak on behalf of my parents to the man who killed their son. I'm up here because this will likely be the only chance I have to address the man who took my brother's life. I'm not here to talk about the financial hardships we've had to endure since Rory's death—the funeral costs, the travel costs, me quitting my job to be closer to my family—all that shit is unimportant. I'm not even here to explain how hard it was to tell my five- and six-year-old sons they don't need to get their favorite uncle Rory any Christmas presents this year. I'm here to tell Wilbanks that I'm fucking livid my best friend of twenty-two years is gone.

"After everything Rory has been through, after everything my family has been through in the last few years, it's sickening to stand up here, talking about him being dead for absolutely no reason. He's dead because he was in the wrong place at the wrong time. He's dead because there are psychotic people like Jonathan Wilbanks who roam our streets.

"Wilbanks, my father says he's forgiven you. He's a better person than I am. My mother says that she'll learn to forgive you. She, too, is a better person than me. But I'll never forgive you, man. I don't have to. Instead, I'm going to wake up every morning knowing that you're stuck in a box, counting down the days till the end of your own miserable existence."

Wilbanks stared at his shackled feet.

I questioned his manhood for several more bars. Then I insulted his friends and family in front of his friends and family. One of his friends stood in protest. I told him to meet me in the hallway or sit the fuck down. The judge had the bailiff remove him. He understood my anger during what he called "an emotional process." I threw the paperwork I was holding at the back of Wilbanks's head and dared him to look at me one more time. He wouldn't.

At the conclusion of the trial that saw Wilbanks sentenced to life without the possibility of parole, and his accomplice sentenced to twenty-seven years, I was approached by the assistant district attorney of Santa Clara County. I'd lost my composure a bit toward the end there, but he told me he was impressed with the way I handled myself during the lengthy trial process and asked if I'd ever thought about a career in law. I hadn't, but thought it could be a fresh start. Maybe justice was my calling. He wrote me a recommendation to attend the University of Southern California's concurrent online Master's of Social Work and Law program, to which I was accepted. I was then hired on to work as a victims advocate for the Santa Clara County DA's office.

After a year or so of reliving my trauma vicariously through other victims of violent crime, my mental health was shot. I dreaded going to work to see what grisly files were sitting on my desk. There are only so many murder and rape trials a guy can sit through before it breaks him. Beyond that, I felt like I was playing for the wrong team. I went into work wearing a suit and tie and watched as my colleagues saw to it that young men who looked just like me had the book thrown at them. Meanwhile, affluent white men were often let off with little to no punishment. Brock Turner, the Stanford swimmer who was convicted for violently raping another student behind a dumpster, was given a sentence that essentially amounted to a couple months in jail. Aaron Persky, a judge that I'd sat in front of several times at work, explained that a multiyear sentence "would have a severe impact on [Turner]." That was not the type of system I wanted to work for. I was still having a hard time reconciling my military service and being a member of a military-industrial complex that had ruined the lives of other poor brown people on the other side of the world.

One day, without much forethought, I put in my two weeks' notice. I was broken—again. Eventually, I'd land work as a social worker and took my bleeding heart to Catholic Charities, a nonprofit that's funded by the diocese and state grants. I worked in their programs for battered women and refugees seeking asylum but would eventually help run their homeless veterans housing program.

It was incredibly difficult to convince landlords in the Bay Area to rent to my troubled clientele, most of whom had dual diagnoses, meaning they had both substance-abuse issues and mental health issues. Eventually I learned that if I offered to pay above-market rates and included several additional behavior clauses in the rental contracts, I could talk my way into a set of keys. But even when homeless veterans were successfully housed through our program, the triumphs were short-lived. The newly housed veterans regularly found themselves back out on the streets or behind bars within months.

Weeks before Christmas, I was pulled into the office with the program coordinator. I was notified to tell all of my clients they'd be receiving thirty-day notices to vacate. Our program was being shuttered and no longer providing housing subsidies to the homeless veterans who I'd spent the previous year advocating for and winning over.

Less than six months after Rory's death, I received a Facebook message that Jonam, my former college classmate, was killed during his first deployment overseas. While on patrol with his men, a donkey strapped to an overturned cart was blocking the road. Despite not expecting enemy contact, Jonam ordered his men to stay vigilant as he approached the helpless beast. The burro was saddled with an improvised explosive device, killing Jonam instantly. Like Rory's death, it just seemed like a waste.

Over the years, I eventually fell out of touch with everyone I served with. Everyone except Allen. He kept in constant contact with the others, so I didn't have to. Not knowing that I had little desire to reminisce about our time overseas and the people I spent that time with, he'd provide me with the occasional update.

Two of the guys we served with, who were both New Jersey state troopers, found themselves behind bars soon after returning to civilian life. One was caught selling a stolen AK-47 that he'd smuggled home from Iraq. The other was convicted of sexually assaulting sex workers on duty. Hardly surprising.

I was surprised when I got the phone call from Allen that Hawkes, the abrasive but lovable Irishman, had fallen to his death off the roof of a ten-story building. There were rumors that he jumped. Others said he was thrown over the side in a fight. Some said it was a tragic accident. I didn't know Hawkes *that* well, but I enjoyed his company during our deployment. Hawkes was a man of multitudes, so all theories were totally plausible, and no matter which one was the truth, they all led to the same sad destination.

I was heartbroken when I got the phone call from Allen that Smitty, the NCO with an infectious smile, had died in a fiery DUI crash on the Jersey Turnpike. His smiles were how I'd like to remember Smitty, and until this day I have a photo hanging on my fridge of Smitty grinning ear to ear.

The phone call that hurt most was the one I'd gotten from Allen the day his daughter Sierra was born. Sierra was a totally healthy baby girl, he reported. But he himself had fallen seriously ill at the hospital. Allen told me that what were initially thought to be the side effects of a lack of sleep and stress turned out to be the symptoms of late-stage stomach cancer. He was given around a year to live. Just like the day I was born, Sierra's birth was a bittersweet moment for her own father.

I called Allen when I could, but he rarely answered because he was sick from the chemo. He'd call me back whenever he was feeling up to it. Our conversations were usually short, but he remained upbeat. On one occasion, he ended the call by telling me he loved me. When I reciprocated, he said, "Oh, dude, I was talking to my wife. But it's nice to know you feel that way." I laughed until I cried.

As the year progressed, the phone calls became fewer and further between until they all but stopped. The first time I drove to San Francisco to visit him in the hospital, he was sleeping when I arrived. I sat in the hallway, occasionally peering through the window, watching him grimace in his sleep. On my next visit, he called me. But when I answered, it was his wife on the line. Allen had passed away that morning. I pulled over to the side of the road and cried some more.

Between the distance, work, grad school, raising two children, worrying about Allen, and the court proceedings of my brother's murderers, my bandwidth for anything or anyone else was low. Brahim and I spoke on the phone periodically. He still used prepaid phones like he did in Iraq, so his number was constantly changing. He didn't use e-mail or social media. He didn't say why, but I suspected it was because he was wary he'd out himself or the loved ones he left behind to people who wanted them dead. They no longer had the protection or assurances the US military had given them years earlier. Brahim kept me updated on the latest happenings in Iraq for a time.

When the US withdrawal from Iraq was complete in 2012, Brahim and I talked about what this meant for his country. He displayed a cautious optimism but didn't trust the Iraqi Army—which we spent the better part of a decade funding and training—to do its job. I understood his reservations. I'd seen firsthand how Iraqi Security Forces continually failed under the slightest amount of pressure. And that was with the backing of the United States. It was difficult to believe the unit stood a chance when we left.

Like the drawdown of coalition forces from the Middle East, Brahim and I slowly began to drift apart. *If I gave our friendship away, I couldn't lose him like I'd lost Rory and Allen*, I thought.

In the first month of 2014, ISIL (the Islamic State of Iraq and the Levant), the growing terror group established while I was in Iraq several years earlier, had seized Fallujah. Then, only a few months later, I watched on the news as ISIL declared a caliphate, a reign of Muslim rule, before leading a violent offensive on Mosul. Around five hundred thousand Iraqis fled during the conflict, and after only six days, ISIL defeated the Iraqi Army and captured the city.

The bodies of Iraqi soldiers were hung from underpasses entering into the city, heads were put on pikes that lined the roads, and burned remains were left out in the streets as a warning to anyone who dared challenge the new governance. It was medieval brutality.

Days later, ISIL attacked Hawija and Al Zab, then executed fifteen Iraqi Security Force members as they pushed their way toward Kirkuk. The display of ultraviolence worked; the Iraqi Army laid down their arms and abandoned Kirkuk. The Peshmerga, a Kurdish militia and occupants of Kirkuk and Iraqi Kurdistan, seized tanks and Humvees left behind by the Iraqi military but were still unable to hold off the Black Flag. Thousands of civilians fled, and many more were killed. ISIL was the new controlling government entity in Eastern Iraq.

Over the next several weeks, I called each of the numbers Brahim had previously given me over the past year or so. Each one was disconnected. I reached out to every taxi company in the Phoenix metropolitan area, but none of them would confirm if he even worked there, let alone give me any of his personal information.

In my heart, I knew he went back home. I would've done the same. I *did* do the same when a different kind of evil showed up to my doorstep. Brahim would call me if and when he needed to, and I would be there to answer it when he did.

At their height, the Islamic State controlled a third of Syria and nearly half of Iraq. In 2015 the Islamic State's reign of terror expanded into eight more countries. They bombed a Russian passenger plane over Egypt, killing 224 people, and 130 more were killed in a series of coordinated attacks in Paris. A year later, a man who pledged his allegiance to ISIL killed forty-nine people in a nightclub in Orlando. Then in 2017, a suicide bomber detonated himself during an Ariana Grande concert in Manchester, England, killing another twenty-two people. More recently, the Islamic State claimed responsibility for an attack on a Russian concert hall that left 140 people dead.

In 2017, with the help of their allies, the Iraqi military took back control of Kirkuk and restored a new democratic central government, but not before thousands of people were murdered and irreparable damage had been done. By the end of the conflict in Iraq, nearly half a million Iraqis would be dead. ISIL would add at least another thirty thousand names to that list by the time their reign was over.

Much like the Nazi regime that terrorized the world decades earlier, the caliphate kept impeccable records. Among the ruins, inspectors, soldiers, and journalists found birth certificates and applications to join ISIL's ranks. Investigators also unearthed lists of approved reading materials, medical reports, driver's licenses, certificates and diplomas for graduating ISIL training camps, marriage licenses, real estate contracts, weapons lists, and every other document one could think of.

They also found death and execution certificates.

Over two hundred mass graves and twenty thousand bodies linked to the atrocities of the Islamic State have been uncovered, with many more still being found regularly. With limited funding from the Iraqi government and international bodies, it may take decades to discover the rest and even longer for families to find the closure they seek.

I wasn't seeking closure, but it was given when I received a call that Brahim's remains were found in Kirkuk.

EPILOGUE

IN SOME WAYS, America and Iraq aren't dissimilar. And although we haven't been in a civil war for the better part of two centuries, Americans continue to find themselves at odds with one another. John Steinbeck wrote about the disconnect and disparity in the US following the Great Depression. He critiqued the people who claimed to be the greatest Americans. "They're the same ones that burned the houses of old German people during the war. They're the same ones that lynch Negroes. They like to be cruel. They like to hurt people, and they always give it a nice name, patriotism or protecting the constitution." Hate is as American as apple pie. It's inviting to those who are empty. It's easily shared and it feels like sustenance. As a society, we'll keep ingesting it until we're sick.

But despite all the ugliness that's been on display in high definition—the police brutality, the anti-immigrant sentiment, the violence against the LGBTQ community, women losing their bodily autonomy—I still believe America is the land of promise. It's a place where young men like Rory, an eccentric Black kid, can pursue his artistic and offbeat passions. It's a place where folks like Allen can aspire to start a family on a quiet, tree-lined street in a sleepy Northern California suburb. America is a place where immigrants like Brahim can find salvation away from their own war-torn homes. (The sad irony that America is often the purveyor of the foreign policies that make those homes war-torn was not lost on me as I wrote that sentence.)

Through the lives and the deaths of Rory, Allen, and Brahim, I've learned that being an American has nothing to do with fighting conflicts in foreign lands halfway around the world. If we had never stepped foot in Iraq, nothing here at home would've changed in the slightest. In fact, we'd very well likely be better off as a nation. Because of the dubious nature of America's purpose in Iraq, you might posit that all the lives lost there were recklessly thrown away. And maybe you'd be right.

We didn't free the people of Iraq. There were no weapons of mass destruction, and we weren't there to install a democracy. We destroyed their country, killed half a million people, and set the country back decades, if they ever recover at all. Being a participant in all that will be something I spend the rest of my life trying to rectify, a wrong I'll forever try to right.

The fight to uphold American ideals is in our own homes and on the streets outside, places where tragedies, like the ones Rory and Allen found, find us more readily than in any war zone. But sometimes those streets can lead us on compelling journeys to intersections of tragic endings and auspicious new beginnings, to places where fate brings us together and pulls us apart again.